Conan Doyle

RONALD PEARSALL

Conan Doyle

A BIOGRAPHICAL SOLUTION

RICHARD DREW PUBLISHING
GLASGOW

First published 1977 by Weidenfield and Nicolson

This edition first published 1989 by
Richard Drew Publishing Ltd
6 Clairmont Gardens, Glasgow G3 7LW
Scotland

British Library Cataloguing in Publication Data

Pearsall, Ronald
  Conan Doyle: a biographical solution.
  1. Fiction in English, Doyle,
      Sir. Arthur Conan
  I. Title
  823′.912

  ISBN 0-86267-255-4

Printed and bound in Great Britain

CONTENTS

1
A CATHOLIC
EDUCATION

Arthur Conan Doyle was born in Edinburgh in 1859, the son of Charles Doyle, civil servant, and Mary Doyle, née Foley, who were married in 1855. Mary Doyle had a great pride in her forebears, and had managed to convince herself that she was descended from the Plantagenets. In due course she communicated her beliefs and findings to young Arthur, and his early memories include being put to the question on heraldry. Charles Doyle also had an impressive ancestry and could, if the will was strong enough and the wine was flowing freely, associate himself with D'Ouilly, D'Oyly and D'Oel, though firm facts were hard to come by, for the Doyles were Catholics with their roots in Ireland, and genealogical records were incomplete.

Charles Doyle had come to Scotland from London about 1850, and had been deposited with the Foleys, also expatriate Irish Catholics. Doyle's father, John, had left Dublin in 1817 to settle in London as an artist, and was to make his name as HB, caricaturist. His caricature was urbane and polite, far removed from the brutality and bawdy of most other cartoonists of the Regency, and he specialized in political satire. In appearance he was not unlike the Duke of Wellington, and he was often saluted in the park under the impression that he was the duke.

His staunch belief in Catholicism did not prevent him being accepted into the houses of the rich and powerful and he numbered among his friends and acquaintances Disraeli, Thackeray and Sir Walter Scott. He married Marianna Conan, sister of Michael Conan, an artist and journalist who reported the art scene from Paris, and they had seven children, two girls and five boys, James, Henry, Richard, Francis and Charles. It was a richly talented family, and three of the boys established themselves in positions commensurate with their abilities.

The most famous proved to be Richard, born in 1824, one of the most brilliant illustrators and cartoonists of the century, who brought to the pages of *Punch* great originality in his whimsy and his sophisticated pseudo-naïvety, and in his use of 'outline' drawing without shading of any kind. Richard was the man who designed the cover of *Punch* that remained unaltered until long after the end of World War Two, to be replaced by vulgar trendiness. Whatever the Doyles born of the union of John Doyle and his wife Marianna were, they were not vulgar.

Francis died before he was sixteen. James was known as 'The Priest' and was the scholar of the family, writing *A Chronicle of England* and *The Official Baronage of England*, which took him thirteen years and became an authoritative text-book of the College of Arms. The *Chronicle* was illustrated in colour, and in quality the colour reproduction rivalled the work of George Baxter. Henry began as a painter and art critic, and was sufficiently competent to be commissioned to do murals of the Last Judgment for the Roman Catholic church at Lancaster. He was also a portrait painter, and Cardinal Wiseman sat to him, but he achieved his greatest fame as director of the National Gallery of Ireland from 1869 onwards.

He had a flair and a perception not then common to gallery directors, and during his term he obtained, often at Christie's sale room in London, many fine paintings, including those by artists resolutely out of fashion. Among his best buys was Rembrandt's *Sleeping Shepherds*, for which he paid £514 in 1883; he also bought a portrait head of an old man by the same artist. A painting by Fra Angelico was bought at Christie's for £73, and he also purchased works by Bellini, Correggio, and Ruysdael and saw the merit in Richard Wilson, a landscape artist who was then thought dull and who has only been re-evaluated since World War Two. He also invested in English portrait painters such as Reynolds and Gainsborough before their prices soared, thanks to American investment in such pictures, and built up a sturdy collection of Irish paintings, sufficiently good to remain on the walls of the National Gallery of Ireland and not to be demoted to the cellars, the fate of English gallery purchases of the same period.

Charles could not compete with this array of brilliant brothers. He entered the Civil Service and spent most of his life in the Edinburgh Office of Works, painting in his spare time, dreamy and remote, and fathering a family he could ill afford. On £240 a year, plus about £60 from selling pictures, he and his wife lived in genteel poverty, bolstered up by their awareness of their heritage and discomfited by knowledge that Charles was the failure of the brood.

The first of the children was Annette, who as soon as she was able was sent out to be a governess in Portugal, remitting all her salary home and dying young. Arthur was the second, with the name Conan added to please his great-uncle and godfather. Looking back, Arthur described the poverty as hardy and bracing. Encouraged by his mother, he escaped into the world of romance through the agency of a library. So rapidly did he devour its stock that he was informed that books could not be changed more than twice a day.

Occasionally reality broke in. Between the ages of seven and nine the young Doyle was sent to a local Edinburgh school which he described as like something out of Dickens, with a harsh cane-wielding master. Sometimes the grand Doyle relations came from the south to see the ne'er-do-well brother and his wife. Once Thackeray came and dandled the boy on his knee; it was hardly compensation for poverty of the kippers and curtains variety. No one in the house starved. For the poor of Edinburgh life among the Doyles would have seemed unimaginable luxury.

For Catholics anxious to give their children a respectable education there were two public schools, Downside run by Benedictines, and Stonyhurst, in Lancashire, run by Jesuits. The preparatory school for Stonyhurst was Hodder, a mile away, and Doyle entered this in 1868, spending two years there and five years at Stonyhurst. Doyle's great-uncle Conan had warned that the Jesuits had their little quirks, and as if to prove it Doyle's parents were approached and told that if their son was given over to the Church the fees of £50 a year would be remitted. Although this was a fifth of the father's income from his job, Mrs Doyle refused, and at no time was the young Arthur Conan destined for the Church, making the selection of Stonyhurst pointless. As a power house of the Catholic Church it had its niche, but as an educational establishment it left much to be desired.

This was true of most public schools of the period, and matters had changed little since the poet Cowper had written: 'Great schools suit but the sturdy and rough.' Fortunately Doyle was sturdy, and probably rough as well. He was certainly noted for his untidiness, and his determination to go his own way. He would have profited from the individualized education given by adventurous masters such as

Edward Thring of Uppingham, headmaster from 1853 to 1886. Thring's principle was the need to adjust school education to develop the capacities of each boy, a concept totally alien to the Jesuit masters or, to do them justice, the masters of Harrow, Eton or Winchester.

There was not much difference in intention between the Jesuits of Stonyhurst and Rugby under Dr Arnold. 'He is perfectly educated who is taught all the will of God concerning Him, and enabled through life to execute it,' declared Arnold. Stonyhurst was at one with him on this, and with most of the other schools in the belief that education should be based on the classics, though this was disputed by many theorists. In *Essays on a Liberal Education* (1867), Henry Sidgwick, Professor of Moral Philosophy at Cambridge, commented: 'It is curious in contemplating English school life as a whole, to reflect how thoroughly we believe in natural exercises for the body and artificial exercises for the mind.' This was felt by some public school masters. E.E. Bowen of Harrow wrote: 'In classical study alone, we profess to learn principles first and then advance to facts ... It is truly a painful sight to see a boy sit down to master a set of clumsy rules, of which he will never use the half, and never understand the quarter.'

Stonyhurst was strictly orientated towards the classics, publishing its own *Latin Grammar*, with Virgil, Cicero, Livy, Tacitus, Horace and Homer drummed into its pupils, and with geography and mathematics for light relief. Indoctrination was systematically carried out through 'catechism'. English was taught by 'Reading and Spelling: by Heart: Dictation: Composition: Analysis and Sentences'.

The old Catholic colleges were brought into being by the determination of Queen Elizabeth I to stamp out Catholicism, which meant that if Catholics wanted an education for their sons they were obliged to send them overseas. Douay was founded in 1568, and Saint-Omers in 1592. People who sent their sons to these establishments were guilty of high treason, and if the boats were stopped in transit the boys were thrown into prison. The Napoleonic wars forced the Jesuits at Saint-Omers to seek a safer place for their charges, and although Bavaria was contemplated it was decided, as Catholics were no longer persecuted, to return to England, and Stonyhurst was opened in 1794.

It brought back many curious traditions, such as six classes, Rhetoric, Poetry, Syntax or Upper Grammar, Middle Grammar, Rudiments or Great Figures, and Figures or Little Figures. Rhetoric corresponded to the Sixth Form, Poetry to the Fifth, Syntax to the Fourth, and so on. The various rooms at Stonyhurst were called Study Place,

4

Shoe Place, Washing Place, Strangers' Place, and new boys were in-
culcated into strange rites to fit them into the antique scheme.

Stonyhurst was a ramshackle building unlived in for nearly half
a century, and most of it was derelict and uninhabitable. Parts were
destroyed, lead statues in the gardens were melted down and the lead
used to repair the roof, and additions were made, not with great enthusiasm or taste because it was believed that after the Napoleonic
wars the school would return to Europe. Many of the boys were Irish,
and when the Jesuits opened colleges there Stonyhurst suffered. In
1829 there were only 120 students; by Conan Doyle's time there were
rather less than 300.

Building operations were carried out over the decades, and not until
1851 was there a proper washplace for the boys. Until then they had
to be content with a row of taps with a trough below to carry off the
dirty water. 'There was no accommodation for brushes, sponges, or
soap, which had to be kept in another room on the floor above,' declared the historian of Stonyhurst College in 1901. In 1852 a large
covered playground, the Ambulacrum, was opened, a new 'Sodality
Chapel' was opened in 1859, and shortly before Doyle arrived at the
school an 'underground magnetic chamber' was built to facilitate instruction in meteorology and magnetism. Stonyhurst College was not
completely rebuilt until long after Doyle had spent his five years there.
He described it as 'that grand medieval dwelling-house'.

His seven years at Hodder and Stonyhurst he called 'seven weary
steps ... I do not know if the Jesuit system of education is good or
not; I would need to have tried another system as well before I could
answer that'. In 1889 he wrote to a friend that he would never send
a son of his to Stonyhurst: 'They try to rule too much by fear – too
little by love or reason.' The fear was physical and psychological. The
boys were always under scrutiny by spies 'whose presence secures that
training in orderliness, self-control and obedience to law, that is a
chief object in education'. This practice, which even they confessed
was 'un-English', was defended by the Jesuits on the grounds that
such supervision by prefects and masters prevented the immorality
so noteworthy a feature of Eton, Harrow or Winchester, and that it
was 'possible to meet in great measure the special dangers of boarding-
school life without any prejudice to liberty and manliness'.

Discipline was kept by using a method called the 'penance-walk',
in which a boy was compelled to walk in silence and isolation up and
down the playground for up to an hour, and corporal punishment

was inflicted with an instrument shaped like the sole of a slipper, called a 'ferula', and by the boys a 'tolly'. 'One blow of this instrument', recalled Doyle, 'would cause the palm of the hand to swell up and change colour.' The maximum punishment was what was called 'twice-nine' (nine on each hand), minimum nine, except for small boys who took six. The birch was the ultimate deterrent. Doyle admitted that he was often beaten, not because he was more vicious than his companions but because he 'had a nature which responded eagerly to affectionate kindness (which I never received), but which rebelled against threats'.

The regimen was austere, and boys were expected to stay at Stony-hurst for Christmas, the time being passed with amateur dramatics. Dry bread and watered milk constituted breakfast, and the day ended with a supper of hot milk, bread, butter and often potatoes. There was fish on Fridays. During the afternoons there was a snack called bread and beer, described by Doyle as 'horrible swipes'. On this curiously unwholesome diet the fifteen-year-old Doyle was five feet nine inches tall and 'pretty stout'.

The English public schools put great store in compulsory games, considering that it would quell any unhealthy urges of the flesh, and Stonyhurst was no exception, though even when enjoying themselves the boys knew that the spies were among them and there would always be a priest within earshot to report on any hastily spoken oath. As with the names of classrooms and forms, Stonyhurst brought to Britain a variety of distinctive sports, the main objection to which was that no other school had heard of them and therefore could not compete with Stonyhurst. Cricket had been incorporated in the list of sports in 1860, but other Stonyhurst sports such as 'trap' and 'cat' were not known elsewhere. 'Cat' was a form of rounders which was believed to have been taken from sixteenth-century Oxford to Europe when the Jesuit schools started there.

Even cricket had its Stonyhurst counterpart, with a stone as wicket, boys who 'fagged' instead of fielded, a semi-circular crease, and an obligation to slog the ball (at every stroke the bat had to be raised above the horizontal). 'There and back' constituted one run. This Stonyhurst cricket had its exotic spin-offs – 'common innings' and 'tip and run', not to mention 'double puffing'. These variations did not disappear until 1886 (by which time Doyle was writing his first Sherlock Holmes story). There was also a Stonyhurst football, with a small ball and goals seven feet wide. Modern fourth-division association football teams facing re-election would welcome one of its rules – there was no limit on the number of players.

By the time Doyle went to Stonyhurst what was contemptuously called 'London' cricket was well established, and it was now possible to draw up fixtures with other schools. However, religious discrimination still held sway and in June 1874, when Doyle was at Stonyhurst, the Protestant paper *The Rock* attacked the masters of Rossall school for permitting a cricket match with Stonyhurst. 'All these commminglings with papists act as so many enticements to idolatry, and the masters who do not see this are unfit to manage a Protestant school.' The Stonyhurst cricket uniform of white flannels, pink shirts, and blue caps was a source of suspicion.

Notwithstanding the various inconveniences of being a pupil at a Catholic seminary, Doyle did well at cricket, and would certainly have made his mark at association football had it been in existence at Stonyhurst then (it was introduced in 1884). He was so full of his prowess that he wrote home saying that he would like to enter some cricket club in Edinburgh, and thought that he 'could take a place in the eleven of any club in Edinburgh'.

Instruction in the classics and mathematics passed him by, and he does not appear to have made any use of the 'underground magnetic chamber'. 'I can say with truth that my Latin and Greek, which cost me so many weary hours, have been little use to me in life, and that my mathematics have been no use at all,' he recollected in his autobiography.

As he prepared to go out into the savage ungodly world, the Jesuits did not think much could be made of Doyle. He would not be an ornament to any monastery. When he was asked what he would like to be and he replied that he wanted to be a civil engineer, the questioner declared that the civil part would be difficult. For any position it would be necessary to go through university, and therefore to matriculate, but before the examinations Doyle managed to get to London, at Christmas 1874, staying with Richard Doyle, the ageing *enfant terrible* of *Punch*. He went to the Lyceum and saw Henry Irving in *Hamlet*, and to the Haymarket Theatre for *Our American Cousin* (the play President Lincoln was watching when he was assassinated). He did the usual small boys' round, including the Tower of London, and particularly liked the armoury where the weapons of the British Army were stored. He thought the 67,000 Martini-Hentry rifles wonderful, but perhaps less so than the racks, thumb-screws and other instruments of torture. He saw the Crystal Palace at Sydenham with its life-size models of prehistoric creatures, the animals at the Zoological Gardens in Regent's Park, and Madame Tussaud's wax-works, then in Baker Street. He was very taken with the 'room of Horrors, and the images of the murderers'.

He returned to cram for the matriculation examination, and passed very creditably. In 1875 he went for a year to a Jesuit school at Feld-kirch in Austria to brush up his German, and during this time he tobogganed, played football on stilts and learned to play the bombar-don in the school band. He broke his return to Scotland with a visit to his great-uncle Conan in Paris, who had given Doyle his middle name but nothing much else.

In later years Doyle remembered the Jesuits as keen, clear-minded and earnest, and although hard and narrow they were also fearless as well as 'uncompromising bigots'. He himself was of too rugged a nature to be more than temporarily thwarted by the efforts to make adolescents conform. The physical chastisement did not bother him, nor did the psychological pressures, and whatever the Jesuits did they curbed the sexual malpractices that were commonplace elsewhere by constant vigilance. So far as one can gather there were no homosexual groups at Stonyhurst where every prefect had his favourite and the prettier boys were fought over by their elders (who sometimes com-peted with the masters for their favours). If there was a fagging system, giving rise to the abuse of privilege, no one mentioned it in connection with Stonyhurst.

Doyle left Stonyhurst a healthy animal, with his imagination stirred by Walter Scott and Macaulay, and the only token of a literary bent his editorship of the school magazine during his last year. He did not look back on it with the dread that Sir Oliver Lodge, who was later a formative influence on him, did. 'My schooldays were undoubtedly the most miserable part of my life', Lodge wrote in his autobiography, referring to his years at Newport Grammar School in Shropshire, which had much the same syllabus as Stonyhurst. Unlike many of his contemporaries, Doyle passed through the test of the Victorian boarding-school apparently unscathed.

Morally admirable Stonyhurst might have been, but in many ways it was a kind of ghetto, harbouring deep suspicion and often hostility towards the world outside which was looked on by the Jesuits as a hotbed of contamination. This bred a sense of superiority which could often, under experience, turn to a sense of inferiority; the boys were encouraged to look upon themselves as an élite which was too high-minded to contend for the honours of life. Consequently there was no shame in being obscure in later life. In 1894 the Bishop of Newport explained why Stonyhurst had not produced a prime minister or more notables, by claiming 'that a considerable number of men who un-doubtedly would have made their mark in the learned professions, the services and literature, have lived and died in comparative obscurity as Jesuit fathers'.

So far as Stonyhurst was concerned, its most famous pupil was Charles Waterton (1782–1865), the naturalist who explored South America, and in the 1901 history of the school Doyle and his contem-porary the *Punch* cartoonist Bernard Partridge were not mentioned as past luminaries. The authors preferred 'author, traveller, and civil servant' Miles Gerald Keon, now totally unknown; a minor anti-quarian of Exeter, Dr Oliver; and a family of actors, the Vandenhoffs, whose only claim to fame is that the father sent his son back to his old school. Another of Doyle's contemporaries at Stonyhurst was Father Thurston, who gained distinction as a fervent opponent of spiritualism. It must have seemed to ambitious boys that their school was devoted to producing a race of celibate nonentities.

The transition from Stonyhurst to Edinburgh University was abrupt, and there was none of the smooth accepted progress from school to university that marked the privileged English, though had he been English the lowly income of the Doyle family would have weighed more heavily against the young man. Edinburgh University was not in the least like Oxford or Cambridge, but more akin to a polytechnic. There was no living in, no university organism, no inter-linked colleges, and the teaching was carried out in a brusque busi-ness-like fashion. The professors sold their knowledge, the students paying their money directly to them and receiving their money's-worth in instruction, not a penny more and not a penny less. Outside the lecture room there was no fraternization between teachers and taught.

It was decided that Doyle would be a doctor. It was a no-nonsense career at which a competence would be difficult not to earn. Edin-burgh had a name for medicine, and in 1876, the year that Doyle entered the university, it had introduced the degree of M.B. instead of M.D. to bring the university into line with English systems, en-abling graduates to practise almost anywhere. The Faculty of Medi-cine became greatly enlarged; the number of students went up from

543 in 1861–2, to 1,070 in 1876–7, to 1,898 in 1887–8, with some improvement in the facilities offered. The increase in the number of students meant that the professors delegated some of their work to student-assistants, so that the standard of teaching was inclined to be uneven.

Although there were fewer great characters among the professors, things were easier for the impecunious student. The Students' Club opened in 1876 in its own rooms opposite the university, and provided dinners for its members, two courses for a shilling, though it was not until 1887 that University Hall was founded to provide 'the long felt need in Scottish universities of college life as understood in England with its social advantages and avoidance of the drawbacks of solitary life in lodgings'. Doyle lived at home, so the misery of a garret room in the wynds was avoided, but being so tied he could not ignore the very evident inability of his father to provide the wherewithal to keep a family, still increasing in size.

Doyle's time at the university was embittered by lack of money. When he had returned from Germany he had found that there was a long list of bursaries and scholarships open for competition, and crammed hard, winning a bursary of £40 for two years. Unfortunately there was a clerical error, and he learned that this particular bursary was only open to arts students. Nor did he get the next highest, which had already been awarded, and was fobbed off with £7. This obliged him to do outside work and compress his university course. Although he did not receive his M.B. until 1881, he had already by that time done a good deal of doctoring. In 1879 his father went into a nursing-home.

By the time Doyle arrived at university the truly great men of British medicine had retired. Syme, who held the chair of Clinical Surgery 1833–69, was the foremost surgeon of his day. J.Y.Simpson (Midwifery, 1840–70) was a pioneer in the use of anaesthetics, and Joseph Lister (Clinical Surgery, 1869–77) was about to move to King's College Hospital, London. The men with whom Doyle dealt, largely at a distance, were comparatively minor figures, even though Professor Rutherford provided a model for Professor Challenger, and Joseph Bell, surgeon at the Edinburgh Infirmary, was transmuted into Sherlock Holmes. Among the other professors Doyle mentioned, and who were unquestionably used as bases of characters, was Balfour, described by Doyle as a hard rugged old man with the face and manner of John Knox. Balfour did botany, and was known as 'Woody

Fibre'. Doyle and his fellow students did not like botany, and he referred to his 'long weary grind at botany, chemistry, anatomy, physiology, and a whole list of compulsory subjects, many of which have a very indirect bearing upon the art of curing'.

Botany was regarded as one of the most uninteresting of the set subjects, and learned by rote. Dr Crichton-Browne described a class held by Balfour in which a student was asked to say what order a poppy belonged to, and although he pulled the flower to pieces he was none the wiser. Only when he was asked a question the answer to which had been previously learned did the student manage the text-book reply. There was more cribbing at examinations on botany than on any other subject, and two or three professors perambulated the examination room to prevent cheating, looking out for notes on shirt-cuffs or thumbnails. On the principle of Poe's 'The Purloined Letter' one student took with him to the examination room Balfour's *Class Book of Botany*, and on receiving his paper referred to it quite openly. He passed with commendations.

Doyle also remembered the chemist Alexander Crum Brown, who held the chair for nearly thirty years, memorable for his fear of his own experiments. He sheltered when he was about to explode some mixture, but it usually failed to ignite and the class shouted 'Boom!' Charles Wyville Thomson, zoologist, had recently returned after being scientific head of the *Challenger* expedition, but he died when Doyle was halfway through his five years' tuition. They were characters, far more distinctive than the Jesuit teachers of Stonyhurst, and they rooted themselves in Doyle's mind. Their knowledge was awesome to Doyle, even when it had little relevance to medicine as it was practised, and their attitudes, a mixture of pragmatism, callousness and gentle dottiness, impressed the unworldly youth, though Rutherford's sadistic delight in vivisection was not embodied in the more amiable personality of Professor Challenger when he made his debut in *The Lost World* forty years later.

When he went out into the world as a doctor Doyle found out that botany and chemistry were of even less importance than he had supposed. His first berth was with Dr Richardson in the summer of 1878. Richardson was a small-time G.P. running a practice among the poor of Sheffield, and Doyle remained with him for only three weeks. An advertisement in the medical papers eventually landed him a job with Dr Elliot at Ruyton-of-the-Eleven-Towns in Shropshire. Elliot had a quiet country practice, and Doyle made himself useful, at one time assisting to remove a lump of iron from a man's head, the result of an old cannon exploding. But the kind of doctoring he was doing did not correspond with the romantic vision of the calling. 'There are men and classes of men', said Robert Louis Stevenson, 'that stand above the common herd; the soldier, the sailor and the shepherd not infrequently, the lawyer rarely, rarelier still the clergyman, the physician almost as a rule. He is the flower (such as it is) of our civilization ...' 'What profession is there equal in true nobleness to medicine? He can abolish pain, relieve his fellow mortals from sickness; he is indisputably usefullest of all men,' declared Carlyle, himself an ex-graduate of Edinburgh University and a kind donor of bursaries despite his comparative poverty (though his bursaries did not go to medicine).

'I believe', said Dr Johnson, 'everyone has found in physicians great liberality and dignity of sentiment, very prompt effusions of beneficence and willingness to exert a lucrative art where there is no hope of reward.' There were Victorian doctors like this, but far too many of them were male versions of Mrs Gamp. They pretended omniscience, but mainly dabbled in the dark, refusing to recognize medical discoveries and jealously guarding their own 'cures'. Dr Hoare, Doyle's next post, was a Birmingham doctor in a fair way of business who made £3,000 a year by diligently dealing out pills, ointment and medicine at 1s. 6d. a time, with visits 3s. 6d. Doyle acted as dispenser, sometimes making up a hundred bottles in an evening.

There was little specialization, a gulf between surgery and medicine, and an abyss between the 'learned physician' who took a literary, fastidious and meditative interest in his profession and the experimental scientist. The first clinical laboratory was not opened until 1885, and then not in Britain but Munich. So much was being discovered by the experimentalists that the ordinary G.P. became defeatist, preferring to stick to his old hoary concepts of what was wrong. The most widely held view of the role of doctors at the time Doyle was first practising was called 'expectant medicine'. Doctors were conscious of their own ignorance, and the mysteries of nature, and contented themselves by putting their patients under diet and nursing in the hope that they would get better, relying 'on the tendency of all equilibriums to recover themselves under perturbation'. For idealistic young men just entering their profession the cynicism came as a deadly blow.

'Expectant medicine' encouraged laziness, and placed a premium on an irresistible bedside manner. The phenomenon of infection was understood, and so was the importance of hygiene and the role of heredity in certain transmitted diseases, but far too often they were not acted upon. The old school scorned the new-fangled stethoscope and thermometer, preferring to rely on their intuition, their powers of observation and their gimmicks. Many doctors, even those knighted for their services, contented themselves with prescribing placebos, others were noted for the zest with which they filled their patients with drink. When Sir Edward Clarke, a prominent lawyer, went to see Sir William Jenner because he was feeling ill, Jenner's advice was brisk and succinct: 'Drive home at once, take the earliest train you can to Brighton, take a quiet lodging, on no account look at a book or newspaper, walk about on the sea-front till you are tired out, and then go in and sleep, and drink every day two glasses of the best champagne you can get.' Clarke had been a teetotaller for four years, but he followed the instructions and got better. He was fortunate. Patients of doctors who followed the doctrines of expectant medicine either recovered or died.

Hospital consultants were no more informed. Sutton, the pathologist of the London Hospital, was accustomed to prescribe 'a bottle of Jamieson and a pretty nurse'. 'None will be surprised that far more spirits were consumed in his ward than in any other,' commented Dr A.T. Schofield drily. 'Nevertheless, he effected some marvellous cures, so wonderful are the powers of the human constitution.' Samuel Fenwick, also a London Hospital consultant, always carried a small stoppered bottle in his pocket. When seeing a new patient for the first time he asked the patient to put out the tongue and dabbed it with the stopper of his little bottle, whereupon he pronounced with great gravity the word 'rheumatism'. One celebrated surgeon, Walter Rivington, was so absent-minded that he was once stopped walking home from his hospital, thinking that his day was over, when in fact he had one patient under chloroform in the theatre, another being anaesthetized and several others waiting for his knife. Well-known doctors had little faith in their contemporaries. Sir William Gull was called in as consultant, and noticed a symptom missed by the attendant doctor; he pointed it out, and the doctor was agitated, saying that the patient was not only a patient but a friend and he was doubly distressed. 'Pray calm yourself,' said Gull. 'It might have been worse. If you had discovered the symptom you might have treated it.' This sort of sarcasm deprived Gull (recently accused of being Jack the Ripper), who was a first-rate doctor, of the presidency of the College of Physicians. When a prominent surgeon of the 1870s, Sir James Ferguson, was referred to the work of the Austrian physician Niemeyer during a case he was involved in at King's College Hospital, he retorted: 'I do not see how anything said by an Old Testament prophet can have any bearing on a case like this.'

Such was the situation in medicine when Arthur Conan Doyle became Dr Doyle. Some were seeing the failure of systematic drugging and that filling a patient full of alcohol made him or her, logically, an alcoholic. There was a widespread interest by adventurous medical men in electricity as a cure, in hydropathy, in gymnastics, in massage and in hypnotism. Astute doctors were making several thousands a year using homeopathic methods. It was a free-for-all, in which the patients were the only ones to suffer. Hospitals, except for the rich, were dreadful. It was suggested that over the portal of every hospital gate should be the inscription 'Feel full of hope, all ye who enter here' but no one ever had the nerve to do it. The hospital was, wrote W.E.Henley,

> Where life and death like friendly chafferers meet
> Through a loud, spacious and draughty gloom.

There was never any indication that Doyle had any revolutionary ideas about medicine, or that he thought he was especially privileged to carry the banner of Hippocrates. After three years at Edinburgh he put his thoughts in order for his mother. He thought it would be a pity to involve himself in a country practice or – a conventional opening for any newly qualified general practitioner – act as a medical officer on board ship. 'Let me once get my footing in a good hospital and my game is clear,' he declared. He would 'observe cases minutely, improve in my profession, write to the *Lancet*, supplement my income by literature, make friends and conciliate everyone I meet, wait ten years if need be ...'

This is what the young Doyle thought of as success, and his mother enthusiastically agreed. Their relationship was always close, and the absence of his father in the nursing-home released the bonds of a too strict Catholicism. Eventually Mrs Doyle adopted Protestantism. Unlike the Doyle relations, she was adaptable, and what was good enough for Arthur was good enough for her. Her brother-in-law, Richard, sketched her when she was young, a personable girl with wide-spaced eyes and tidy hair parted in the middle in a severe style.

Her advice and precepts were never slow in arriving on Doyle's door-step, as a schoolboy, as a struggling doctor or as a famous writer. Sometimes he regarded them, sometimes he did not, but they were always motivated by sturdy common sense and a determined regard for her son. Throughout his life he referred to her as 'The Ma'am', a formidable little lady who lived until 1921.

Doyle graduated, not brilliantly. As he said himself, he was a sixty per cent man; that was all that was necessary to set oneself up with a brass nameplate.

2
THE
SOUTHSEA YEARS

None of Doyle's part-time jobs was particularly lucrative. Dr Hoare of Birmingham paid him two pounds a month, and another job, on an Arctic whaling ship, earned him two pounds ten shillings (£2·50) a month, plus three shillings (15p) a ton 'oil money'. Doyle went on this seven-month adventure in 1880, finding that his main duties were to be a companion for the captain and to break up any fights among the seamen. He was already showing the signs of insensitivity that were to baffle his admirers, and the sangfroid with which he watched the slaughter of the seals demonstrated to the seamen an admirable lack of squeamishness. It was brutal work he admitted, but it gave work to seamen, dockers, tanners, curers, chandlers, oil-sellers and leather merchants.

He nearly drowned in the icy waters before the ship left the seals for the whales, and although Doyle was signed on as surgeon he joined in the hunt, and was so enthusiastic that the captain offered to make him harpooner as well as doctor. 'The lancing, when the weary fish is killed with the cold steel, was more exciting [than harpooning] because it is a more prolonged experience,' he wrote long afterwards, noting with surprise that the whale 'appears to have but little sensibility to pain, for it never winces when the long lances are passed through its body'. As the whale entered its death throes, Doyle gloried in the contest. 'Who would swap that moment for any other triumph that sport can give?' Sport?

His time at sea toughened Doyle up, physically and probably mentally. For a man in his early twenties he was storing up a formidable battery of experiences, and his whaler types crop up time and again in his stories, sometimes dressed up in army uniform. His ventures into the sub-world of the Birmingham slums gave him insight into the way the very poor lived, though he never made very much of it. A doctor was almost the only member of the middle classes who could gain entrance to the lowest sections of the population, without the patronizing that went with the late-Victorian hobby of slumming. Soon after graduation he was away to sea again, to Africa on the 4,000-ton cargo steamer *Mayumba*, which carried up to thirty passengers. Most of the passengers were bound for Madeira, but there were also some negro traders whom Doyle did not like.

It was a stormy voyage, and Doyle had to cope with sea-sickness on board, but eventually the ship reached the tropics, called at Sierra Leone, Liberia and Nigeria where Doyle went down with fever. He soon recovered, explored the mangrove swamps and went alligator shooting, as well as swimming round the ship in shark-infested waters, emulating the natives. It was the right kind of life for an adventurous young man of means, but it did not lay any ground for a future in medicine, and when he returned to England his London relatives got together to decide what to do with him and to offer all assistance short of actually giving him money to assist his mother and family. The London Doyles were art-orientated, and although being a doctor was respectable it lacked the Bohemian sparkle.

Doyle himself had had the very commendable idea of taking short-term employment and getting enough money together to buy a practice of his own, but a sense of reality impelled him to believe that this was easier dreamed about than done. Nor had he succeeded in attracting to himself a comfortable situation in a hospital. The Doyles, better versed in the way of the world, had a better idea – patronage. They would send to their nephew their ailing friends. For this, the young man needed to have only one qualification besides a degree. Like them, he had to be a Catholic, and there was no question, after his indoctrination at Stonyhurst, that he was. But at Stonyhurst Doyle had been lukewarm, and at university he had, like many of his fellow students, become an agnostic. After Darwin's *Origin of Species* of 1859 and the subsequent flood of books pouring scorn on traditional cosmology there did not seem any choice.

The London Doyles had family solidarity, the consciousness that they, with their alien faith, had to keep together to combat the forces of infidelity that were sweeping the land. Thirty years before, Richard Doyle had resigned from *Punch* when it launched a savage attack on Roman Catholicism in England, and by putting principles before self-interest he established a line of conduct for his brothers and their families to follow. With Charles in a nursing home, there was no guarantee that Mary Doyle would keep Arthur to the straight and narrow. Charles had been unsuccessful, but he had not betrayed the true faith. However, it seemed that not only had Charles failed to make a name for himself in the great world outside Edinburgh, but had also failed in the attempt to inculcate his son in the ways of righteousness. To their horror, Conan Doyle told his aunts and uncles that he had lost his belief in Catholicism, and all thoughts of helping him in his career were stifled.

A chance was offered to him by a Dr Budd, whom Doyle had known slightly at the university and whom he had met since in Bristol, when Budd was already insolvent, hopes of taking over his doctor father's patients not having materialized. A telegram from Plymouth offering Doyle a job at £300 per annum was a certain bait. Budd claimed to have seen 30,000 patients in a year, with takings at more than £4,000. He did this, as Doyle soon found out, by packing the customers in and using the whole gamut of quackery, self-advertisement and reckless prescription of drugs, some of them useless, some of them dangerous, and some of them killers. His patients thronged his waiting-room, the staircase, with the overflow in the coach-house, while Budd carried out his performance.

There were hundreds of doctors like Budd who capitalized on the vulnerability of the poor and on the complacency of traditional medicine: young men who had emerged from medical school callous and self-centred without any other thought than to make a handsome living from the ignorant and frightened three-and-sixpenny public. They had their parallels among the upper echelons of doctors, who made a more than handsome living from the ignorant and frightened two-guinea public (and were not afraid to proclaim it).

In the early stages of their relationship it was easy for Budd to pull the wool over his colleague's eyes, but Doyle expressed his growing puzzlement to his mother, who advised him to break with Budd as their association would ruin her son's reputation. However, it was several weeks before Doyle did anything, and then it was on account of his carelessness (or Budd's unscrupulousness). Budd got hold of a letter from Mrs Doyle in which he was freely criticized, and he resolved to end the uneasy partnership by suggesting that Doyle went into practice on his own, towards which he would offer a pound a week.

Doyle had no option but to agree, though he found Budd amusing and his roguery comical – so much so that Budd occupied a central position in his 'novel' *The Stark Munro Letters*, which Doyle admitted was openly autobiographical. With less than £10 to his credit and the promise of a pound a week from Budd Doyle took a steamer from one naval port, Plymouth, to another, Portsmouth. On his first night in Portsmouth Doyle became involved in a street brawl when he tried to protect a woman who was being kicked by a rough.

He attacked the job of finding premises and setting up as a G.P. with commendable gusto, renting Bush Villa in Southsea for £40 a year plus rates, ordering £12 of ointments, powders, pills and tinctures, and spending about £4 on furniture – two small tables, three chairs, an umbrella-stand, curtains, a bed, a fender, a toilet set, a carpet and three pictures. Priority was given to the consulting-room, and Doyle camped out in the rest of the house, using a box as combined chair, table and larder. He cleaned his brass plate himself, cut down food to the minimum, and estimated that he could live on less than a shilling a day while he waited for his practice to build up.

No servants were possible on this kind of money, not even a £12 a year general maid, but his younger brother Innes was brought down to act as housekeeper/companion, while his mother sent down sheets, pillows and blankets. He was relying on Budd's pound a week, but instead he received a truculent letter from his one-time colleague declaring that his maid had cleared some torn papers from the grate and seeing mention of his name had taken them to Mrs Budd, who had stuck the pieces together and found one of Mrs Doyle's inimitable letters, referring to Budd as a bankrupt swindler. The prospect of a pound a week faded into the distance, but Mrs Doyle dug into her own scanty savings to replace the Budd money.

There was no steady stream of patients, and Doyle had a rooted abhorrence to using the system adopted by Budd, who gave free consultations but charged for medicine, whether it was needed or not. During the first six months Doyle lost a stone in weight, and was obliged to do business through barter, with an epileptic grocer who provided butter and tea for services rendered during and after a fit. When things were bad Doyle pawned his watch. Matters did improve sufficiently for him to bring in a housekeeper, and he went out to get custom, joining football clubs, bowling clubs, political and literary clubs, and cricket clubs. His prowess at sport, his captaincy of the

Portsmouth Cricket Club, his ruggedness on the football field, brought him in a class of patient which would never have visited him otherwise.

He was a man for all Portsmouth seasons, a big fish in a small pond, reading papers on Gibbon and Carlyle at the Portsmouth Literary and Scientific Society, keeping his name in front of the locals by letters to the editor in favour of vaccination and vivisection, and scoring goals and making runs – depending on the time of the year. His income went up, though not indexed to his popularity and his willingness to serve on innumerable committees. The first year he made £154, the next £250, and the following about £300. To give this figure some kind of reality, this was four times the wage of a skilled craftsman – a mason, a printer, a tailor or a carpenter, but it was not very near the figure which he told his mother he was aiming at – £1,000 a year. Even so he could keep a servant and support his brother Innes, and no longer needed to cut down on food and smoking.

The young, handsome doctor, penniless as he might be, was the target for Portsmouth match-makers, but although modestly susceptible he conducted himself in accordance with a respectable middle-class profession. His love affairs were in a minor key. There had been a Miss Jeffers, 'a little darling with an eye like a gimlet', and a Miss Welden, who weighed in at more than eleven stone, and who eventually went to Switzerland, but both before and during his Southsea period medical high jinks were not on the agenda. In 1885 brother Innes went off to public school.

Dr Pike, a colleague with whom Doyle had struck up a friendship, had in his charge a young boy who was suffering from cerebral meningitis. The mother was staying in a boarding-house where it was difficult to nurse her son, and Pike wondered if Doyle was interested in taking the patient in. Doyle agreed, and although the boy died he became acquainted with a sister, Louise, a quiet gentle girl, whom he married in August 1885, soon after receiving the degree of M.D. from the University of Edinburgh.

It was a comfortable rather than a passionate marriage, and, as Doyle related in his autobiography, 'there was no single occasion when our affection was disturbed by any serious breach or division, the credit of which lies entirely with her own quiet philosophy'. The union did not affect his considerable role in Portsmouth life, and throughout the ten years when she was well and the ten years when she was ill she remained very much a background figure. Her arrival brought some mitigation to his financial circumstances, as she had £100 a year in her own right.

Louise appealed to his protective instincts. Nicknamed 'Touie', she was a home-loving girl, with the round face, full lips and big eyes that painters such as Millais transmitted into the Victorian stereotype of maidenly modesty. She adored needlework and was fond of the custom of reading aloud together. As with all genteel girls, she played the piano, not well enough to be ostentatious but ably enough to be agreeable. The piano was bought on hire-purchase, and, as with most middle-class households, was a token of cultural respectability to Arthur, Louise and his mother-in-law, who moved in with them.

Notwithstanding his many public duties, Doyle found time to write. His metier was the adventure story, occasionally with a touch of the macabre and occult, but the stories brought him in no more than £50 a year. It was a pleasant hobby, but there did not seem much chance of writing providing more than back-up money. *London Society*, *All the Year Round* and *Boy's Own Paper* served as outlets for his apprentice work. His breakthrough had come in 1883 when *Cornhill* accepted a story, 'Habakuk Jephson's Statement', based on the *Marie Celeste* mystery, for which it paid twenty-nine guineas.

The young author was gratified by the reception of the story as a documentary, and it was convincing enough for it to be officially denied. However, unlike Byron, Doyle did not wake up one morning to find himself famous, and it soon appeared that the acceptance by the prestigious *Cornhill* was a flash in the pan, for the editor James Payn returned further effusions, though his writing was so notoriously bad that Doyle had difficulty in getting the gist of his rejections. *The Narrative of John Smith* was an early attempt at a novel, and was lost in the post on its first outing. In 1884 he began another novel, *The Firm of Girdlestone*, crammed with reminiscences of university days and something of a muddle, and although it did get into print eventually it was a book with which Doyle was never pleased.

In his *Some Literary Recollections* (1885) James Payn put his finger on the kind of book Doyle had written:

The proper construction of such a work comes by experience, and never by intuition: when a young writer attempts [a novel] he succeeds at best in writing a narrative and not a novel; he takes a character, generally more or less himself, and describes his career from the cradle to the altar, which he considers to be equivalent to the grave. It is, in fact, an autobiography of a person of whom no one has ever heard, and the only chance, therefore, of its success is that the incidents in the hero's life should be of a striking kind.

Almost as if he was going out of his way to confirm the truth of Payn's thumbnail sketch of a first bad novel, Doyle ended *The Firm of Girdlestone* with the hero and heroine 'going down the vista of the future, gathering wisdom and happiness as they go'.

With his interest in everything that was going on, from far-off colonial wars to the pros and cons of vaccination, it would have been remarkable if Doyle had not involved himself in the parlour occult – spiritualism. His first exposure to the movement that was eventually to rule his life was in Birmingham in 1880 when he went to hear an American medium, and he took it up again in Portsmouth, which was on the periphery of the circuit of the professional spiritualists and had its own trance medium in the person of J.Horstead, who somewhat unfortunately lived in Asylum Road.

J.Horstead was a run-of-the-mill medium whose main messages came from 'John Wesley', though occasionally Lord John Russell came through and spoke in glowing terms of Gladstone. It was Horstead's aim to bring home-bred spiritualism to Portsmouth, and he began a circle that numbered between thirty-five and forty. The circle languished after a year or two, and J.Horstead returned to the obscurity from which he had briefly emerged. So far as spiritualism was concerned, Portsmouth returned to the dark.

The main defect of Horstead and his colleagues was that they were tame. Nothing sensational happened at the meetings, and the general public demanded sensation and not polite exhortations, even if they were inspired. Mr Corsterphine of Glasgow, writing in the spiritualist periodical *The Two Worlds* in 1889, summed it up perfectly: 'Much of the success of the spiritual movement will depend upon the phenomenal – the people seem anxious for it. They have been lectured, preached to and at, and the literature has been scattered broadcast among them, but the cry is "Show us our dead!" '

In the 1880s, when Doyle began devoting some time to it, spiritualism had reached a feverish pitch. Although it was not realized at the time, the decade saw the decline of the more extravagant manifestations, and materializations, the hereafter made manifest through the agency of mediums, were not so numerous and not so impressive, simply because the spirit of enquiry was abroad. In 1882 the Society for Psychical Research was formed, and a fake medium might well find himself or herself held up to ridicule in its proceedings or journal. Uncovering bogus mediums was also a favourite hobby of newspaper reporters.

Seances could contain sceptical spies and *agents provocateurs*, and fraudulent mediums who had made a good living from working on the grief and susceptibilities of the bereaved could never be sure that they were not heading for a dramatic exposure. The Society for Psychical Research was very keen to sign up materialization mediums for investigation, but was disappointed. The only professional medium never detected in fraud, D.D. Home, had retired, and those remaining preferred to be found out by amateurs, went into retirement themselves or departed for Australia, where there was an eager gullible market for their wares.

The Society for Psychical Research turned its attentions from the more flamboyant aspects of spiritualism to surveys of hallucinations, poltergeist phenomena and extra-sensory perception, and in so doing built itself a reputation for probity and careful research. Doyle was an early member, and was influenced by its clear-sightedness and non-sensationalism, though his own inklings were towards the dramatic. It did not seem possible to get this without embracing the spurious as well.

During his time at Portsmouth Doyle became acquainted with a General Drayson, who held seances at his home. Doyle was invited to join in, and this he did, with a degree of caution. Drayson had been a teacher at the naval college at Greenwich and had reached 'certain conclusions regarding the movements of the earth that were at variance with recognized scientific traditions' (the words are those of the Rev. John Lamond, Doyle's first biographer). The medium at these seances was a railway signalman's wife, whose speciality was the production of apports, the sudden appearance of objects, preferably unlikely, such as the block of ice a foot long that appeared at a seance held by a celebrated medium, Mrs Guppy, in 1869.

The successful apport should be something that is patently not in the seance room, so that sleight of hand is ruled out. However, fraudulent mediums had many ways of introducing apports into their meetings, concealing fruit and such like beneath (if they were women) their voluminous clothing or in secret drawers in the table, trick guitars and other tools of the trade.

Doyle was sufficiently impressed by his first systematic foray into spiritualism that in 1887 a letter from him describing results obtained through a medium appeared in the spiritualist journal *Light*, and the tone was sufficiently constructive for F.W.H.Myers to contact him. Myers was a foundation member of the Society for Psychical Research, born in 1843, educated at Cheltenham and Trinity College, Cambridge, a poet and a man of wide culture. Like Doyle, he could lose his objectivity when his own interests were at stake, and the impetus that drove him into psychic research was the desire to be reunited with his dead lover. Nevertheless, within his limitations he was assiduous and painstaking, as can be seen in his monumental *Human Personality* with its hundreds of case histories and examples.

Myers asked Doyle if he would help in the researches being carried out by the society, but already Doyle's eyes were fixed on his future role, 'to break down the barrier of death, to found the grand religion of the future', as he wrote in the notebook he kept during his Southsea days. During this period he read widely in the copious literature of spiritualism and allied metaphysics. The *Reminiscences* of the American High Court Judge Edmunds seemed to Doyle 'an example of how a hard practical man might have a weak side to his brain'. But he was impressed by the number of reputable scientific men who had leapt into spiritualism. As he later wrote in *The New Revelation* (1918): 'When I regarded spiritualism as a vulgar delusion of the uneducated, I could affect to look down upon it; but when it was endorsed by men like Crookes, whom I knew to be the most rising British chemist, by Wallace, who was the rival of Darwin, and by Flammarion, the best-known of astronomers, I could not afford to dismiss it.'

Doyle was a great name-dropper, but was unable to differentiate between major names and second-raters, between men who were activated by purely scientific motives and those who had an ulterior motive. Sir William Crookes was in his fifties by the time Doyle became first interested in spiritualism, and had long risen, having discovered the metal thallium in 1865 and for years having pioneered electric lighting. Crookes was anxious to believe and was easily hoodwinked. It has been maintained that he deliberately allowed himself to be taken in because of his attachment to a young pretty medium, Florence Cook. 'As a believer Mr Crookes is all very well,' said the conjurer J.N.Maskelyne, 'as an investigator, he is a failure.' Alfred Russel Wallace was not the rival of Darwin, though he arrived at the theory of natural selection independently. He was a natural historian and only that, and lacked the insight and breadth of vision of Darwin. Camille Flammarion (1842–1925) was a popularizer of astronomy with quaint ideas, making his mark in 1862 with *The Plurality of Inhabited Worlds*. He and his kind were obsessively interested in the question of whether there was life on Mars, and Wallace entered into this controversy. Spiritualism was an umbrella movement that sheltered a lunatic fringe which fervently seized upon wild speculation and made it into fact.

The support given to spiritualism by Crookes, Wallace and Flammarion weighed heavily with Doyle. He looked up to them as founts of knowledge, not as human beings as fallible as anyone else, and he attacked those scientists who had come out against spiritualism with indignation, as though he personally had been insulted. 'Their action in this respect was most unscientific and dogmatic,' he complained.

Not all the Southsea seances encouraged Doyle to carry on investigating the hereafter. At one, a long and detailed message came through from a commercial traveller who had been killed in a recent fire at a theatre at Exeter. The spirit implored the sitters to write to his family who lived at a place called Slattenmere in Cumberland. Intensely excited, Doyle did as was asked, but the letter was returned, as he ironically admitted, through the dead letter office. This failure disgusted him, though it is curious that he confessed that he had not bothered to find out if there was a real place called Slattenmere.

A spiritualist clergyman known to Dr James Crichton-Browne had also received spurious messages, and had come to the conclusion that 'there must be lying spirits whose mission is to deceive mankind'. At one seance, he was requested to make a maiden lady living nearby 'more religious'. When asked why, the 'spirit' replied that she had just ten days to live and would die from 'ossification of the heart'. 'And the extraordinary thing', the clergyman told Crichton-Browne, 'is that the old lady is still alive and well ...'

Doyle asked General Drayson what he was to make of false and sometimes vicious messages, and the excessive banality of 'genuine' spirit messages. Drayson had a pat answer: 'Every spirit in the flesh passes over to the next world exactly as it is, with no change whatever. This world is full of weak and foolish people. So is the next. You need not mix with them, any more than you do in this world. One chooses one's companions.' One went to one's club, and shut out the low mean spirits. Victorian spiritualism was a mirror-image of Victorian materialism.

During his Southsea period Doyle was at a seance which impressed him sufficiently to recount it many years later. A 'Dorothy

Poslethwaite' was contacted, who allegedly had died in Melbourne five years earlier when she was sixteen. She had been at school with one of the seance sitters, and spelled out by tilting the table the correct name of the headmistress of the school. This struck Doyle as undeniable evidence, and he was willing to accept other information, that Dorothy existed in a sphere 'all round the earth', that she knew Mars was inhabited by an advanced race and that the Mars canals were artificial.

Although in later life Doyle claimed that he treated spiritualism in the Southsea days with objectivity and scepticism, it does appear that the seeds of conversion were being sown. The rejection of Catholicism had left a void which uneasy Deism could not fill. He was never flippant on the subject of spiritualism, unlike, for example, his former editor James Payn. Among his multitudinous jobs, Payn had a regular spot in the *Illustrated London News*, and in January 1894 he observed: 'It seems curious that a messenger from the other world – who, it must at least be granted, is not so common as a telegraph boy – should be despatched to us, in cases where there is no urgency, nothing important to be communicated and (one is sorry to be obliged to add) sometimes with false information.'

There were others who found a good deal of honest fun to be had out of spiritualism. In *Punch* in March 1906 there was a characteristic specimen under the heading 'Messages from the Spirit World':

Jones Tertius, happening, one day last week, to stand for a few moments in the passage outside the door of the Head's study, on the other side of which Tomkins Minor was engaged in a discussion with the Doctor on the propriety of appearing in afternoon school wearing an imitation high collar manufactured out of cardboard, heard a succession of resounding raps. In a subsequent conversation Tomkins Minor (who appeared broken by his experiences) said he hoped he might never visit the room again.

When rendering 'Dear heart, I only love thee' to a party of friends at her semi-detached villa in the Brixton Road, Miss Elizabeth Spinks was interrupted by loud raps on the division wall and in consequence completely broke down at the eighth bar ('Oh, could I gently whisper'). Miss Spinks has since removed to Balham, and she refuses to go near her former residence.

When fulfilling a Bridge engagement a few nights ago, a gentleman of moderate means, during the course of the game, heard mysterious raps, apparently coming from beneath the table, and slightly anterior to his opponent's declaration. The gentleman came away completely broken by his experiences. He refuses to go near the house now.

Long-winded as this is, it shows how *Punch* mirrored the opinions of the middle-class man in the street. The easiness with which spiritualism could be mocked encouraged believers to look inward, be secretive and regard their religion as a private cult. Certainly Doyle does not appear to have involved himself too deeply for some considerable time after he left Southsea, nor, despite the invitation of Myers, did he participate very much in the Society for Psychical Research.

There were other diversions and interests. There was sport, there was his practice – given a boost by his appointment as consultant to an insurance company – there were his literary evenings, there was his wife, and soon a daughter, and there was his writing. Despite setbacks and the accumulation of rejection slips, he persevered.

3
ENTER
SHERLOCK HOLMES

In the course of his voracious and indiscriminate reading, Doyle chanced to come across some detective stories. He found them nonsense, depending for any interest not on character nor the remorseless logic of events, but on the long arm of coincidence. If the plot was faltering the writer happily brought in a one-armed Chinaman or a mysterious lady in black. Doyle decided to try one himself. The first essential for the detective was an outlandish name, and Doyle picked out Sherrinford Holmes. Sherrinford was not quite right, and he was rechristened Sherlock. Ormond Sacker was even worse for the name of the narrator, and he was renamed Dr John Watson.

The first vehicle for Sherlock Holmes was to be entitled *A Tangled Skein*, but eventually this title was discarded and *A Study in Scarlet* substituted. When it was completed, Doyle sent it to Payn, editor of the *Cornhill*, for serialization. Payn told him that it was both too long and too short for his magazine, but Doyle did not lose confidence and the manuscript went first to Arrowsmith, then to Warne, and then to Ward, Lock & Co., which offered £25 for sole copyright.

It is surprising that Payn did not recognize the potential of *A Study in Scarlet*. Admittedly it was not stylish, but, as Somerset Maugham commented in his notebook for 1941, that really does not matter:

One fusses about style. One tries to write better. One takes pains to be simple, clear and succinct. One aims at rhythm and balance. One reads a sentence aloud to see that it sounds well. One sweats one's guts out. The fact remains that the four greatest novelists the world has ever known, Balzac, Dickens, Tolstoy and Dostoievsky, wrote their respective languages very indifferently. It proves that if you can tell stories, create characters, devise incidents, and if you have sincerity and passion, it doesn't matter a damn how you write.

28

Doyle's style hardly altered for forty years. He sat down and wrote, unworried by the hesitations and concern for literary propriety that make 'artistic' novelists of his time (such as George Moore) almost unreadable. He was never brainwashed by 'fine writing', whereas people like Payn, old literary hands who had been through the machine, were.

Payn himself was the worst kind of professional writer. Born in 1830, first in print in 1852 while still an undergraduate, he settled in the Lake District, contributing regularly to Dickens's weekly *Household Words* and *Chambers's Journal*. He moved to Edinburgh in 1858 to act as joint editor of *Chambers's*, and to London in 1861. His most popular novel, *Lost Sir Massingberd*, known jocularly as *Found Sir Missing Bird*, was serialized in *Chambers's Journal* in 1864, and in 1883 he took over the influential magazine *Cornhill*.

It was poetic justice that Payn in his reminiscences should have had a little quiet fun at the expense of those publishers' readers who had turned down books destined to be best-sellers. Not that there was any sign that Ward, Lock & Co. knew what they had acquired, for when Doyle wrote to ask if they could raise the offer they refused. The ultimate insult was to hold the book for a year and then push it out in *Beeton's Christmas Annual* at the end of 1887. Literature was a difficult oyster to open, Doyle had written to his mother. It did not seem that it was very nutritious, for Doyle had *The Firm of Girdlestone* going the rounds, and this novel did not seem likely to provide much money either. As he waited for *A Study in Scarlet* to appear he turned his attention to thoughts of a historical novel which would set him up as a serious novelist.

The publication of *Beeton's Christmas Annual* went unremarked, though the edition sold out and Ward, Lock & Co. proposed a second edition, perhaps illustrated by Doyle's father. Charles Doyle produced six black-and-white drawings, though he was not the ideal man to illustrate a modern novel, being always preoccupied with fairies, pixies and the creatures of nightmare. Nor did he have the fluent technique so evident in the work of the professional magazine illustrators, especially now that he was ill and old.

Having sold the copyright outright, there was no money in a second edition for Doyle, nor was there in an American edition. Absence of copyright laws meant that American publishers could select what English authors they liked without the annoyance of parting with money, and this state of affairs existed until 1891. Anthony Trollope, author of the Palliser novels, complained that he 'never got a farthing from the Americans, save £50 for *Ayala's Angel*'.

A Study in Scarlet may not be the best of Doyle's books, though some would claim it to be, but, considering what came later, it is perhaps his most important. Structurally it is a mess, with a centre section that is melodrama of the most off-putting kind. The basic plot was taken from Robert Louis Stevenson's *The Dynamiter*, published in 1885, and although the partial setting in America may have been responsible for the strong American interest, it was an America that only existed in Doyle's imagination. But it did not matter, for the novel bubbles with life from the time the sturdy Dr Watson seeks out his possible flat-mate.

Doyle began planning his historical novel, *Micah Clarke*, in July 1887. Narrated in the first person and set in the late seventeenth century, its centrepiece is the battle of Sedgemoor. It encouraged comparison with Blackmore's *Lorna Doone*, which also has the background of the Duke of Monmouth's rebellion, but whereas *Lorna Doone* is a pleasant romantic novel with historical accompaniments Doyle's intention was more serious – to be readably sociological and to write the definitive novel which, for some reason, Lord Macaulay had omitted to do. The inspiration was Macaulay. But Macaulay, though he had a penchant for *interpreting* fact to suit his own standpoint, did not *manipulate* fact to speed the story or add to the interest. Doyle's own opinion of what the seventeenth century was really like led him to distort the character of a historical figure, the Duke of Beaufort. One might as well write a historical novel dealing with the late nineteenth century in which Queen Victoria marries John Brown and Gladstone runs off with one of the prostitutes he rescued.

It was an early instance of Doyle knowing best, of his intuitive certainty that, as he put it in the preface, he, and only he, was vouchsafed information about the 'actual condition' of the England of the time. In a letter to his mother, Doyle wrote that *Micah Clarke* had taken five months to write, but two years to research. After its completion he approached Payn of *Cornhill*, who told him that he was wasting his time trying to synthesize fact and fiction, but Longmans were interested after Andrew Lang had given it a favourable report. *Micah Clarke* was published in 1889.

Doyle wrote in his autobiography that he 'fairly let himself go upon the broad highway of adventure' in *Micah Clarke*; the novel received a good deal of critical acclaim among those who found it delightfully old-fashioned in the manner of Stevenson, whose *Treasure Island* had appeared as a serial in *Young Folks* and in book form in 1883, and whose *The Black Arrow* (1888) had capitalized on the same market. Stevenson himself had deplored its 'tushery', having no doubt that it was a pot-boiler. Doyle saw *Micah Clarke* not as a capital adventure yarn but as a logical successor to the two historical novels he admired most, Reade's *The Cloister and the Hearth* and Tolstoy's *War and Peace*. Reade, declared Doyle, had 'collected his rough ore and ... then smelted it all down in his fiery imagination'. He went on to say that it was a good thing to have the industry to collect facts. 'It is a greater and a rarer one to have the tact to know how to use them when you have got them. To be exact without pedantry, and thorough without being dull, that should be the ideal of the writer of historical romance.'

The more destructive critics denied that Doyle had the tact to deal with facts, and threw up their hands with horror when he manipulated events to suit his purposes. B.A.Crackenthorpe, writing in the *Nineteenth Century* in 1895, might well have had Doyle in mind when he castigated historical novelists who 'without the inspiration of the giants, without their fine instincts for selection and rejection, follow them closely, dogging their footsteps, shadowing their movements in the crowded market-place, eager to learn where they acquire their materials and how they use them when acquired'.

In 1889 Doyle's daughter Mary Louise had been born, and the responsibility of having a family of his own to support placed him in a quandary. There were a number of options open to him. To carry on as a general practitioner; to specialize in some branch of medicine; to persevere in the vein of *Micah Clarke*; or to write entertainment fiction. The study of the eye he thought might prove profitable, though he had hopes of *Micah Clarke*, which, he wrote to his mother, should be an income in itself. *A Study in Scarlet* had not caused much of a stir, and there was no guarantee that a follow-up would do any better.

But the United States had seen in Doyle a writer to be cultivated, and in 1889 he was invited by the Philadelphia publisher Lippincott to write a successor to *A Study in Scarlet*. Over dinner at Greenwich, *The Sign of Four* was projected. It was here that Doyle met Oscar Wilde, signed up by Lippincott to write *The Picture of Dorian Gray*, a marvel of Victorian decadence and hothouse morality. Doyle and Wilde, the innocent and the knowing, in unlikely juxtaposition. And Doyle's cup was full when Wilde told him how much he had admired

Micah Clarke, the hearty heigh-hoing and hurtling bullets of which find few echoes in Wilde's own work.

Sherlock Holmes, now backed with US dollars, might do very well, but he was not a character who would make his creator a master author. Undaunted by the reservations of the critics of *Micah Clarke*, Doyle launched himself on another historical novel, *The White Company*, and this was followed fourteen years later by a sequel, *Sir Nigel*. In his autobiography Doyle commented that together 'they form the most complete, satisfying and ambitious thing I have ever done'. Once again, Doyle turned to Payn.

Payn, so unenthusiastic about the first Sherlock Holmes novel, agreed to publish *The White Company* in the *Cornhill*, recognizing that he had made a mistake about *Micah Clarke*, though quality was not of much interest to him, only what went down well with the general public. *The White Company* was more deeply researched than the earlier historical novel, and Doyle claimed in an interview in the *Bookman* in 1892 that he had read no less than 150 books in preparation, though one book, W. Longman's *Life and Times of Edward III* (1869), gave him most of the background information he needed. On its completion, he wrote in his autobiography: 'I knew in my heart that the book would live and that it would illuminate our national traditions.'

Heroic, chivalrous, the novel was a written equivalent of the Victorian historical picture, with ancient terms littered throughout the text to show that Doyle had done his homework; terms such as caitiff, devoir and jongleur, all in one sentence. Most of the critics did not think it would illuminate the national traditions. It was no doubt a capital yarn, but no more, suited to high-spirited youngsters, and Doyle was exasperated by the critics' obtuseness. 'They do not realize', he complained to his mother in November 1891, 'how conscientious my work has been.' It was some satisfaction to see that the English public was not put off by faint praise; the three-volume edition sold out, and more than fifty editions in one volume followed, proof that Doyle had found a formula.

1890 was an important year, but Doyle was still cautious, and in October he joined a number of English and European doctors in a trek to Berlin where Robert Koch, a bacteriologist, had found a wondrous cure for tuberculosis, the so-called lymph-innoculation cure. In 1883 Koch had gone to Egypt and India in search of the cholera germ; he had found it, and a grateful government rewarded him with £5,000. Koch was something of a *prima donna*, and Doyle was unable to get near him. He had obtained a commission from W.T.Stead to do a pen-portrait of Koch for his *Review of Reviews*, but it seemed that his journey was a waste of time and only the help of an amiable American enabled him to form for himself a cogent picture. Doyle came out against Koch; the whole thing was experimental and premature, he told the *Daily Telegraph*, and it turned out that he was correct.

On the train to Berlin Doyle had spent a good deal of time chatting with a Harley Street skin specialist, Malcolm Morris, who told him that he was wasting his time in Portsmouth and that London was the place to be. He advised Doyle to study the eye for six months in Vienna, and then set up in London, where he would have sufficient patients, lead an enjoyable social life, and still have time for literature.

The vision stimulated him. His mother thought the change would be for the better, and there was no difficulty winding up the practice, too small to sell and therefore pointing up the fact that as a general practitioner Doyle was a failure. The Portsmouth Literary and Scientific Society gave him a farewell dinner. It, and the sportsmen who found Doyle a welcome addition to any team playing any sport, were sorry to see him go. Although Doyle was now in his thirties, he still set great store by the views of his mother, recognizing that his wife would never have the worldly wisdom or insight to make a judgement on his career. He could trust his mother; she had willingly put her son's welfare ahead of her own, or even her husband's, as when she refused to let Doyle be taken over body and soul by the Catholic Church at school. Only in her last years – she died in 1921 – did Mary Doyle refuse to sponsor her son, and that was after he had become a spiritualist.

The young daughter was left with her grandmother, and Doyle and his wife made for Vienna, arriving there on 5 January 1891. Although he had acquired some German during his later schooldays, the Jesuits had not included in their curriculum the technical terms needed for the study of the eye, and Doyle soon found himself out of his depth. He was more interested in selling a story he had written to pay for the Vienna trip, 'The Doings of Raffles Haw', a feeble yarn about modern alchemy.

The Doyles enjoyed skating, Viennese society, and the glittering decadence of the Austro-Hungarian Empire, but 'The Doings of Raffles Haw' did not raise sufficient cash for the hoped-for six months' stay. They were back in England, travelling via Venice, Milan and Paris, within three months. They took rooms in Montague Place, and for £120 a year Doyle obtained the use of a front room and part use of a waiting-room for an anticipated practice at 2 Devonshire Place. It was a practice that did not materialize.

The White Company was running in the *Cornhill*. Research and tact with facts were seeming to pay off. Meanwhile the two Sherlock Holmes novels were sleepers. The much-vaunted research and care that had gone into his historical novels were not in evidence there; and they were not needed. The clumsy structure, the almost criminal carelessness, the off-hand quality of some of the writing were unimportant. Doyle had done more than find a formula – he had popped a needle into the vein of the public, introducing an antibiotic against the ills of the *fin de siècle*. He gave the reading public an archetype, a hero figure who was absolutely new and unique, far removed from the hearties and vainglorious oafs with which he had peopled his 'serious' novels. It is now traditional to regard Sherlock Holmes as a real person, Dr Watson as his Boswell, and Doyle as a somewhat tiresome in-between, part stenographer, part literary agent. Holmes made Doyle uneasy; he had created a monster who was more real than himself, though this was not immediately apparent. It has become more evident as the years have gone by, as *The White Company* and associated historical bygones gather dust on the shelves of second-hand bookshops.

The contradictions and confusions contained in the Sherlock Holmes saga have been the cause of much scholarly amusement on the part of the Sherlockians. Though *A Study in Scarlet* and *The Sign of Four* were written in quick succession, it seems remarkable that a young author setting out on a career should not at least have reread his manuscripts and ironed out any discrepancies. One of the most careless errors concerns Dr Watson's celebrated wound. In *A Study in Scarlet* he is 'struck on the shoulder by a jezail bullet, which shattered the bone'. In his first meeting with Watson, Holmes observes that Watson's left arm has been injured, and 'he holds it in a stiff and unnatural manner'. In *The Sign of Four* Watson refers to his wounded leg, through which he has had the self-same jezail bullet (a jezail is a long and heavy Afghan musket). 'Though it did not prevent me from walking, it ached wearily at every change of the weather.' Subsequent stories locate the wound in the leg, though Holmes speaks of a 'damaged *tendo Achilles*'. By the time of *The Hound of the Baskervilles*, the wound causes no more trouble. Watson is a fair runner, and 'reckoned fleet of foot'.

There was also confusion about Holmes's waking day. *A Study in Scarlet* gives him regular habits: 'It was rare for him to be up after ten at night, and he had invariably breakfasted and gone out before I rose in the morning.' By the time of *The Hound of the Baskervilles*, not only Watson's wound has vanished but Holmes is 'usually very late in the mornings'. *A Study in Scarlet* makes Holmes an ignoramus about philosophy and literature. Later Holmes speculates endlessly on philosophy and philosophical systems, and quotes from the most obscure of authors. In *The Sign of Four* Holmes asks Watson who Thomas Carlyle was; subsequently he pontificates at some length on the dour Scots philosopher, learnedly assessing his connection with Richter. From not knowing anything about the solar system, Holmes later discourses on the most erudite of astronomical topics.

Strongly characterized as were Holmes and Watson, subsidiary characters are not so consistent, as if Doyle could not remember what they looked like, as if they were mere props. One of the most permanent of these minor personalities is Inspector Lestrade, present in thirteen of Holmes's cases. Introduced in *A Study in Scarlet* as a 'little sallow, ratfaced, dark-eyed fellow', he is transformed in *The Hound of the Baskervilles* into a 'small wiry bulldog of a man'. He also has, like many of Doyle's characters, a limp, provided so that Holmes can spot his footprints amidst a host of others. Although the physical requirements for a Victorian policeman were not too rigorous, there was little scope for a small man with a limp.

There can be few writers of stature who have been so casual about their characters (even to Mrs Watson calling her husband 'James' when everyone knows his name is John), and if Doyle had had a clear picture in his mind of Lestrade when he invented him, what caused such an astonishing lapse? If he wanted, for the purpose of the plot, a detective with the qualities of a wiry bulldog it would have been more logical, and no disadvantage to the story-line, to bring in a policeman with a different name.

Only in retrospect were such contradictions noticed, for at the time it was believed that *A Study in Scarlet* and *The Sign of Four* were routine productions of no great consequence. The class of reader who bought such books would be looking for an easy read. Not for them puzzlement that a doctor should be so ignorant of poisons that he would let Holmes speculate that the pills that killed the villain of *A Study in Scarlet* contained 'South American arrow poison', presumably curare, which is harmless taken internally.

Then there is the curious business of Watson's dog, a bull pup, which could be either a young bulldog or a bull terrier. When Holmes and Watson are discussing whether they can tolerate each other's habits, Watson mentions that he has a pet. Holmes does not object, but perhaps Watson has mystic insight into Holmes's sensitive temperament, for the pup is never mentioned again.

But, as Somerset Maugham said about style, consistency did not matter. Doyle did not write for learned snail-watchers who would build a hide about each contradiction, and chatter to each other over their latest findings. There may be some uncertainty about Holmes's habits, but there is a commendable zest and certainty in building up the picture of the individual himself. Doyle did not baldly state that Holmes was a man apart, but demonstrated it. Early in their acquaintance, Watson records Holmes's dicta on the acquisition of knowledge:

You see, I consider that a man's brain originally is like a little empty attic, and you have to stock it with such furniture as you choose. A fool takes in all the lumber of every sort that he comes across, so that the knowledge which might be useful to him gets crowded out, or at best is jumbled up with a lot of other things, so that he has a difficulty in laying his hands upon it.

This is not a particularly novel sentiment, but how directly Doyle, through the mouth of Holmes, states it. Shortly afterwards Holmes reveals his methods, through the somewhat unbelievable medium of an article called 'The Book of Life' in a magazine: 'From a drop of water a logician could infer the possibility of an Atlantic or a Niagara [could he?] without having seen or heard of one or the other. So all life is a great chain, the nature of which is known whenever we are shown a single link of it.' He goes on from the general to the particular: 'By a man's fingernails, by his coat-sleeve, by his boot, by his trouser-knees, by the callosities of his forefinger and thumb, by his expression, by his shirt-cuffs – by each of these things a man's calling is plainly revealed.' Watson describes the article as twaddle, and for the first time Holmes reveals to him his profession, though he draws a specious distinction between the consulting detective (himself) and the government (presumably the Metropolitan Police) and private detectives.

Doyle may have slipped up in detail, but never with the spirit of place. Although his knowledge of London in 1886 was no more than that of the occasional visitor, his accuracy in drawing the decaying inner suburbs showed that he had taken in the essence of such places, perhaps bolstered by his knowledge of the London equivalents in Portsmouth and, above all, Birmingham. Number 3, Lauriston Gardens, was the archetypal seedy setting. It 'wore an ill-omened and minatory look. It was one of four which stood back some little way from the street, two being occupied and two empty. The latter looked out with three tiers of vacant melancholy windows, which were blank and dreary, save that here and there a "To Let" card had developed like a cataract upon the bleared panes.'

The description, terse and unsensational, is as explicit as a Victorian wood engraving, and throughout the first section there is no hint of overwriting, no forced purple passages, the customary defects of first novels (though it must be remembered that *A Study in Scarlet* was preceded by the mysterious novel about Mr Smith that was lost in the post). Certainly his apprenticeship in short stories helped him to keep his matter trimmed to the bone, and his models encouraged brevity – Bret Harte and Stevenson.

There is not much detecting in *A Study in Scarlet*. Holmes deduces that Watson is a military man who has seen service in Afghanistan, that a visitor is an ex-sergeant of the Royal Marines and that a cab and not a carriage was at the scene of the crime, but one of the minor feats is more impressive because it occurs in passing. On the wall of the murder house the word RACHE is scrawled in red. The police jump to the conclusion that this was destined to be RACHEL, the writer being interrupted in his work. Holmes believes that it is *Rache*, German for revenge, a blind 'to put the police upon a wrong track'. 'The A, if you noticed, was printed somewhat after the German fashion. Now, a real German invariably prints in the Latin character, so that we may safely say that it was not written by one, but by a clumsy imitator who overdid his part.'

This was to become the kind of classic clue for detective-story writers of the following generation, but at the time it seemed very novel, ingenious without exceeding the bounds of probability. Verisimilitude in detail helped the reader to overlook some of the wilder flights of fancy. To trap the murderer, Holmes puts an advertisement in the newspaper, and the bait is taken, but by 'a very old and wrinkled woman' who hobbled into the apartment, dropped a curtsy, blinked with 'her bleared eyes'. She is not what she seems, but a young man in disguise. Somehow he managed to convince the eagle-eyed detective that he was a woman, standing an arm's length away, without benefit of theatrical lighting or professional make-up in 'the sudden blaze of light'.

The ability of a person to disguise himself or herself at will was one of the conventions taken over from earlier writers and dramatists, such as Shakespeare, and Doyle frequently made use of it for a plot twist or variation. In his last Sherlock Holmes novel, *The Valley of Fear*, the whole story turns on disguise. But in real life disguise is not so easy, and in particular the quick changes often demanded are impossible to carry out. Convincing make-up is not, as Doyle seemed to think, removed in a trice by a few deft movements with the wrist and a splash of water.

Throughout the gestation and production of the early work, Doyle did not conceal his preference for the historical novels. But he had a sneaking suspicion that there was a lot of mileage in Sherlock Holmes. It occurred to him that a single character, Holmes, running through a magazine series, would bind the reader to that particular magazine. Each instalment would be complete in itself, so that if a reader missed one issue it would not matter. For the first time he used an agent, A. P. Watt, and through him *Strand* received the short Sherlock Holmes story, 'A Scandal in Bohemia'. But before the legend is explored, it may be interesting to trace the antecedents of 'the first consulting detective'.

4
DETECTIVES
AND DETECTION

The word detective was coined in 1843, but he existed long before then in fact and fiction. There is detection of a type in the Bible, and in *Zadig* (1747) Voltaire allows the title character to deduce that a missing bitch recently had puppies, limped in the left foreleg, and had long ears. A missing horse was five feet high, with small hooves, a tail three and a half feet long, and was shod with silver shoes. Zadig had not seen the bitch or the horse, and was flogged for his presumption, though he later told the uncomprehending how he had come to these conclusions – the teats and ears of the bitch dragging in the sand, the horse brushing off leaves at five feet, the tail wiping away dust at three and a half feet. Marks on the stones gave him the data about the shoeing. Voltaire had taken the fragment of deduction from a romance published thirty years before.

William Godwin's *Caleb Williams* (1794) has detective-story elements with the planting of clues by the villain to incriminate someone else (a knife found in the innocents' lodgings, the broken blade of which fits a piece left in the stab-wound of a murdered man). The *Mémoires* of Eugène Vidocq were published in 1828. Vidocq was the son of an Arras baker, whose till he frequently robbed, served in the army, was an acrobat and was sentenced in 1796 to eight years in the galleys for forgery. He escaped, joined a band of highwaymen, whom he betrayed to the authorities, and then became a police spy, in which role he was so useful that when a Brigade de Sûreté – *sûreté* means security, warranty, precaution, and is not a French equivalent of Scotland Yard – was formed in 1812 Vidocq was made its chief. He was suspected of organizing the burglaries he solved so brilliantly, and was dismissed from office. He started a card index system, and was one of the first policemen to take impressions of footprints. He was also skilled in disguise, and this gave the idea that it was easy to change one's appearance at will with the minimum of trouble and the maximum of effect. As an old man Vidocq visited London; his ability to present himself in a form unlike his natural self was illustrated by a comment in *The Times* that his height was five feet ten inches 'when perfectly erect', whereas his true height was five feet six.

Vidocq was a powerful influence on French crime fiction and popular sensational novels, and Eugène Sue and Dumas both picked up hints from him for their various purposes, though Vidocq's main claim to fame is his impression on Edgar Allan Poe (1809–49), who, in five short stories, laid down the framework of the detective story and created many of the fixtures and fittings. Doyle's debt to Poe is incalculable, and he admitted it. 'You want strength, novelty, compactness, intensity of interest, a single vivid impression left upon the mind,' he commented in his *Through the Magic Door* (1907). 'Poe is the master of all.' These are the five qualities so much in evidence in the Sherlock Holmes short stories.

T.S. Eliot also admired Poe, but with reservations. 'The variety and ardour of his curiosity delight and dazzle: yet in the end the eccentricity and lack of coherence of his interests tire.' Poe called these stories 'tales of ratiocination'. The best known is perhaps 'The Murders in the Rue Morgue' (1841), a locked-room mystery in which the murders are committed by an orang-outang. It is not so far removed from *The Sign of Four*, where the murderer is a pygmy, no larger than a child, as agile as a monkey. And the echoes continue into the short stories, into 'The Speckled Band', a locked-room mystery where a window is replaced by a ventilator, and an orang-outang is replaced by a snake.

Poe's brain, continued Doyle, 'was like a seed-pod full of seeds which flew carelessly around'. The detective stories were 'admirable ... so wonderful in their masterful force, their reticence, their quick dramatic point'. But he only gives full marks to 'The Murders in the Rue Morgue' and 'The Gold Bug'. 'The Gold Bug' is a puzzle story, in which the interest centres around the decipherment of a code on a piece of paper left by the pirate Captain Kidd. Poe's hero did this by reference to the fact that the most common letter in the English language is the letter 'e'. In one of the most closely reasoned of the Sherlock Holmes short stories, 'The Dancing Men', Doyle uses the same means of solving a code. 'As you are aware,' says Holmes, 'E is the most common letter in the English alphabet and it predominates to so marked an extent that even in short sentences one would expect to find it most often . . . But now came the real difficulty of the inquiry. The order of the English letters after E is by no means well-marked, and any preponderance which may be shown in an average of a printed sheet may be reversed in a single short sentence . . .' Doyle ingeniously tackles the problem by having the code delivered to Holmes in short sections. One message contains five symbols, of which two are decidedly 'e's, and he finally breaks the code by a process of elimination.

The most influential of all Poe's stories was 'The Purloined Letter', probably published in 1844. This is a document of tremendous importance stolen from the usual unnamed royal personage. There is a suspect, but because he is a minister he cannot be arrested off-hand, and his apartments have to be searched in secret. Eventually Poe's detective hero Dupin is called in; he sees the document immediately, in full view, soiled and crumpled, so obvious that the police have ignored it. It is the kind of paradox that detective-story writers were to love, from G. K. Chesterton to Agatha Christie, who in *The Murder of Roger Ackroyd* had the narrator as murderer.

Surprisingly, Doyle did not specifically mention 'The Purloined Letter'. It decidedly did not come in the class of Poe stories that Doyle was unhappy about, in which perspective and proportion were lost and horror and weirdness predominated. But here, also, Doyle took many of his themes from Poe. His most powerful and striking Sherlock Holmes tales are those where there is an element of the awful and a hint of the supernatural, for instance the spectral creature in *The Hound of the Baskervilles*. Doyle, in the Holmes stories, never crosses into the supernatural, but only suggests it; Poe was not so cautious, and his terrors do not yield, as they do in Doyle, to rational explanation, though he could be as adept at times, as in 'Thou Art the Man': the rotted corpse of a murdered man sits up in a makeshift coffin and says to the murderer 'Thou art the man'. In this case the corpse has whalebone rammed down his throat, and is doubled up into a case the spectators believe contains wine. When the top is opened the corpse seems to sit up, while the voice is supplied by ventriloquism. Doyle never did anything quite like this, but at no time did he ever pretend that the macabre side of Poe's talent had no influence on him. His work, Doyle recounted, 'turns the thoughts too forcibly to the morbid and the strange'.

One of Poe's main legacies to Doyle was in the relation of the hero to what was going on around him. Dupin, no matter how curious or horrific the circumstances are, is cool and collected. So is Holmes, on all occasions, though he becomes quietly excited when he is on the trail. He is an outsider, unaffected by girlish sentiment, his vision and senses unblurred, while his clients sob and sweat all around him, falling apart in panic or despair. Not that Holmes admires Dupin (it was subtle of Doyle to have one fictional character commenting on another one, and by doing so making them both seem real).

In *A Study in Scarlet* Holmes explains to Watson that he knows all about him from observation. 'You remind me of Edgar Allan Poe's Dupin,' says Watson. Holmes is displeased: 'Now, in my opinion, Dupin was a very inferior fellow. That trick of his of breaking in on his friends' thoughts with an apropos remark after a quarter of an hour's silence is really very showy and superficial. He had some analytical genius, no doubt; but he was by no means such a phenomenon as Poe appeared to imagine.'

Holmes was no more complimentary to Lecoq, the brainchild of Émile Gaboriau (1833–73), who did much to popularize courtroom drama and the cut-and-thrust of accused and accuser. Lecoq was a master of disguise and a shrewd observer, but unlike Dupin and Holmes he was part of the system, an instrument of law and order and not an amateur. The private detective was an Anglo-American convention, though still rare enough. When Dickens or Wilkie Collins wanted a detective in their fiction they preferred an official one, such as Inspector Bucket in *Bleak House* (1853) or Sergeant Cuff in *The Moonstone* (1868), both based on real-life detectives, Inspector Field and Inspector Whicher. Bucket is a sympathetic plodder, the kind of policeman later to be used with relish as a butt for the amateur, but in Sergeant Cuff Collins created a type of character whose appearance in a later detective story would have been a puzzle. He had the look and the habits of one of the perennial amateurs:

A grizzled elderly man so lean that he looked as if he had not got an ounce of flesh on his bones in any part of him. He was dressed all in decent black, with a white cravat round his neck. His face was as sharp as a hatchet, and the skin of it was as yellow and dry and withered as an autumn leaf. His eyes, of a steely light grey, had a very disconcerting trick, when they encountered your eyes, of looking as if they expected something more from you than you were aware of yourself. His walk was soft; his voice was melancholy; his long lanky fingers were hooked like claws.

Collins not only created a new kind of detective, but he also adapted traditional fiction forms for the new genre. 'The Biter Bit' is a witty and succinct detective story told in the form of police reports and letters passing between an inspector, a sergeant and a new detective recruit. This was published in 1859, and in Dickens's periodical *Once a Week* of 1862 a novel by Charles Felix called *The Notting Hill Mystery* was serialized, also told in the form of letters and reports with an insurance investigator as narrator.

The 1860s also saw the Irish horror-story writer Sheridan Le Fanu trying his hand at a puzzle novel in *Wylder's Hand* (1864), but no one had really succeeded since Poe in making the detective story not only interesting but gripping. Even such a sterling story as 'The Biter Bit' was merely readable, a way of passing half an hour. Excellent as it is, *The Moonstone* has too little detection, though the theme of a stolen jewel was to serve as a staple not only for Doyle but for his hosts of imitators.

There were murder mysteries in abundance, the blood and thunders poured out from the cheap presses for a barely literate working class, and the hardly more interesting specimens in the weeklies and monthlies. In 1865 the anonymous *Mystery of the Bloody Hand* came out in *London Society*, in which the murderer hacked off the victim's hand. The most likely person is accused, but the appearance of a phantom hand to the heroine leads her to its burial place beneath the true murderer's barn. *Found Dead*, an anonymous serial in *Chambers's Journal* in 1868, appealed solely to a subdued fascination with the gory. They were hardly more sophisticated than the penny dreadfuls – horror stories put out in penny parts – initiated in 1841 by Edward Lloyd, a newspaper proprietor, or the sadistic torture-ridden novelettes of G.W.M.Reynolds (1814–79), who also started his own newspaper, *Reynolds' News*.

Strenuous efforts were made to suppress sensation-seeking shockers, but it was mournfully realized that the public taste was far worse than was anticipated by those who were passionate for working-class literacy; Lloyd, and what was known as the Salisbury Square school of literature, gave mystery fiction unsavoury overtones, unless it was healthy outdoor adventure or associated with the occult. Bulwer-Lytton's *The Haunted and the Haunters* was thoroughly respectable, though it has many of the characteristics of a hack mystery story.

One of the barriers to the acceptance of crime fiction was the tendency in the earlier writers such as Gaboriau to glorify the criminal at the expense of society. In the magazine *Nineteenth Century* in 1881 John Ruskin wrote: 'All healthy and helpful literature sets simple bars between right and wrong.' Popular crime fiction had none of this lack of ambiguity. It was 'essentially Cockney literature, developed only in the London suburbs, and feeding the demand of the rows of similar brick houses, which branch in devouring cancer round every manufacturing town'.

Another factor that weighed against crime fiction was the power of the circulating libraries, in particular Mudie's, of New Oxford Street, started in 1842. Mudie was both distributor and censor, and he had a vested interest in the purity of the books he was purveying, for a lubricous book in the wrong hands could mean the cancellation of a subscription.

The nineteenth-century novel was expensive, and it often came out in three volumes. The first true three-decker was probably Scott's *Kenilworth* of 1821. Mudie was in favour of three-deckers, because a subscriber would have to take out three subscriptions in order to borrow a novel in its entirety. When there were books coming out, not to have read which was social death, the eager readers stumped up their extra guineas. The authors were anxious to oblige, for so powerful was Mudie that when the publisher Bentley approached Rhoda Broughton he offered her £750 for her novel *Second Thoughts* if it filled two volumes, but £1,200 if it made three. When another woman novelist, Adeline Serjeant, presented Bentley with *The Story of a Penitent Soul* there was only sufficient material for a one-volume book. Nevertheless, the book was set in print, but when the circulating libraries refused to have anything to do with it the printing was brought to an abrupt halt. Only when Miss Serjeant agreed to issue the work in two volumes did the libraries relent.

To give some idea of the importance of Mudie's Select Library, it is interesting to see that Mr Mudie bought 1,000 copies of Mrs Henry Wood's *The Channings*. The second largest order came from W.H.Smith & Son – 104 copies.

No form of novel suffers so much from padding as the detective novel, and the terser the better. Even if a writer had the ability to carry out a long detective novel and had a niche for it in a serial form in magazines, the necessity of making the end of each instalment cliff-hanging destroyed any coherent and logical story-line. It was all right for a mystery novel to be chopped up in this way, but not for a detective novel.

In 1886 a hitherto unknown Australian writer, Fergus Hume (1859–1932), wrote a best-seller, *Mystery of a Hansom Cab*. Hume was born in England, educated in New Zealand where he studied law, and then went to live in Melbourne. He visited a local bookshop and asked which books sold most. He was told the detective stories of Gaboriau, and having bought all his books 'determined to write a book of the same class; containing a mystery, a murder, and description of low life in Melbourne'. The Australian publishers would not touch it, so Hume had it published at his own expense, selling the copyright for £50 to a syndicate called the Hansom Cab Publishing Company. This must have done very nicely, for within ten years it had sold 375,000 copies in Britain alone.

Doyle did not think much of it. It is 'one of the weakest tales I have read,' he wrote to his mother, 'and simply sold by puffing.' Hume wrote well over a hundred books, and was turning them out more than forty years after what he called 'Cab'. As late as 1920 a gathering of literary men considered it one of the four best detective stories of all time (the others were *The Moonstone*, Bentley's *Trent's Last Case* (1913) and *The Hound of the Baskervilles*).

If the authors of these books have anything in common it lies in the unashamed lack of realism. With the possible exception of Wilkie Collins, who had Dickens to inform him on such matters, they had no experience of police procedure and methods or acquaintance with crime and criminals. It has been said that the Sherlock Holmes stories have been recommended by budding police forces as essential reading to recruits in their detective departments, but even the most enthusiastic would hesitate to name Holmes as the typical sleuth, official or otherwise. To treat fiction as a text-book is to assume that Doyle anticipated certain techniques. In his preface to one of the reissues of *The Sign of Four*, Len Deighton draws attention to the fact that Holmes made his appearance before the publication of the classic *Criminal Investigation* by Hans Gross; but this is to overlook considerable material otherwise available and the fact that Gross's book was anticipated by the work of Alfred Taylor (1806–80), for forty-six years Professor of Medical Jurisprudence at Guy's Hospital.

Investigation techniques were by no means so elementary in the pre-Holmes period as is often thought. As we have seen, Vidocq pioneered the systematic examination of footprints, and fingerprints had long been used as methods of identification. In ancient times an impression of a monarch's thumb had established his credentials, and a relic of this is preserved in the formal confirmation of a legal document by 'delivering' it as one's 'act and deed'. In 1823 J.E.Purkinje read a paper before the University of Breslau, proving that fingerprints were permanent and advocating a system of classification. In India, Sir William Herschel wished to use fingerprints in the courts to prevent false personation, and the Bengal police, under the administration of Sir E.R.Henry, used fingerprinting for the detection of crime long before such methods were taken up in Europe. Sir Francis Galton wished to introduce fingerprinting, and pointed out that this was successfully done in the United States for the identification of Chinese immigrants. Galton wrote a book on the subject in 1892. The anthropologist Welker took impressions of his fingerprints in 1856 and 1897, proving that they do not change with age.

Perhaps fingerprints are the most obvious and widely publicized police method, and they are not mentioned often in the Holmes stories, though the plot of one of them turns on the use of an innocent man's fingerprints, obtained by asking him to put his finger on a blob of sealing wax for a perfectly respectable reason. Microscopy was more in Sherlock Holmes's line, but in his discoveries of the importance of identifying tobacco ash and other natural and unnatural substances he had long been anticipated: by for instance Dr Emil Pfaff, whose *The Hair of Man, Its Physiological, Pathological and Legal Importance* (1866) appeared more than twenty years before *A Study in Scarlet*, which allegedly heralded the scientific detective. The optical microscope itself reached a pitch of perfection during the Victorian period, with the introduction of the binocular microscope around 1860.

In his book on hair, Pfaff recounts a case in which the Holmes method was carried out with exemplary success. A man was wounded by an unknown assailant, who in flight dropped his cap. Upon examination, two hairs were found sticking inside the cap. They were light grey, but had a number of cells that were jet black, and from further examination the detective was able to put out a call for 'a man of middle age, of robust constitution, and inclined to obesity: black hair intermingled with grey hair, recently cut; commencing to go bald'.

The analysis of dust had reached extreme sophistication, and a passage from Gross's *Criminal Investigation* (which predates the Holmes *short* stories) might almost be from the mouth of Holmes himself:

The dust of the desert will contain little besides pulverized earth, sand, and small particles of plants; the dust of a ballroom, crowded with people, will in great measure proceed from the fibres from which the clothes of the dancers are woven; the dust of a smith's shop will be for the most part composed of pulverized metal; and that upon the books of a study nothing but the reunion of the particles of earth carried in on particles of paper. Examining more closely, we find that the coat of a locksmith contains a different kind of dust to that on the coat of a miller: that accumulated in the pocket of a schoolboy is essentially different from that in the pocket of a chemist; while in the groove of the pocket-knife of a dandy a different kind of dust will be found to that in the pocket-knife of a tramp.

It had long been recognized that experts should be called upon in case of need, not only chemical analysts but mineralogists, zoologists and botanists. The nineteenth century saw the introduction of many new poisons, and in the trial of Palmer at the Old Bailey in 1856 the forensic expert Taylor was brought in. The poison used was strychnine, not much known though first discovered in 1818. Dr Lamson used aconitine in 1882, while Dr Pritchard preferred the non-vegetable poison antimony. If experts were brought in, there was no problem determining the exact poison used, and in real life the police would have called in a professional rather than rely on a dilettante such as Holmes.

Several of the Holmes stories are concerned with handwriting and ciphers, and Doyle was no innovator here. As early as the seventeenth century Camillo Boldo had published a book on graphology, and in the eighteenth century an anonymous book was published in Paris with the title *The Art of Judging the Character of Men by Their Handwriting*. Ciphers and cipher-breaking had a long pedigree. The most obvious one – broken by Holmes in 'The Dancing Men' – the substitution of letters by other letters or symbols, is known as the Julius Caesar cipher. The most difficult to break, the 'multiplication' or 'square' cipher, was described as early as 1580 by Vigenère Blaise.

One of the most ingenious ways of transmitting secret messages is through playing cards. Each card bears a letter of the message, and the recipient has merely to arrange the pack in a prearranged sequence while the sender shuffles the pack after he has written his message. It is surprising that Doyle did not use this for a Holmes story, surprising because there is no doubt that he had thoroughly digested Gross's book on criminal investigation in which the playing card method is described. Those who know their Sherlock would immediately see that one of the firearm cases Gross describes in detail provided the entire plot of the late Holmes story 'Thor Bridge'.

Holmes sometimes accuses himself of stupidity when he fails to spot what to him (but no one else) is an obvious clue, but there is no evidence that he ever had any doubts about the scientific method (though he once chivalrously had a kind word to say about womanly intuition). Often he mocks the police for jumping to conclusions when they should have behaved more circumspectly, but forensic experts in real life were no less apt to use intuition as a substitute for knowledge. An interesting case occurred in 1851, the Norwich murder, where fragments of a woman's body were dispersed over the countryside. The bits were gathered together, and a doctor who reckoned he knew about such matters declared: 'The well-filled under-structures of the skin, its delicacy, the neatness of the foot, that of a person not accustomed to toil or to wear coarse heavy shoes, the clear well-trimmed nails of both hands, and feet, led him to fix her age between sixteen and twenty-six.'

Eighteen years later a Mr Sheward confessed to the murder of his wife. It was she he had killed and cut up. Her age had been fifty-four.

The aim of Doyle was not to write a primer on detective techniques, and although it is clear that he was not the originator of such methods, as is often claimed, his handling carries conviction. Doyle established the rooms in Baker Street and their contents, the firm relationship between Holmes and Watson, and the firm reality of the London of the 1880s and 1890s, with its butchers, bakers and candlestick-makers, the 'pale, taper-faced man with sandy whiskers' (Doctor Percy Trevelyan of 'The Resident Patient') and the 'smart young City man, of the class who have been labelled Cockneys' (Hall Pycroft of 'The Stockbroker's Clerk'). But except for a muddled entrance by a rival in one of the stories in *The Case-Book of Sherlock Holmes*, there are no more private detectives. Was Sherlock Holmes the only consultant detective in London?

Certainly he was the only one with a range of talents. There were agencies, such as one in Wych Street (where Aldwych now runs) with the telegraphic address 'Sleepless', but they were largely used in divorce cases, breach-of-promise cases, and in tracing missing persons, mostly on behalf of solicitors. In many cases, lawyers did their own investigating. The private detectives operated in the shadier areas of life, occasionally receiving publicity when a particularly juicy divorce case was reported in the newspapers. 'A person named Simpson' made his entry in one sensational divorce case.

There are few instances of official detectives running to the private opposition for help, and if there were able private detectives they would not have received the cooperation of the Metropolitan Police that so often fell to the lot of Holmes. The detective police were quite able to carry out their own investigations and bring the criminals to justice. The qualities looked for in a detective were

the vigour of youth, energy ever on the alert, robust health and extensive acquaintance with all branches of the law. He ought to know men, proceed skilfully, and possess liveliness and vigilance. Tact is indispensable, true courage is required in many situations, and he must be always ready on emergency to risk his health and life; as when dangerous criminals are to be dealt with, fatiguing journeys to be undertaken, persons stricken with infectious diseases to be examined, or dangerous post-mortems attended. He has moreover to solve problems relating to every conceivable branch of human knowledge; he ought to be acquainted with languages, he should know what the medical man can tell him and what he should ask the medical man; he must be as conversant with the dodges of the poacher as with the wiles of the stock jobber, as well acquainted with the method of fabricating a will as with the cause of a railway accident ... He should be able to pick his way through account books, to understand slang, to read ciphers, and be familiar with the processes and tools of all classes of workmen.

Thus the opinion of Gross. It was a lot to ask of any man.

In addition a good detective should build up a body of informers. This was crucial to the solving of crime, and had been since the Bow Street Runners, the 'robin redbreasts', had been formed. The New Police formed by Sir Robert Peel had rejected the Bow Street Runners and their mode of operation – secrecy, infiltration and the acceptance of 'blood money'. They were a somewhat corrupt detective force, as far removed from the police inspectors of Doyle's imagination as Holmes himself. For many years the New Police, known as the 'lobsters', the 'bobbies', the 'coppers', the 'peelers' and the 'crushers', had no detective police force, though in 1833 a Parliamentary Commission advised the setting up of a plain-clothes force of three inspectors and nine sergeants. Later six constables were brought in as 'auxiliaries'. Eventually there were 108 men in plain clothes in the Metropolitan Police out of a total force of 6,000. One of the earliest mentions of policemen in plain clothes was in 1845 in the Salt Hill murder near Windsor, in which the miscreant was caught by the use of the new-fangled telegraph.

There was no need for a finely honed sophisticated machine. There was a well-defined criminal class; after a crime had been committed the police looked around to see who was on 'ticket of leave' (a form of parole) and in most cases it was, all agreed, a fair cop. Much of the crime was petty, and could be solved by the most obtuse Sergeant Plod. There were clever criminals, and there was a love/hate relationship between the cream of the profession, the burglars, and the police. As distinct from a 'low thief', a burglar was known as a 'right man', a 'good man', a 'family man' and 'cracksman'. In France he was also elevated, as *la haute pègre*.

Sherlock Holmes came on the scene when the validity of the concept of the criminal type was being argued. This was largely an Italian theory, and its chief propagandist was Dr Lombroso. A criminal could be recognized by certain moral and physical traits – receding forehead, big jaw and projecting chin, asymmetrical skull, protruding ears, cold, glassy and ferocious eyes, good eyesight but defective senses of hearing and smell. The moral characteristics were vanity, stupidity and lack of conscience. It was too simple, and Britain was among the first countries to recognize the weakness of the system, which had arisen from the human desire to pigeon-hole threats to a shaky society.

Most sorts of crime feature in the Sherlock Holmes stories, provided that they are asexual (the jealousy stories have more in them of hurt pride). Crimes by professionals, unless executed by master criminals, are rare; there is little random violence, unlike real life. The murder cases are intricate; this became a dominant trend in detective fiction in which lesser crimes are ignored. Only a murder, preferably mysterious, could retain a reader's interest throughout a novel. Factual murders were less accommodating, as they were overwhelmingly sordid, matter-of-fact and emotional, offering an immediate suspect who in nine cases out of ten did the crime – a husband, a wife, a lover or a combination of these. A professional criminal who committed murder in the pursuit of his trade was an outsider, no longer a cracksman or a family man, but a common bungler.

For cases outside the ordinary there was a formidable body of expert help available, especially in the less emotional crimes such as forgery and fraud. Notwithstanding the advances of forensic science, a murderer who killed a stranger without a reason could stand a good chance of escaping judgement. The perfect murder became an obsession with later detective-story writers. But the Victorians, and the Victorian writers, wanted none of it.

5
HOLMES
TRIUMPHANT

Doyle owed the publication of his historical novels to the perspicacity of literary men who had a clear idea, as Ruskin had, of what constituted if not a good at least a respectable novel. The publication of his first two detective novels was due to chance. If he had turned down the contemptible £25 offered by Ward Lock, Sherlock Holmes might not have been projected into Baker Street. If the law of copyright had not been so full of holes the Americans would not have obtained *A Study in Scarlet*, and therefore Lippincott would not have had occasion to commission *The Sign of Four*. The publication of the Sherlock Holmes short stories was directly due to the acumen of George Newnes, a man who had started life in the fancy-goods trade. They did not need an Andrew Lang or a Payn to give them their blessing.

In 1712 a tax of a halfpenny per sheet was imposed on newspapers; in 1815, when the average price of a newspaper was sevenpence, it was fourpence a sheet. In 1855 the tax was finally repealed, and there came a flood of cheap newspapers. The introduction of wood pulp made for cheaper newspapers still, and between 1875 and 1885 the circulation of newspapers in England trebled. Machinery was introduced, and capital outlay was offset by previously undreamed-of circulation and advertisements. The evolution of the half-tone process to reproduce photographs also gave newspapers a new look though it was the weeklies that profited most from this innovation. Almost overnight, the weeklies began to look modern, though *Punch* did not condescend to make use of the half-tone process for ten years after it was generally introduced in 1882.

With massive circulations a new kind of journalism was needed to cater for an unknown public which did not have the same interests as, for example, the traditional reader of *The Times*. Liveliness and immediacy were more important than grace and cleverness, and the interview was introduced, in newspapers and in the weekly press. There was also an increasing interest in the woman reader. In 1880 the *Lady's Pictorial* was started, followed by *The Lady* (1885), *Woman* (1889) and the *Gentlewoman* (1890). News weeklies were already on the market. The *Illustrated London News* was founded in 1842, and new-comers could not expect to compete with it; a news weekly meant having correspondents abroad or expensively travelling and the use of profit-reducing agencies.

It was necessary to have a gimmick. George Newnes (1851–1910) found one when he started *Tit-Bits* in 1881, the first of a long succession of periodicals designed to amuse and instruct. The son of a Congregational minister, Newnes (knighted in 1895) began life in the fancy-goods trade, but seeing an unsuspected gap in the market he started a vegetarian restaurant in Manchester for the purpose of raising capital for his weekly. With the low cost of paper and printing, it was not difficult to get sufficient cash.

As the name implies, it was a compilation of snippets of the believe-it-or-not order, interspersed with crisp factual articles. It was chock full of information, carried jokes and puns, ran a lively correspondence column and competitions for prize tit-bits, and was the first periodical to insure readers against railway accidents. It was an immediate success, and encouraged Alfred Harmsworth to start *Answers to Correspondents*, soon known as *Answers*.

Answers and *Tit-Bits* provided pin-money for many writers who were just starting a career, including H.G.Wells, whose scientific background enabled him to ask suitably intriguing questions, to be duly answered a week or two later. Sometimes he was able to provide both the question and the answer, and so pick up a double fee.

Tit-Bits was the first outpost of the Newnes empire, and it gave him a stable base. In 1891 he began *The Strand Magazine*, modelled on the American *Harper's* and *Scribner's*, with a simple formula – a picture on every page, exciting stories, interviews with people in the news, and factual articles of the kind so much enjoyed by the readers of *Tit-Bits*. The first issue sold 300,000 copies, and this figure soon rose to more than half a million.

As H.G.Wells wrote in his *Experiment in Autobiography* (1934), 'the last decade of the nineteenth century was an extraordinarily favourable time for new writers and my individual good luck was set in the luck of a whole generation of aspirants'. Wells saw that the predominance of Dickens and Thackeray and their succesors and imitators was passing. 'For a generation the prestige of the great Victorians remained like the shadow of vast trees in a forest, but now that it was lifting, every weed and sapling had its chance, provided only that it was of a different species from its predecessors.'

The weeds and saplings enjoyed a favourable season, fostered by enthusiastic publishers – not only the school of Newnes but dilettantes like the Astor family who, wrote Wells, had 'a taste for running periodicals at a handsome loss'. It was the ideal time for writers such as Doyle. Greenhough Smith, the editor of *Strand*, was not only willing to consider work but touted for it, just so that a promising author would not be snapped up by a rival. It was through his agent that Doyle submitted his first Sherlock Holmes short story, 'A Scandal in Bohemia'. It was not one of his better stories, and there was little detection in it, but Smith liked it. Doyle contracted for a series of six at thirty guineas each; for a follow-up of six more he asked for fifty guineas each, and in the climate of the time he got it. He reckoned on writing 3,000 words a day – he could earn more in a couple of days than a working man could earn in a year.

A week after sending off 'A Scandal in Bohemia' he had completed 'A Case of Identity'. Ten days later he sent off 'The Red-Headed League', and a week later 'The Boscombe Valley Mystery'. That was 27 April. On 4 May he felt ill, and collapsed at home. It was a severe bout of influenza. Nothing concentrates the mind more than the possibility of death, and nothing clears it more than the prospect of getting better. He made his decision:

I determined with a wild rush of joy to cut the painter and to trust for ever to my power of writing. I remember in my delight taking the handkerchief which lay upon the coverlet in my enfeebled hand, and tossing it up to the ceiling in my exultation. I should at last be my own master. No longer would I have to conform to professional dress or try to please anyone else. I would be free to live how I liked and where I liked.

His apprenticeship in life had ended, and the boom years were beginning.

The response to Sherlock Holmes in *The Strand* was shattering, even to those who had recognized his potential, and it was not long before he was regarded as a real person. Visitors in trouble went to Baker

Street and sought, without success, number 221 B. Dr Watson, though known to be haphazard with dates, could surely not have made a mistake about his address? Probably it was thought that the bungler Doyle had made one of his silly transcribing errors. In one of the stories, Watson had let slip that 221 B Baker Street had a bow window, so hopefuls looked for a house with a bow window. There was none.

It was not the first time, nor the last, that a fictional personage had been regarded as real, though this illusion usually evaporated in the cold light of day when the book had been put back on its shelf. Dickens's characters were treated as real. Hardened critics sobbed when Little Nell died, and when Walter Savage Landor, the poet, read about her death he threw his cook out of the window.

Holmes, as described in *A Study in Scarlet*, had something of the lean-ness and bird-like qualities of Wilkie Collins's Sergeant Cuff. 'In height he was rather over six feet, and so excessively lean that he seemed to be considerably taller. His eyes were sharp and piercing, save during those intervals of torpor to which I have alluded; and his thin, hawk-like nose gave his whole expression an air of alertness and decision. His chin, too, had the prominence and squareness which mark the man of determination.' This terse and vivid description was sufficient for the *Strand* illustrator Sidney Paget, and his depiction of Holmes became authoritative in the same way that Tenniel promul-gated the definitive version of Alice in Wonderland. Doyle was not altogether happy about Paget's vision. In his autobiography Doyle saw Holmes as having 'a thin razor-like face, with a great hawk's-bill of a nose, and two small eyes, set close together on either side of it'. Although this gives the impression that Holmes had two sets of eyes, no doubt giving him exceptionally acute and stereoscopic vision, it is clear that Doyle considered Paget's version too pretty, though later, as in 'The Boscombe Valley Mystery', he went along with the more romantic image: 'His brows were drawn into two hard, black lines, while his eyes shone out from beneath them with a steely glitter. His face was bent downwards, his shoulders bowed, his lips compressed, and the veins stood out like whip-cord in his long, sinewy neck.'

The outdoor Holmes was different from the indoor Holmes. At times he seemed a parody of the aesthete, and at a concert described by Dr Watson he behaved in a manner that must have intensely irri-tated his neighbours: 'Gently waving his long thin fingers in time to the music, while his gently smiling face and his languid, dreamy eyes were as unlike those of Holmes the sleuth-hound, Holmes the relentless, keen-witted, ready-handed criminal agent, as it was possible to conceive' ('The Red-Headed League').

Doyle was no music-lover, and he was describing the manner in which he thought a music-lover reacted to music. In this respect, he was the plain man, at one with his readers who looked on classical music with a mixture of awe and contempt, prevented by innate prejudice from enjoying it. The aim of Doyle was to indicate that Holmes's tastes were rarefied and not of the common order. He did this clumsily, and was high-faluting in the worst possible way. When Doyle was asked about music in 1920 for the purpose of a symposium in *John O'London's Weekly* he was both arrogant and defensive: 'Most music annoys me – especially in restaurants and other inappropriate places. I always feel that there is music which would move me greatly, but I never quite seem to get it. Yet I have an average ear and a good memory for music.'

The aesthetic element in Holmes was also hammered home by the references in the early Holmes stories to his use of narcotics, particularly cocaine. It was an understood thing that the aesthetes took drugs, but in the 1890s it was not realized that addicts could be hooked. A taste for cocaine was an expression of the aesthetes' desire to be different, to increase their sensibilities and to demonstrate their superiority to the common herd. Drug-taking was not so heinous as it was later to be, and few looked askance at Coleridge's and De Quincey's use of laudanum or Rossetti's addition to chloral hydrate.

Doyle probably selected cocaine as Holmes's drug because it was novel and mysterious, introduced into medical practice in 1884 by the Austrian oculist Köller. It was superior to morphine, which Holmes also took, because it was only used by top people, unlike morphine which had been extensively used in China to wean the opium-smoking population, estimated at thirteen million, from their disgusting habit (the result was to create a nucleus of morphine addicts). The new 'non-addictive' drug heroin was not widely known at the time, and Doyle's ignorance on this score probably prevented Holmes taking up heroin.

Whereas a cocaine addict was interesting, an opium addict was wretched and carried no kudos. When Watson visited an opium den in the East End in 'The Man with the Twisted Lip' and found Holmes there in disguise there is no record that he had any passing thoughts that Holmes was extending his tastes. The opium den itself was a stereotype, later to be a stock in trade of Edgar Wallace, in which the addicts sit around in curious attitudes like participants in a charade. Watson, and Doyle, thought that opium-smoking was a simple matter of putting opium into the pipe and puffing away, whereas the addict has to go through a complicated procedure to make the opium smokable. On this occasion, Holmes pre-empted Watson: 'I suppose, Watson, that you imagine that I have added opium-smoking to cocaine injections and all the other little weaknesses on which you have favoured me with your medical views.'

Doyle was often asked on whom Holmes was based. He always expressed his debt to Poe's Dupin, and also to Dr Joseph Bell of Edinburgh, born in 1837. Bell was both flattered and surprised when this became known to him, and he sent Doyle ideas for plots which were not, Doyle admitted, very practical. Bell considered that Doyle's medical education had taught him to be observant. In his autobiography Doyle illustrated Bell's methods, identical with those of Holmes. A civilian patient visited Bell, and the doctor reasoned that the man had been an N.C.O. in the army, was recently discharged, had been in a Highland regiment, and had been stationed in Barbados. It was magic to the man, but Bell explained all to his students. Although respectful, the man had not removed his hat. Had he been out of the army some time he would have relinquished this army habit. He was clearly Scottish, and had therefore been in a Highland regiment (not necessarily – he could easily have been in the Royal Artillery, the Royal Engineers, or in one of the many non-combatant corps such as the Land Transport Corps). An air of authority in a person clearly of the non-officer class made him an N.C.O., while as his complaint was elephantiasis Bell decided that this fitted in with service in the West Indies (the disease can be known as Barbados leg).

Again, as with service in a Highland regiment, this was assumption rather than deduction. Elephantiasis is a tropical disease not restricted to the West Indies. The Doyle anecdote implies that the analysis was carried out on the man's entrance (he had his hat on). Yet elephantiasis rarely attacks the parts of the body on view, hardly ever the face, often the legs and the scrotum. If it were the scrotum, it seems most indelicate of Bell to draw attention to it while showing off his acute observation. This confusion between assumption and deduction marks many of the Sherlock Holmes stories; it is only deduction if the reader can be made to believe that it is, by suspending his critical faculties.

There is no way of finding out whether the anecdote concerning Dr Bell is authentic or whether Doyle was recreating the kind of question and answer method that he remembered from his days as a medical student. Other than Bell, the character Holmes most resembled was Sergeant Cuff in Wilkie Collins's *The Moonstone*. Doyle had read Collins, and had compared him with Gaboriau. The theme of the stolen jewel was repeated in *The Sign of Four*. Collins had not capitalized on his creation of Sergeant Cuff; without a platform such as *The Strand* there was no point in it.

Most fictional characters are taken for what they are – inventions of the author based on memories, unconscious and conscious, of people known, seen or read about. Sherlock Holmes, even when it was accepted that he did not exist, seemed more real than most other creatures of fiction, and Doyle offered bait by assigning a provenance. If he was so annoyed by others taking an inordinate interest in Holmes, he was partly to blame, both decrying and fostering the myth.

There is little doubt that Holmes possessed characteristics that Doyle had, and was given a social background not dissimilar to that of Doyle. Holmes also had characteristics that Doyle would have liked to have had. Holmes was almost always right. Doyle often *thought* he was right, when he was merely being a conventional middle-class Victorian, just, in fact, like Dr Watson. There is a good deal of Doyle in Dr Watson, and when he was deploring the extravagant attention paid to Holmes Doyle tended to upgrade the patient, kindly Watson, though in a backhanded way. 'In the course of seven volumes,' he reminisced in his autobiography, '[he] never shows one gleam of humour or makes one single joke,' adding shrewdly: 'To make a real character one must sacrifice everything to consistency.'

There was a good deal of Dr Watson not only in Doyle but in the readers of *Strand*. They were largely middle class or improved working class anxious for acceptance, and they were inclined to share Watson's attitude to Holmes, compounded of respect, awe and friendship, yet without a hint of servile kowtowing. Holmes had upper-class qualities, but was approachable; the humble and the aitch-less knew that they would get a fair polite hearing from Holmes, and that he would not patronize them. He was an oracle, and was free from the petty defects of the mass of mankind, a hero figure who was increased in stature, and not diminished, because he operated in a clearly described environment that all could recognize. Holmes was chivalrous, and his sense of justice was impeccable. Most intelligent people knew that this was rare, and the newspapers were full of cases of injustice, brought to light by the new-found zest of popular journalism.

The certainty of Holmes was a great comfort to readers who were dimly aware that the old order was coming apart. Victorianism had begun to crumble in the 1890s, and even those who had deplored the excesses and suffocating hypocrisy of the sixties and seventies were concerned about the possible aftermath. Anarchy, chaos, the possibility of war with America, the immorality of the decadents – Holmes was an antidote to all these, demonstrating that God was in his heaven and all was right with the world as he scourged wrongdoers, within the law and outside it.

Despite his predilection to drugs, Holmes was largely free from the temptations and frailties of his readers, human attributes which would hinder the full exploitation of his potential and clog the thinking mechanism. This meant no sex. In *The Sign of Four* Holmes explained why: 'Love is an emotional thing, and whatever is emotional is opposed to that true, cold reason which I place above all things. I could never marry myself, lest I bias my judgment.' In the first of the Holmes short stories, 'A Scandal in Bohemia', Watson amplified on this:

All emotions, and that one particularly, were abhorrent to his cold, precise, but admirably balanced mind. He was, I take it, the most perfect reasoning and observing machine that the world has seen: but, as a lover, he would have placed himself in a false position. He never spoke of the softer passions, save with a gibe and a sneer ... Grit in a sensitive instrument, or a crack in one of his own high-power lenses, would not be more disturbing than a strong emotion in a nature such as his.

Yet Holmes knew about feminine psychology, and on one occasion he rated feminine intuition higher than his own considered judgment. In 'The Man with the Twisted Lip' he stated that he had seen too much 'not to know that the impression of a woman may be more valuable than the conclusion of an analytical reasoner'. And although the chief appeal of Holmes was to male readers, his sympathy with the many ladies in distress who arrived at 221B Baker Street would have commended itself to those women who had picked up *Strand*.

As a concession to romantic taste, there was one woman in Holmes's life, Irene in 'A Scandal in Bohemia'. She was 'always *the* woman. I have seldom heard him mention her under any other name. In his eyes she eclipses and predominates the whole of her sex.' True she was an adventuress, but had reformed on her engagement. When the case was over, Holmes was contented with her photograph in lieu of a fee. Not that Holmes did not have the wherewithal, for in 'Charles Augustus Milverton' he implants himself in the affection of Agatha, a housemaid, to gain information, and in the space of a few hours, disguised as a comely young plumber, he comes to an arrangement with her.

Small incidents like this helped to make Holmes sympathetic to a reader who was basically suspicious of cool celibates, just in case celibacy was a cover for homosexuality, a talking point throughout the 1890s and especially in 1895 when the Oscar Wilde trial broke surface. Holmes had elected not to be a womanizer, though it was clear from his lightning conquest of Agatha that he could have gone through the card had he had the inclination. However, irrespective of *Strand* readers, the Victorians were conditioned to believe that celibacy was a factor in supernormal intelligence. Long lists were drawn up of celebrated bachelors, including Jesus Christ, Kant, Newton and Beethoven. It was not known, or overlooked, that Newton was a crabbed introvert and that Beethoven had certainly not been chaste in his youth (his deafness was due to syphilis). It was reasoned that they were geniuses because they were celibate.

The appeal of Holmes was not confined to the middle-class reader of adventure stories. The puzzle element attracted the intelligentsia who had so far been catered for by word games such as acrostics and who would, eventually, fall under the spell of the crossword puzzle (invented in 1924). The plotting was looked upon as the key element in the success of the Sherlock Holmes stories, at least by writers anxious to jump on the bandwagon and flood the popular market with their counterfeits. They did not realize that the detective work was only interesting if the people concerned were interesting, and the background was convincing. G. K. Chesterton, who in Father Brown created one of the best of the Holmes competitors, pointed this out in a pertinent article in the *Illustrated London News* in 1920:

First of all, there is evidently a very general idea that the object of the detective novelist is to baffle the reader. Now, nothing is easier than baffling the reader, in the sense of disappointing the reader. There are many successful and widely advertised stories of which the principle simply consists in thwarting information by means of incident. The Bulgarian governess is just about to mention her real reason for concealing herself with a loaded rifle inside the grand piano, when a yellow Chinaman leaps through the window and cuts off her head with a yataghan.

Chesterton went on to say: 'The true object of an intelligent detective story is not to baffle the reader, but to enlighten the reader; but to enlighten him in such a manner that each successive portion of the truth comes as a surprise. In this, as in much nobler types of mystery, the object of the true mystic is not merely to mystify, but to illuminate.' He was contemptuous of the hack writer who makes the characters stock figures because greater depth would be wasted on the form. 'In other words, he does the one thing which is destructive in every department of existence – he despises the work he is doing.' The sensational story-teller 'does indeed create uninteresting characters, and then try to make them interesting by killing them'.

Conan Doyle was not free of the defects of the bad writers. He was inclined to be perfunctory, and he had mixed feelings towards Holmes. But he played fair with his readers. He never fobbed the reader off, as Temple-Ellis did, where the hero explains: 'I know that I ought to have done thus-and-thus, but some impulse which I cannot explain prompted me to do the exact opposite.' 'Such behaviour', commented Dorothy Sayers in 1931, 'is mere perversity and a determination to make the plot occur in the teeth of all common sense.'

Once Holmes had begun to grip, and was the only personage capable of boosting the circulation of the *Strand* by more than a hundred thousand by his presence in its pages, it did not matter much about the quality of the detection or, indeed, if there was or was not a plot. In the first dozen of the *Strand* stories, published by Newnes in 1892 as *The Adventures of Sherlock Holmes*, 'The Five Orange Pips' has little to commend it except the title, 'The Engineer's Thumb' is melodramatic rubbish, and 'The Noble Bachelor' might well have featured in the pages of *Girl's Own Paper* in an undistinguished week.

One of the ingredients that helped to underpin Holmes was Doyle's unerring sense of place. He had just moved from Southsea, and was intoxicated with the romance of London, the poetry of the streets. The 1890s writers made much of this, whether they were poets or writers of fiction. There were the *London Voluntaries* of W. E. Henley, Laurence Binyon's *London Visions* and Arthur Symons's *London Nights*. Richard le Gallienne spoke of:

> London, London, our delight,
> Great flower that opens but at night,
> Great city of the midnight sun
> Whose day begins when day is done.

The most diverse of novelists bayed their praise of London. Arthur Morrison in his *Tales of Mean Streets* (1894), George Gissing in *New Grub Street* (1891) and Somerset Maugham in *Liza of Lambeth* (1897) all explored the picturesque possibilities of London. Many authors lived in the more unsavoury parts of the metropolis, wallowing in the curious allure of the seedy. Kenneth Grahame, later to achieve fame as the author of *Wind in the Willows*, lived in a tiny top flat off the Embankment, attuned to the river and drinking coffee at a low stall, rubbing shoulders with poets, cabbies and the Thameside riff-raff. The poet W.B.Yeats had rooms over a cobbler's shop off the Euston Road, glorying in its scruffiness as he pursued his researches into black magic.

London was an exciting place in the nineties, intensely alive, and although the rhapsodizing now sounds somewhat ridiculous, London at night seemed magical:

> Lamp after lamp against the sky
> Opens a sudden beaming eye,
> Leaping a light on either hand,
> The iron lilies of the Strand [Richard le Gallienne]

As Holbrook Jackson wrote in his influential *The Eighteen Nineties*: 'Where, in the past [poets] found romance only in wild and remote places among what are called natural things, they now found romance in streets and theatres, in taverns and restaurants, in bricks and mortar and the creations of artificers.' W.E.Henley saw beauty in Trafalgar Square:

> Trafalgar Square
> (The fountains volleysing golden glaze)
> Gleams like an angel market. High aloft
> Over his couchant Lions in a haze
> Shimmering and bland and soft ...

In his *London Visions* Laurence Binyon was no less enthusiastic:

> All is unreal; the sound of the falling of feet,
> Coming figures, and far-off hum of the street:
> A dream, the gliding hurry, the endless lights,
> Houses and sky, a dream, a dream!

London had something for everyone, a variety of facets to appeal to all. It was becoming a fun city, with dozens of theatres and hundreds of music halls. 'A New Spirit of Pleasure is abroad amongst us,' said Richard le Gallienne. He saw a change from a stolid into a volatile nation. Much of this was not due to a change in conditions, but a change in attitude; people were waking up from the sluggish dreams of Victorianism, and were determined to enjoy themselves without guilt or restraint. The most typical sign of the times was the incredible popularity of a music-hall tune, 'Ta-ra-ra-boom-de-ay', sung by Lottie Collins with a dashing display of petticoat, which for four years, between 1892 and 1896, became the mashers' national anthem.

What was especially novel about the hedonism of the 1890s was that all classes partook of it. Even the poor found that their pennies bought more, and were able to grasp the fruits of a capitalism that by some fluke had worked. All classes had more leisure time. The Bank Holidays Act of 1871 had laid down free days for all, and the working week was gradually being reduced. For many, Saturday was no longer a full working day. Compulsory education had given the working classes a new self-respect, and self-development was an aim pursued by both costermongers and clerks.

Few who lived through the 1890s were consciously aware of the change of attitude. Writers dimly realized that they were allowed more leeway, and Rudyard Kipling looked back sardonically at the novelists of a previous age:

> We asked no social questions – we pumped no hidden shame –
> We never talked obstetrics when the Little Stranger came ...

Nor did Conan Doyle, but he too breathed in the spirit of pleasure, the joy in being alive in the greatest city in the world. There were parts of London he did not like, the anonymous ribbon-building, the tracts without individuality, the still squalid ghettoes of the old East End. They might serve as copy for Gissing but not for Doyle – unless they were picturesque.

Doyle often selected the seedy unfashionable areas of London as settings, described by Watson in 'The Red-Headed League':

We travelled by the Underground as far as Aldersgate; and a short walk took us to Saxe-Coburg Square [there is no such square] ... It was a pokey, little, shabby-genteel place, where four lines of dingy two-storied brick houses looked out into a small railed-in enclosure, where a lawn of weedy grass and a few clumps of faded laurel bushes made a hard fight against a smoke-laden and uncongenial atmosphere.

The terse precision of such description is in agreeable contrast to the long-winded scene-setting of Doyle's 'serious' novels, where he felt obliged, as Eric Ambler shrewdly noted, to pass on every last scrap of the special knowledge he had acquired in his researches to his reader. For a parallel one must turn to the crime fiction of Raymond Chandler, whose descriptions have the same admirable brevity.

Weather plays a considerable part in the atmosphere of the Holmes stories:

It was in the latter days of September, and the equinoctial gales had set in with exceptional violence. All day the wind had screamed and the rain had beaten against the windows, so that even here in the heart of great, hand-made London we were forced to raise our minds for the instant from the routine of life, and to recognize the presence of those great elemental forces which shriek at mankind through the bars of his civilization, like untamed beasts in a cage. ('The Five Orange Pips')

Doyle fully exploited the magic of horse transport:

We dashed away through the endless succession of sombre and deserted streets, which widened gradually, until we were flying across a broad balustraded bridge, with the murky river flowing sluggishly beneath us. Beyond lay another broad wilderness of bricks and mortar, its silence broken only by the heavy, regular footsteps of the policeman, or the songs and shouts of some belated party of revellers. A dull wrack was drifting slowly across the sky, and a star or two twinkled dimly here and there through the rifts in the clouds. ('The Man with the Twisted Lip')

Doyle had a way with the vivid phrase: 'Outside the stars were shining boldly in a cloudless sky, and the breath of the passers-by blew out into smoke like so many pistol shots' ('The Blue Carbuncle'). He could easily have used a cliché, such as 'shining brightly', and a lesser writer would certainly have substituted 'blew out like smoke' for 'blew out into smoke', an inspired transmutation instead of a tired metaphor. In 'The Beryl Coronet' Doyle depicts a winter morning in Baker Street:

It was a bright, crisp February morning, and the snow of the day before still lay deep upon the ground, shimmering brightly in the wintry sun. Down the centre of Baker Street it had been ploughed into a brown crumbly band by the traffic, but at either side and on the heaped-up edges of the footpaths it still lay as white as when it fell. The grey pavement had been cleaned and scraped, but was still dangerously slippery, so that there were fewer passengers than usual. Indeed, from the direction of the Metropolitan station no one was coming save the single gentleman whose eccentric conduct had drawn my attention.

How graphic it is! And exactly visualized, with the brown crumbly band of slush contrasted with the 'grey pavement'. The use of passenger in the sense of one who passes is a felicitous touch, and the jerk into reality with the mention of the Metropolitan station adds the final touch of immediacy.

Fog does not feature in the Sherlock Holmes stories so much as one would imagine, and when fog is used it is often to contrast the cosy muddle of the Baker Street rooms with the mysterious and subtly threatening world outside. One of the best descriptions occurs in 'The Copper Beeches': 'A thick fog rolled down between the lines of dun-coloured houses, and the opposing windows loomed like dark, shapeless blurs, through the heavy yellow wreaths. Our gas was lit, and shone on the white cloth, and glimmer of china and metal, for the table had not been cleared yet.'

All these examples occur in the first dozen stories in *Strand*, when Sherlock Holmes was beginning to get his stranglehold on the reader. But economical and persuasive description is not enough, and if one looks through the stories it is surprising what a high percentage of the wording is conversation, especially the client explaining the problem and Holmes explaining the answer. Doyle always made the clients' accounts convincing; their words key in with the character briefly sketched. It was in the clients explaining their predicaments that Doyle was at his most masterly. They had to say just enough to make their cases intriguing, without indicating the true facts, and any red herrings built into their accounts had to accord with their characters, their place in society and their attitudes towards the phenomena that drove them to seek Holmes's advice. Sometimes a case came via one of the Scotland Yard detectives, such as Hopkins or Lestrade, sometimes a case began with an object, such as the battered billycock hat handed to Holmes by a commissionaire at the opening of 'The Blue Carbuncle'.

The first series of short stories was collected as *The Adventures of Sherlock Holmes*. The second series was collected as *The Memoirs*, and there was no reduction in the standard of story-telling though there was still inconsistency and carelessness. The story of 'Silver Blaze' was set on Dartmoor, possibly the worst place in England for a racing stable. No trainer would set his horses across the granite-strewn and uneven moor, ill-served with the kind of terrain favoured by responsible owners. Newmarket yes, Dartmoor no. In 'The Stockbroker's Clerk' Doyle uses one of his favourite themes – the mysterious job offered to a client to get him out of the way. Although connoisseurs can pick out the line these stories take, Doyle is always at his best in them.

'The Gloria Scott' is the one about the bad man who tries to reform, but fate takes a hand and lays him low, while 'The Musgrave Ritual' (perhaps the most intriguingly titled of the Holmes saga) is an exasperating blend of imagination and improbability, with a butler of twenty years' standing being dismissed on the spot for looking at an old family document and a set of instructions in the 'Ritual' that fail to make sense. 'The Musgrave Ritual' helps build up some of Holmes's more eccentric habits – his keeping cigars in the coal-scuttle, tobacco in the toe of a Persian slipper, and correspondence transfixed by a jack-knife in the centre of the wooden mantelpiece. Watson also tells the reader of the detective's quaint indulgence in indoor revolver shooting, picking out the initials VR on the facing wall.

'The Reigate Squires' is a workmanlike piece, but 'The Crooked Man' is something of a disappointment, with a revengeful man and his weird pet, which turns out to be nothing more menacing than a mongoose. 'The Resident Patient' starts well, but has a tame dénouement, while 'The Greek Interpreter' is mainly noteworthy for the introduction of Holmes's brother Mycroft, with the international crooks of minor interest.

The detective work, good, bad and indifferent, had the effect of binding the stories together, and even when the working-out was slipshod, the characterization of Holmes and Watson encouraged the reader to overlook inconsistencies and unwarranted assumptions. Then, in 'The Final Problem', Doyle tired of Holmes and killed him off. Holmes and master criminal Professor Moriarty struggle together near the falls of Reichenbach in Switzerland, and both plunge to their death. Doyle had got the idea when he went with his wife for a short holiday in Switzerland. It seemed a suitable place to end the career of Holmes.

'The difficulty of the Holmes work', he wrote in his autobiography, 'was that every story really needed as clear-cut and original a plot as a longish book would do. One cannot without effort spin plots at such a rate.' And Holmes was not worth the effort. Doyle set out 'to do some work which would certainly be less remunerative but would be more ambitious from a literary point of view. I had long been attracted by the epoch of Louis XIV and by those Huguenots who were the French equivalents of our Puritans ...'

Readers of *Strand* and posterity did not give, and have not given, a button for the epoch of Louis XIV and the boring misadventures of the Huguenots as laid out, in all their detail, in *The Refugees*. During his Norwood period, Doyle also wrote a short novel of suburban life, *Beyond the City*, a book dealing with evil possession called *The Parasite*, and a historical novel of Napoleonic times, *The Great Shadow*. None of them caused any stir, though Doyle was proud of the Napoleonic book. *The Refugees* had the mark of gloom on it almost from the start; writing to his mother in December 1891 he predicted that it would be 'conscientious, respectable and dull'. The wish to be a writer of serious books was becoming an obsession; anything was better than being identified with 'a lower stratum of literary achievement', to wit, detective stories.

By this time, Doyle was earning £1,600 a year – at least £20,000 almost tax free in present-day currency. On this he ran a very comfortable establishment in South Norwood. There was no bookishness about him. Anthony Hope, author of the first of the Ruritanian cloak-and-dagger romances, *The Prisoner of Zenda* (1894), said that Doyle looked as if he had never heard of a book in his life. The novelist Eden Phillpotts recalled a big-hearted friendly man who loved cricket and billiards, and Jerome K. Jerome found Doyle 'big bodied, big souled, and big hearted'.

Doyle was both proud of being a writer and ashamed of it. He had the ordinary man's aversion to artiness, and was at pains to dissociate himself from aestheticism as epitomized by Oscar Wilde. He was suspicious of intellectualism, which he equated with pretension, and although he met George Meredith and Meredith expressed his admiration for Doyle's work, Doyle was more guarded about the other's novels, which he considered difficult. He liked to have about him plain men who spoke their minds, and who would not overawe him with long words. This possibly arose from a sense of inferiority, and his life-long interest in sport from a need to compensate. The writer as he-man reached its apotheosis in Ernest Hemingway, but Conan Doyle ran him close.

For some obscure reason, this obsession by writers with being he-men is now known as machismo. Its most recent representative is Norman Mailer. It arises from uneasiness that a writer might be, from the nature of the calling, a cissy. Doyle was expecially vulnerable, as were many who had emerged from public schools which were devoted to sport and where anything savouring of the artistic was treated with contempt (especially by small boys). Then there was the example of his father, who was artistic in the worst possible way to a Victorian – Charles Doyle could not make a living at it, and his pursuits prevented him from earning enough money at a mundane job to keep his family in comfort. Only in late life did Conan Doyle appreciate the small but very real talent of his father.

Although Doyle looked as if he had never heard of a book in his life, and played up to the image of a typical Victorian hearty, he was obliged to carry out the duties prescribed for a literary man. In particular, he wrote poetry, even if it was the poetry of the he-man, the common man who had no truck with Tennyson and his ilk. The themes were deliberately masculine, owing not a little to the example of Kipling, and the character of Doyle's verse is evident from the titles of his slim volumes – *Songs of Action*, *Songs of the Road* and *The Guards Came Through*.

Songs of Action can be seen as analogues of his historical novels. Typical of them is 'The Song of the Bow', the first verse of which has the kind of heroic bombast handled much better by Shakespeare:

> What of the bow?
>   The bow was made in England:
> Of true wood, of yew-wood,
>   The wood of English bows;
>   So men who are free
>   Love of the old yew-tree
> And the land where the yew-tree grows.

This has something of the quality of an unfunny Edward Lear, suitable for a drawing-room recitation, while 'Cremona' has all the subtlety of a contribution to a school magazine:

> The Grenadiers of Austria are proper men and tall;
> The Grenadiers of Austria have scaled the city wall.

'The Frontier Line' has all the qualities of bad verse, especially the use of proper names to add interest:

> What marks the frontier line?
>   Thou man of Burmah, speak!
> Is it traced from Mandalay,

> And down the marches of Cathay,
> From Bhamo south to Kiang-mai,
> And where the buried rubies lie?

Military and sporting poems make up the bulk of Doyle's poems, and we have a characteristic Doyle hero in Corporal Robert Dick in 'Corporal Dick's Promotion':

> Bearded and burly, short and thick,
> Rough of speech and in temper quick ...

Corporal Dick dies a hero's death:

> Silent and grim on the trampled sand,
> His rifle grasped in his stiffened hand,
> With the warrior pride of one who died
> 'Mid a ring of the dead and the dying.

Soldiers are good fellows all, moulded into men by battle:

> He has learned to joke at the powder smoke,
> For he is the fog-smoke's son,
> And his heart is light and his pluck is right—
> The man who carries the gun.

Doyle is better in his sporting poems, with the officers and other ranks replaced by masters of hounds and grooms and similar low life. None of the grooms and whips, pugilists and beaters have aspirates in their vocabularies. Nor had the common soldiers. This is the start of 'The Dying Whip':

> It came from gettin' 'eated, that was 'ow the thing begun,
> And 'ackin' back to kennels from a ninety-minute run;
> 'I guess I've copped bronchitis,' says I to brother Jack,
> An' then afore I knowed it I was down upon my back.

The same robust tone is preserved in 'The Groom's Story':

> Ten miles in twenty minutes! 'E done it, sir. That's true.
> The big bay 'orse in the further stall—the one wot's next to you.
> I've seen some better 'orses; I've seldom seen a wuss,
> But 'e 'olds the bloomin' record, an' that's good enough for us.

A death on the hunting field was as good a way to go as any:

> A sportin' death! My word it was!
> An' taken in a sportin' way ...

Nevertheless, despite the doggerel and the jogalong metre, the sporting poems have a verve and a vivacity that echo Doyle's interest in sport. .

As a boy Doyle's prowess at sport had been marked, and he did not relinquish it as he grew older. He played football at a highish level when he was forty-four, and cricket into his fifties; it was not a lark, and he dismayed other cricketing literary figures such as James Barrie and A.E.W. Mason by his seriousness. When he was younger he shot, but he later thought that it was unjustified to rear birds in order to kill them and that the slaying of hares and deer might well 'blunt our better feelings, harden our sympathies, brutalize our natures'. It was a humane point of view often held, but rarely put in so trenchant a form by a formidable sportsman who prided himself on his manliness.

As a boxer, Doyle described himself as a fair average amateur; it was an ability he foisted on Holmes. He had a nostalgia for the old prize-ring, the bare-knuckle bouts, and though it is possible to agree vigorously with his comments on blood sports, his defence of prize-fighting was precisely that of the unthinking hearty – 'better that our sports should be a little too rough than that we should run the risk of effeminacy'. His liking for boxing was so well known that in 1909 he was asked to referee the championship between Jeffries and Johnson in the U.S.A.

Doyle celebrated his fascination with prize-fighting in his poem 'Bendy's Sermon'. Bendigo was a Nottingham prize-fighter who became converted to religion and preached at revival meetings throughout the country:

> Bendy's short for Bendigo. You should see him peel!
> Half of him was whalebone, half of him was steel,
> Fightin' weight eleven ten, five foot nine in height,
> Always ready to oblige if you want a fight.

This also illustrates Doyle's lack of ear and faulty technique, for the last line, try as one charitably might, does not scan.

It is difficult to write a poem on golf, but Doyle tried one, replete with technical terms and a sidelong look at the scenery where 'the bracken is bronzing to brown'. It was 'good to feel the jar of the steel / And the spring of the hickory shaft'. As with most sports, Doyle was at home with golf, with a handicap of ten. He did not write about another of his favourite sports, billiards, though it is tempting to imitate the manner of Doyle:

> The white and red, and spot as well, are bounding off the cush,
> It's time to get the cue aloft, to give another push.

That is the ultimate failing of Doyle's verse. Anyone could have written it.

At cricket, Doyle played for the M.C.C. when it was largely a league of gentlemen and got a hat-trick against Warwickshire. He once bowled W.G.Grace. As late as 1904 he got seven wickets for 51 against Cambridgeshire for the M.C.C. He was an early motorist, though not early enough to establish himself in any reference book, a balloonist, and a pre-World War One aeronaut (but as a passenger only). In 1903 he told P.G.Wodehouse that he would like to parachute. Not even the most bigoted anti-Doylist could call him a rabbit.

Although Doyle may have had the appearance of a man who had never heard of a book in his life, there was no doubting his professional approach to writing. In 1892 Henry Irving bought a one-act play on a Napoleonic theme from him for £100, and although an operetta written in collaboration with James Barrie called *Jane Annie* was a failure, it did demonstrate his versatility. Projects became books in the twinkling of an eye. The *Strand* could not take all the material, and he found another outlet in *The Idler*, run by Jerome K. Jerome, the one-time railway clerk who became a celebrity on account of the success of *Three Men in a Boat*. With Jerome the Doyles went to Norway to discover the delights of skiing, which Doyle took to Switzerland and popularized. With the birth of a son, Kingsley, everything seemed to be going well.

1893 was a bad year. His father died, and it was found that his wife had contracted tuberculosis. She was given a few months to live. Doyle took her to Davos in Switzerland, giving up the South Norwood house. It was a bad year for Sherlock Holmes, too. In December 1893 'The Final Problem' appeared in *Strand*. Holmes was dead. Being out of the country, Doyle was prevented from bearing the full indignation of the public, but he received hundreds of letters imploring him to bring Holmes back, black armbands were worn in the streets, and 'Let's Keep Holmes Alive' clubs were started in America.

Renunciation was all very well, and high literary ideals fine, but by disposing of Holmes Doyle cut off a fecund supply of pounds and dollars. Eventually, of course, Holmes was resurrected, though Watson had some tortuous explaining to do.

6
CONSOLIDATION

Much happened in the years between Holmes believed dead and Holmes resurgent. Doyle went from a run-of-the-mill G.P. just turned professional writer to a figure of the establishment, from an eager go-getter with an eye to the main chance to a prematurely middle-aged oracle, whose words carried weight and who could be distressingly pi to those who were disappointed that Doyle was not at all like Sherlock Holmes. There were those, of course, who were pleased to find that not only was Doyle not like his creation, but that he was not like a Literary Giant either.

In 1894 Doyle went to America, giving readings from his books, playing golf and paying respectful visits to the grave of the recently dead essayist Oliver Wendell Holmes and the places associated with Edgar Allan Poe. He was gratified by his reception, misinterpreting it as nation speaking unto nation. The audiences wanted to see the creator of Sherlock Holmes. They were not interested in an alliance of English-speaking peoples, especially as it was likely that Britain and the United States would go to war in the very near future over zones of interest (plans were prepared for this contingency – the Americans expected the British Navy to bombard the eastern seaboard, but they knew they could take Canada).

Doyle was an innocent abroad, telling the Americans what they wanted to hear about their own country and, unlike an earlier lecturer, Charles Dickens, praising them for their even temper, tolerance and hopefulness. He looked crossly back at Britain, and British politicians, who were largely to blame, he thought, for the coolness in Anglo-American relations. 'The centre of gravity of the race is over here,' he wrote to his friend Sir John Robinson.

He had left his wife in Davos, and when he arrived there he found the weather so bad that he contemplated spending the next winter in Egypt, considered to be an ideal place for tuberculosis sufferers. Louise Doyle was not in pain, and was hopeful of a cure. A fictional account of his medical experiences had recently come out in serial form in *The Idler*, and Doyle went to London to arrange publication in book form. Here he met Grant Allen, once a principal of a college for Negroes in Jamaica, later an author of scientific books such as *Physiological Aesthetics* (1877), but who became notorious in 1895 with his novel *The Woman Who Did*, dealing with an unmarried mother who was rather pleased with herself for defying convention. Grant Allen was described by the publisher Grant Richards in 1932 as 'a tall, rather gaunt, beak-nosed, and when I first knew him, red-bearded man ... he had odd and interesting physical habits. For one thing, he was often very ill, and we children had an idea that although he was fed continually – or so it seemed to us – on a diet of oysters and Benger's Food, he would die very soon.'

Richards was right. Allen died in 1899, but not before impressing on Doyle that Hindhead in Surrey had cured him of tuberculosis. Grant Allen was the kind of character who appeared at intervals throughout Doyle's life, a writer of the second rank like Payn and Jerome who by a casual action or remark turned Doyle's life into new channels.

Doyle bought a plot of land at Hindhead, engaged an old Southsea acquaintance named Ball as architect, and set out for Egypt with his family. They settled in the Mena House Hotel, seven miles into the desert from Cairo, and although Egypt provided billiards, tennis and golf it was short on inspiration. The only work he did there was to adapt a novel by James Payn for the theatre, the upshot being a play called *Halves*. However, it was a short gap in the production line. He had been writing the Brigadier Gerard stories, and *Rodney Stone* was on the stocks. For this novel of Regency pugilism and high life, Smith, Elder & Co. paid £4,000 in advance royalties, and *Strand* £1,500 for serial rights.

The Brigadier Gerard stories are bright and breezy, and in them Doyle did not have to parade his research. The brigadier is a brave stalwart fellow who laughs at danger, something of a blockhead who worships Napoleon, with whom he has several meetings. In the first of the stories, 'The Medal of Brigadier Gerard', the hero is sent on an errand by Napoleon carrying a message bearing false information.

The idea is that Gerard, being a clod, gets taken and the information acted upon. The plan goes astray and Gerard carves his way through all his opponents, returning to imperial frowns which turn to smiles when Gerard's simple courage is appreciated. Thus the plot. The writing is riddled with clichés, characterization is wafer-thin, but the story rattles on because Doyle could tell a yarn.

It was not the first time Doyle had glorified war. Later he was to write: 'Wonderful is the atmosphere of war. When the millennium comes the world will gain much, but it will lose its greatest thrill.' There is gory detail in the Gerard stories: 'I drove my sword through his midriff with such frantic force, that the mere blow of the hilt against the end of his breast-bone sent him six paces before he fell, and left my reeking blade ready for the other. I sprang round upon him with such a lust for blood upon me ...'

Rodney Stone was a scamper through the Regency, with a backcloth of Wardour Street historical personages against which Doyle revelled in man-to-man combat and the lure of the prize-fight, manliness incarnate. Prize-fighting, 'the fancy', was difficult to idealize, but Doyle managed it. He had never known the reality, as it disappeared when the Queensberry Rules were framed in 1867. As long as it existed, the prize-ring bolstered up the underworld, and was closely linked with betting and organized vice.

It might seem that Doyle was making every effort to keep away from the vein of ore that he had mined in the Sherlock Holmes stories, desperately trying to prove his versatility. An excursion up the Nile to the Sudan provided material for another story, *The Tragedy of the Korosko*, dealing with a group of tourists captured by the Mahdi. It was the kind of plot Hollywood was to work to death, but Doyle, impressed by the vastness and emptiness of the Nile valley, reacted to the stimulus, and it is possibly his best book since the Holmes stories, with refreshing, tersely drawn characters.

There is also a new tone. The descriptions of death are less hearty, more clinical. One of the tourists has been knifed: 'Brown sat down at the blow and began to cough – to cough as a man coughs who has choked at dinner, furiously unceasingly, spasm upon spasm. Then the angry red cheeks turned to a mottled pallor, there were liquid sounds in his throat, and, clapping his hand over his mouth, he rolled over on to his side.' This is strange fare to put before the reader of romantic fiction, but there is every evidence to suggest that he, or she, came up for more. The fad for the vivid and the explicit was blamed by

Frederick Greenwood on the influence of the new-style reporter. In *Blackwood's Magazine* in May 1897 he wrote of the newspaper-man who 'drenches himself with gore wherever he can find it, on the battle-field, in the murderer's shambles, on the railway track crimsoned by the suicide ... The appetite thus debauched is insatiable; it has wal-lowed in crime ever since.'

If this were so, Doyle in the Brigadier Gerard stories, in *The Tragedy of the Korosko* and in the creepy stories he was writing in the 1890s catered for it. There is more than the bloodthirsty, however, in *The Tragedy of the Korosko*; there is a tone of pessimism and quiet reflection, far removed from the delight in exhibiting the fruits of research, real or assumed, in the historical novels. The shock of his wife's illness found an echo in *The Tragedy of the Korosko*, with a new note of intro-spection and a long look at religion. He realized the implications of Islam, and when the Arab captors pray he muses on the potential power of Mecca:

Who could doubt as he watched their strenuous, heart-whole devotion that here was a great living power in the world, reactionary but tremendous, countless millions all thinking as one from Cape Juby to the confines of China? Let a common wave pass over them, let a great soldier or organizer arise among them to use the grand material at his hand, and who shall say that this may not be the besom with which Providence may sweep the rotten, decadent, impossible, half-hearted south of Europe, as it did a thousand years ago, until it makes room for a sounder stock?

A strange place to let one's hobby-horse run loose – the contempt of the Victorian for the Latin races – but the comment is slipped in cleverly. The love interest is perfunctory and embarrassed, and Doyle's philosophizing about love is jaded and lethargic: 'There is no arguing about love. It is the innermost fact of life – the one which obscures and changes all the others. Pain is pleasure, and want is com-fort, and death is sweetness when once that golden mist is round it.'

Yet *The Tragedy of the Korosko* (the *Korosko* is the boat from which the tourists have been abstracted) shows that given a contemporary theme the story-teller Doyle could forget his preoccupations with great literature.

After their jaunt down the Nile valley, when the Doyles were back in Cairo, war broke out between the British in Egypt and the Der-vishes, and Doyle cabled the *Westminster Gazette* to ask if he could be its correspondent. He kitted himself out, bought himself an Italian revolver and a hundred cartridges, and moved out with the soldiers. It was the first time he had come into close personal contact with warriors, so much eulogized in his novels. He did not think much of the native troops, who were inscrutable, unsporting and unlovable, but the British officers did not let him down: 'The British officer at his best is really a splendid fellow, a large edition of the public schoolboy, with his cheery slang overlying a serious purpose which he would usually die rather than admit.'

Doyle was taken with the camel. 'It approaches you with a mildly interested and superior expression, like a patrician lady in a Sunday school. You feel that a pair of glasses at the end of a fan is the one thing lacking.' His observations on the camel were transferred in almost identical words into the text of *The Tragedy of the Korosko*.

He did not see any fighting. He was to learn that war is largely a question of hanging about waiting for something to happen, and as Kitchener was awaiting several thousand more camels Doyle returned to Cairo, and thence to England, renting a house at Haslemere, then moving to Moorlands, a boarding-house close to the site of his new house.

On 15 March 1897 Doyle met and fell in love with Jean Leckie, thirteen years his junior. He probably met her at a party. It was a difficult position to be in, for unlike many of his literary contemporaries he was an honourable man and had a clear conception of what was right and wrong. His wife Louise was ill, and would die young, in weeks, months or years. She died in 1906, sweet and uncomplaining to the last, and Doyle and Jean Leckie were only lovers in name until they married in 1907. Doyle gritted his teeth. It was a romantic test ostensibly so common in the days of chivalry. The strain was echoed in a poem he wrote later, 'Take Heart', which began:

> When our souls are filled with fear,
>   When the path is dull and drear,
> When the wind is chill and strong,
> When the way is rough and long,
>   Take heart!

Torn between loyalty towards Louise and a passion that he had never felt before, Doyle became edgy, and ready to take offence. Suppressed sexuality could not always be worked off in golf or cricket. His mother knew of the platonic liaison, and in her pragmatic way approved of Jean. Few others knew, least of all literary associates.

Waiting for loved ones had gone out with Tennyson, and in advanced circles traditional moral codes were well and truly buried, with wife-swapping and cultural ménages-à-trois considered of no account. The choice was entirely Doyle's; he did what he thought was right, despite the numbing pain of it all.

There was no doubt that Louise Conan Doyle was not fit, physically or mentally, for the meteoric rise of her husband from a struggling doctor to a wealthy author. She was a tiny woman whose gentleness attracted children and animals to her like a magnet, her daughter Mary remembered. She had a quiet sense of fun, and was the ideal helpmeet for a provincial doctor, a comforter of troubled patients and a solace after a hard day in the surgery.

Jean Leckie was a different matter. The daughter of rich Scots parents living in the Glebe House, Blackheath, she was a horsewoman, rode to hounds, and had trained as a singer in Dresden. She had poise and assurance, and exerted an influence over Doyle which Louise had never managed to do. To complement her musical talents, Doyle took up the banjo.

During the tortuous ten years of waiting, Doyle changed, and he was inclined to over-react to slights, real and imaginary. He joined in literary feuding, the most destructive of amusements, and gossips were stimulated by Doyle's response to the self-advertisement of Hall Caine on behalf of his novel, *The Christian*. The literary life had been kind to Caine. His novel *The Deemster* (1887) was dramatized and ran so successfully that it enabled him to buy Greeba Castle in the Isle of Man and sit in the island's parliament. He amassed a personal fortune of a quarter of a million pounds, and was given a knighthood by writing about God for the glory of Hall Caine.

Doyle wrote to the *Daily Chronicle* that it was tiresome to pick up paper after paper and read Caine's own comments on the gigantic task he had just brought to a conclusion. It was 'unworthy' of Caine. Caine wrote back, protesting that many of the pieces had been written without his knowledge, specifying material in *The Bookman*. He did not need to say that the editor of *The Bookman*, W. Robertson Nicoll, was a close friend of his.

Hall Caine is best known today not as a somewhat sickly novelist but as a comic character, one-time disciple of the Pre-Raphaelite poet/painter Rossetti, an earnest follower of Ruskin ('I have of course the deepest interest in your work,' Ruskin told him, already half-mad), and from the first a very prosy fellow. Rossetti bade him not to use long words, or publish articles in magazines which were 'farragoes of absolute garbage'. In due course, Caine became a habit that Rossetti could not break, and the young man moved in with him in the house in Cheyne Walk, travelled with him to Cumberland, and was with Rossetti when he died in Birchington-on-Sea, Kent, in 1882. If Doyle had had an odd background for a best-selling author, Caine could come close. They were two lions roaring at each other through the medium of the press.

W. Robertson Nicoll, with whom Doyle also crossed swords, was not in the same league as Caine, though he too got the obligatory knighthood dealt out to the second-rate. Nicoll attacked Doyle's domestic novel *A Duet* on account of its alleged immorality, not once but six times, using different pseudonyms and different papers.

A Duet did not do well commercially, though it had a special place in Doyle's affections. Written during the years of waiting for Jean Leckie, it is the story of a couple's courtship and marriage, wistful and tender with something of the artless simplicity of early Wells. It was the triumph of wish-fulfilment, and Doyle had the manuscript bound as a present for Miss Leckie.

He was pleased that both H. G. Wells and Swinburne liked it, and when he discovered that 'O.O.', 'Claudius Clear' and 'Bookman' were one and the same his anger merged into fury, especially when he found out that it was common practice among Nicoll and his ilk. He referred to them collectively as 'the wire-pulling gang', and although this sounds like the title of one of the unwritten Sherlock Holmes stories that intrigue the Holmesians, the personalities involved in mutual back-scratching have long since dropped into oblivion. Nicoll was able to have so many platforms for his sniping because in most cases he ran the periodicals. He was an inveterate founder of newspapers and magazines, usually with a religious slant as he was himself a Nonconformist minister (his best-known venture was *British Weekly*), though he could jump on a bandwagon if one rolled along. Seeing the success of *Strand*, Nicoll started a *Strand* for women, called *Woman at Home*, and recruited most of the magazine journalists around to write for it. The pages included short detective stories by the copiers of Conan Doyle.

Nicoll had done more than attack *A Duet* on account of an immorality that only he could see. In June 1897 he wrote a review of Doyle's *Uncle Bernac* in the *Sketch* under the pseudonym 'O.O.' Nicoll was not fair to *A Duet*, which has that quality rare in Doyle,

charm, but he was almost clinical in his dissection of *Uncle Bernac*:
'It has an air of being very brand-new, of being culled from a hasty
perusal of a few of the best known memoirs of the times; and a book
built of material gathered like that is, of course, a very temporary
erection. Well, if Dr Doyle does not mind, why should we? *Uncle Bernac* is thin, quite unexciting, and does not contain a single surprise
in word or deed.' This has every appearance of being a determined
hatchet-job, and the aspersions cast were directed nicely at Doyle's
Achilles heel – his continual assertions that in his historical books his
research was deep and thorough. Nicoll was one of the few who disputed it; at almost the same time as his cutting review, the *Illustrated
London News* published a bland and vaguely complimentary one of
the book.

Since the early days when the critics had dismissed the historical
novels as stirring tales for young chaps, Doyle had had no fondness
for critics. The half a million readers of the *Strand* were good enough
for him, and as novel and series succeeded each other in its pages
it seemed as if it was a remarkably faithful public. It was certainly
a public with diverse tastes, catered for not only by Doyle's serials
and series but by 'The Dogs of Celebrities', 'Giants and Dwarfs', 'The
Handwriting of Alfred Lord Tennyson', and 'The Training of Performing Animals', all written in the terse economical style of responsible informative journalism. There was little that was topical in
Strand, and a reader who took it and it only would have been unaware
of the changing scene. But even informed readers were shattered when
England became involved in her first major war for nearly half a
century.

Doyle had seen the Boer War coming since the Jameson raid, and
he had a higher opinion of the Boers than the military. They were
grizzled, taciturn and tenacious fellows not so much unlike himself.
However, Doyle did not know how ill-prepared Britain was for war.
Few did.

7
THE
BOER WAR

The motivations of Doyle in wanting to fight in the Boer War are not complicated. He regretted that he had missed the fighting in the Sudan, and as he was now in his early forties the Boer War was perhaps the last time he would have a chance to see battle. He told his mother what he proposed to do, and she was aghast, pointing out that he was the family breadwinner (and the family included her and various other relatives) and appealed to his common sense – there were hundreds of thousands who could fight for one who could create a Sherlock Holmes. Besides, his 'very height and breadth' would make Doyle 'a simple and sure target'.

'Your duty', she continued, 'is at home, and with good pure leaven to raise the tone of the popular taste and feeling!' Doyle was not dissuaded. He replied that it was his duty, and as he had written to *The Times* advising the government to call on 'the riding shooting men' he was honour-bound to volunteer. 'What I feel is that I have perhaps the strongest influence over young men, especially young athletic sporting men, of any one in England (bar Kipling).' The government was not interested in Doyle as a soldier, so he went as a doctor with a team organized by a friend, John Langman. Langman was sending out a hospital of fifty beds, and Doyle helped to choose personnel, which amounted in all, including storemen and cooks, to fifty.

As for the war itself, no one thought that it would last long. It was a direct result of the nineteenth-century carve-up of Africa by the great powers, the finding of gold in the Rand, and mischief-making by a few individuals. Gold had been discovered in the heart of the Transvaal, a small republic of Bible-reading Dutch-descended farmers, and the tiny town of Johannesburg grew into a cosmopolitan centre full of rogues, adventurers and gold-mad miners. Kruger denied the newcomers rights, obstructed mining developments, and heavily taxed them. It was so different from the free and easy anarchy of the Californian gold rush.

The new inhabitants of Johannesburg, the Uitlanders, were ripe for rebellion. In 1890 Rhodes had become prime minister of the Cape. He offered the aid of armed forces under his command to the Uitlanders, attacking from Rhodesia, which he had founded and ran as a private preserve. Six hundred troopers invaded Transvaal in December 1895, but the hoped-for rising did not take place; the troopers were surrounded and imprisoned. This was the Jameson raid (Jameson was Rhodes' administrator in Rhodesia).

This, not surprisingly, led to tension between British statesmen and President Kruger of the Transvaal, especially as the feeling in Britain was that if Rhodes had succeeded in conquering Transvaal he would have been a hero. In 1899 the Uitlanders petitioned Queen Victoria; they felt that they were grossly wronged. British statesmen considered that they had 'suzerainty' over the Transvaal, and pondered over the petition. They despised the Boers, though the Boers had given the British a bloody nose in 1880. No one was greatly interested in peace, and in October 1899 the Boers invaded South Africa, laying siege to Mafeking, Kimberley and Ladysmith. Attempts by the British forces in South Africa to relieve the sieges were soundly defeated.

The Germans were pleased, the rest of Europe only slightly less so, but the Americans were sympathetic, having just won a war with Spain and knowing the problems of empire-building. There was panic in Britain, though some welcomed the war. The commander-in-chief of the British Army, Sir Garnet Wolseley, thought that the English 'best class of society ... can only be saved from annihilation by some such periodical upheaval as a great war'.

Why was there panic? South Africa was a long way off, and Kruger had no fleet. But there was fear lest one of the European powers, seeing the British Army engaged elsewhere, might try its hand. And the British Army was stretched. It was not ready for war. In December 1899 Lord Roberts, another old soldier who was to play a big part in settling the impudent hash of Kruger, wrote: 'I was astonished beyond measure to hear of our utter unpreparedness ... How could this have been permitted? And who is responsible for it?' It was a rhetorical question. Everyone was.

Conan Doyle had seen the great Salisbury manœuvres of 1898, and was shocked by what he had seen, with troops advancing in the close order of the Napoleonic wars, inviting extinction by sophisticated artillery and small arms. One of Britain's key generals, Redvers Buller, had been outmatched by the Duke of Connaught, one of Queen Victoria's sons who was whiling away time in the army.

In times of great danger to the state, the commander-in-chief could call on three auxiliary bodies, the Militia, with a theoretical strength of 125,000, the Yeomanry, the mounted force of the Militia, and the Volunteers, the predecessors of the Territorials. No plans existed for sending these part-time soldiers overseas, or for providing them with transport. When the war started, no one, least of all Wolseley, was interested, but after the 'Black Week' of December when all was going wrong for the British Army the government relented. Wolseley wished to keep the auxiliary forces out of South Africa so that the regular army would gain all the glory.

The British Army was ill-equipped. The establishment of machine-guns was 25 per cent under strength, and the gun ammunition reserve of 200 rounds a gun was exhausted in the first weeks of the war. There was no provision for heavy casualties; the reserve of 5,000 single tents and 100 hospital marquees proved to be ridiculously small. There was no khaki clothing in reserve, only red and blue. Boots had to be called in because the soles fell off in South African conditions.

Despite occasional panic, the outcome of the war was never really in doubt. Kruger's forces amounted to 48,000, most of them irregulars; by the time the war was over, Britain had put a quarter of a million men into the field. Doyle and his hospital personnel sailed from England on 28 February 1900, the day before Ladysmith was relieved, an occasion for national rejoicing as though a famous victory had been won. The party arrived in Capetown on 21 March; on the same day Cecil Rhodes left Capetown for England. Doyle learned that Kimberley had also been relieved, and it looked as though the war would be over before he got a whiff of action. In London he had been given some money for charitable purposes, and Doyle decided to donate some to Boer prisoners penned up on a racecourse. 'There were a few cruel or brutal faces, some of them half caste, but most were good honest fellows and the general effect was formidable,' he wrote later. Other observers were not so charitable. War correspondents descended in hordes on South Africa, commuting between British and Boer positions, writing anything that would make good copy. A joke of the time concerns a young boy who is sternly asked by his father: 'Do you know what happens to boys who tell lies?' 'Yes, Father, they become war correspondents.'

In Britain, there was a chasm between the Little Englanders and the Pro-Boers, each faction paying for its own favourite material. In South Africa there was discomfort and irritation. The Boer was not a senseless peasant, but a formidable foe, a fine horseman and equipped with modern weapons, a match for anyone. Attempts were made to denigrate him. In an interview in *The King* in February 1900, a wounded British officer, Lieut.-Colonel Willoughby Verner, had his say about the enemy:

Are the Boers good shots? Yes; but over-rated. Where their skill lies is in reserving their fire and shooting steadily at effective ranges. I'll explain. You must know that they are cowards – at least those we met were. So long as they can shoot our men down with safety to themselves they are very brave, but they bolt the moment they think there is a chance of their being cut off by cavalry ... The average Boer is a *very* low type – a surly, ignorant, dirty fellow, who knows nothing beyond his Old Testament, in which he contrives to find excuse for his disgraceful treatment of the native.

He was asked about the British artillery: 'Our artillery is in some respects the finest in the world. But, as I have told you, the Boer officers are uncommonly clever. They knew they couldn't come near our artillerymen in general efficiency and fire-discipline, so they decided to beat us in another way – by procuring far heavier guns, of longer range than ours.'

There were apologists more subtle than Verner, but his point of view was shared by many fellow officers, including the generals. War was played by rules; it was a sport in which the other fellow got killed. Major-General Hart conducted his campaign as if he were at manœuvres. He liked to see an advance conducted in well-massed columns, with no nonsense about open order, and this he organized at the battle of Colenso in mid-December 1899, losing more than 500 men while the Boers lost less than a dozen.

All this was ancient history when Doyle went out in early April 1900 looking for action (his hospital equipment had been mislaid). But it was 'Brother Boer's way never to come when you wanted him and always when you didn't'. The missing equipment turned up, and Doyle went back to doctoring after nearly a decade as a professional writer. It was a different kind of doctoring – no sprains, housemaid's knee, influenza and the host of minor ailments dear to the heart of a G.P. Nor was there much in the way of war injuries. What Doctor

Doyle and his colleagues had to combat was enteric fever in Bloemfon-tein, a violent outbreak caused by the Boers cutting off the water supply and the army's reliance on old wells. The outbreak 'was softened down for public consumption and the press messages were heavily censored, but we lived in the midst of death – and death in its vilest, filthiest form'. Doyle praised the nurses, his staff, and the common soldier, who 'may grouse in days of peace, but I never heard a murmur when he was faced with this loathsome death'.

The war moved forward, the water works were captured, and Doyle had an opportunity to go up with the troops. He was eager to compare the officers of his own day with the story-book heroes of Brigadier Gerard's time and the novels of chivalry. He found a parallel in General Pole-Carew, 'spruce, debonair, well-groomed, with laugh-ing eyes and upward-curved moustache'. As for the Grenadier Guards officers: 'Their walk is dainty, their putties are well rolled – there is still the suggestion of the West End.'

He saw the other side of war, the raiding of a farmhouse from which a sniper had been operating: 'A fat white pig, all smothered in blood, runs past. A soldier meets it, his bayonet at the charge. He lunges and lunges again, and the pig screams horribly. I had rather see a man killed. Some are up in the loft throwing down the forage. Others root up the vegetables. One drinks milk out of a strange vessel, amid the laughter of his comrades. It is a grotesque and medieval scene.'

It was difficult to reconcile the poise and *ton* of the officer class with the dirtiness of war, and for almost the first time Doyle was pitchforked into reality. War was not neat and straightforward. A less keen-eyed and observant man could have remained content with the stale stereo-type, oblivious of the incidentals that had nothing to do with the war but which illuminate a way of life. The bar of a hotel is 'fitted with pornographic pictures to amuse our simple farmer friends – not the first or the second sign which I have seen that pastoral life and a Puritan creed do not mean a high public morality'. How different from the clear-cut issues of the historical novel, where the country-dweller has all the virtues associated with the tilling of the soil!

Even the officer class could disappoint, and Doyle lamented the openness with which they expressed their boredom. It would 'be more judicious and even more honourable if [British officers] were less open about the extent to which they are "fed-up" '. Marches were not happy-go-lucky occasions: 'The men are silent on the march; no band, no singing. Grim and sullen, the column flows across the veldt.

Officers and men are short in their tempers. "Why don't you," etc., etc., bleats a subaltern.'

Doyle could be graphic in such a way that one regrets that he was not a war correspondent. 'There comes a shell which breaks high up in the air – wheeeee – tang – with a musical, resonant note, like the snapping of a huge banjo-string, and a quarter of an acre of ground spurted into little dust-clouds under the shrapnel.' A dead trooper is found, and on top of the water-bottle is a red chess pawn. A Sherlock Holmes type problem? No, the trooper had been looting. His effects are tabulated like so many clues – a bandolier, a stylographic pen, a silk handkerchief, a clasp-knife, a Waterbury watch, £2 6s.6d. in a frayed purse. Even in an alien environment the creator of Holmes could note the make of the watch.

While he was in South Africa Doyle met many of the leading generals. Buller was a coarse-fibred man, though a brave soldier. By a skilful choice of anecdote Doyle illustrates Buller's less noble qualities. During the siege of Ladysmith the defenders saved up a few cakes and other luxuries, and these were laid before Buller. 'I thought you were a starving city,' he observed. Roberts's 'light blue eyes were full of intelligence and kindness, but they had the watery look of age.' Roberts was over seventy, and had been called out of retirement to defeat the Boers. Doyle had reservations about Kitchener, the war machine. Kitchener was all of a piece; his family were afraid of him, and it was said that he had never spoken to a private soldier. Once again, Doyle selected an anecdote to express the essence of Kitchener. An officer reported that there was a great dynamite explosion, with forty Kaffirs killed. 'Do you need more dynamite?' wired Kitchener.

It seemed to Doyle that the war was over. On 11 July he boarded a ship for England, and was soon involved in a history of the Boer War. But the war was not over, and a guerilla war continued for two more years, with armies employed to guard the railways, blockhouses built to control the country, and commando raids (the first use of the term) by the Boer farmers against groups of occupying soldiers. Eventually the war was won by the use of concentration camps, where men, women and children died in their hundreds. Even the most fervent of apologists could not talk their way out of this.

The definitive apologia came from Doyle, a sixpenny pamphlet entitled *The War in South Africa: Its Cause and Conduct*. 300,000 copies were sold in Great Britain within a couple of months, and it was translated into many languages including Hungarian and Russian. Profits were distributed generously – to Edinburgh University to give a South African student the opportunity to study there, to the Civilian Rifleman's movement, to the Union Jack Club, to a famine in India, to Japanese nursing, to an Irish old soldiers' institute, to a fund for distressed Boers, to Chelsea pensioners and £300 to sport. Fourpence was given to a crossing sweeper.

The pamphlet was not so one-sided as some of its contemporaries. Doyle conceded that conditions in the concentration camps were far from satisfactory, but protested against widespread accusations of looting, rape, brutality and the use of dum-dum bullets (soft-nosed bullets that exploded on impact, invented in 1897 and taking their name from a military station and arsenal near Calcutta). Doyle refused to believe that they had been used. But there was evidence to suggest that they were. Regrettable things had happened, but the Boers had used trickery, making a mockery of the white flag, had neglected prisoners-of-war and had tortured Kaffir prisoners. It was not exactly six of one and half a dozen of the other; it was more like eight to four. Doyle also made recommendations. The concept of cavalry was obsolete, side-arms were useless, and in future wars more attention should be paid to a civilian militia. The army, still shaken by the defeats the Boers had inflicted, wondered what an amateur was doing, telling them how to do their job. But it was of mere academic interest. The next war would be fought by the book, whether it was against France, Germany or Russia, against generals who knew the rules.

On the boat from South Africa the journalist H.W.Nevinson had become acquainted with Doyle, and noted his 'trustful friendliness'. Nevinson was not alone in thinking that this sterling quality 'may have weakened his power (never very strong, as I was told by men who had worked with him) – his power of judging evidence'. He could be worked on, and used as the unconscious spokesman of a subtle faction. He was an ideal pawn between the soldiers and the politicians in the aftermath of the Boer War.

After every war there is a post-mortem, but in no previous war had so much dirty washing been exposed on its conclusion as the Boer War. Those selected as scapegoats were puzzled and nonplussed, in particular General Buller, who was, wrote Nevinson, 'the kind of man that every Englishman would wish to be if fortune allowed – solid of form, brave above suspicion, silent and indifferent to rhetoric, undemonstrative and unemotional, unyielding in disaster, but under that imperturbable appearance bearing a kindly heart'. It was almost a pen portrait of Doyle. But, according to the German military staff history of the war, he had one great defect: 'Buller was no longer a leader, but merely a fellow-combatant; no longer a general, but a battery-commander. The physically brave man had succumbed morally to the impressions of the battlefield.'

Buller represented a vanishing species, the up-and-at-'em hero, the disciple of the theory of the frontal charge who would have formed a square if he had the chance, the kind of soldier revered and praised in Doyle's historical novels. Indeed, though Doyle probably did not know about it, Buller at Aldershot in 1901 told assembled officers to read historical novels as a basis for acquiring a knowledge of military history. *Punch* picked this up, and envisaged a communiqué based on this proposition: 'We expect to attack in force tomorrow – indeed the movement should have been made today, but I had not finished my study of *Ivanhoe*, and determined to risk nothing by insufficient knowledge . . . I can't find in Scott any rules for working my 4·7 guns, which is rather unfortunate.' Doyle's *The White Company* was sufficiently established as one of the standard historical novels to be mentioned: 'Yesterday made a reconnaissance in the style recommended in *The White Company*, and today we are skirmishing after the instructions contained in *The Last of the Mohicans*. By carefully following best authors, I hope for decisive victory before long.'

Doyle had long relished war as it should have been. He did not spare squeamish readers: 'There was one of those balls that knocked five men into a bloody mash, and I saw it lying on the ground afterwards like a crimson football. Another went through the adjutant's horse with a plop like a stone in the mud, broke its back, and left it lying like a burst gooseberry' (*The Great Shadow* 1893). He revelled in valiant useless charges of cavalry, the shot 'whining like hungry dogs', the commander who leads from the front, and the kind of recruit who 'could stand up to Boney's best'. He could not quite reconcile the image of war as expressed in his books and the reality as experienced, however briefly, in the Boer War. As the author of the interim history of the Boer War, defeat into victory without the necessity of making sense of the long guerilla war carried on by the Boers, he reckoned himself an authority on modern war, and during the uneasy years leading up to 1914 he often speculated about the techniques that would be adopted if and when war broke out, mixing fantasy and common sense in an always stimulating, if not always relevant, brew.

The post-mortem on the Boer War had led to serious evaluation of the army and preparations for war. A Royal Commission was appointed in 1902, 114 witnesses were heard, of whom 22,000 questions were asked. Ammunition supplies always lagged behind demand, naval orders were stopped and ammunition was borrowed from the government of India. There were no long-range guns available, and coastal defence guns at Plymouth were taken. The rifle reserve consisted of 200,000 Lee-Enfields, and it was found that in battle the sighting was incorrect, and gave an error of eighteen inches over 500 yards. The clothing was inappropriate, and all the troops sent out to South Africa had to be reclothed from head to foot. The ammunition pouches were so made that the contents fell out and supplied the Boers.

Regarding the purchase of horses for overseas, 'there was not the symptom of an idea'. Many were unsuitable, and died on board ship. The medical service, fondly believed to have been modernized after the disasters of the Crimean War, was hopeless. Of 8,500 medical men sent out, only a quarter were trained Army Medical Corps men. Medical stores were of inferior quality, and medicine was in cumbrous bottles instead of in pill form ('tabloids'). As for the quality of officers, Lord Kitchener commented: 'There appears to be a want of serious study of their profession by officers, who are rather inclined to deal too lightly with military questions of moment ... In the higher ranks there seems to be a want of that professionalism which is essential to thorough efficiency.'

It was a damning report, but the army authorities still did not want civilian interference, however well meaning. The Army League suggested that attention should be directed at forming a home army with status, with a Militia of 200,000 men, plus the mounted Yeomanry, and the Volunteers (who would take the place of the Militia when the Militia was serving overseas). This was a topic dear to Doyle's heart. In 1900 he had made efforts to start rifle clubs all over the country, and he never lost his belief in the efficacy of a citizens' army, a willing propagandist for the section of the army which agreed with him, a meddling amateur to those who did not.

Whatever the military experts might have thought of him, it was clear that Doyle had won a remarkable propaganda victory with his sixpenny pamphlet. In his own mind he had put the record straight. In April 1902 he was notified that he would receive a knighthood; he demurred, but his mother persuaded him that it was no more than his due, and that refusal would seem a calculated insult to King Edward VII (though other men had refused knighthoods without it being construed as a slight to the monarch). It was not a mark of appreciation for the creator of Sherlock Holmes, though Lord Rosebery took pleasure in his ownership of a first edition of *The Memoirs of Sherlock Holmes*. It was not even a token of thanks for reviving the English historical novel, though Sir Winston Churchill was very enthusiastic about Doyle's contributions in this field. The knighthood was a nod of approval from the establishment, taking into its bosom one of its own.

8
A
TYPICAL
EDWARDIAN

After his return from South Africa in 1900 Doyle went into politics. Even he found it difficult to explain why, though he felt it essential that the present government, which happened to be Conservative, should carry on the war to its logical conclusion. He was an early apostle of unconditional surrender, and a disciple of Joseph Chamberlain and tariff reform. To Chamberlain the introduction of an entirely new and far-reaching tariff system would protect and inspire British businessmen, who were becoming depressed by the inroads the Americans and the Germans were making into international trade. On the other hand, Chamberlain had declared in Leicester in November 1899 that a 'natural alliance' existed between the British and the German Empire – 'both interest and racial sentiment unite the two peoples' – though he rounded on the Germans when their newspapers accused the British of atrocities in South Africa.

Doyle conceived a particular animus against Campbell-Bannerman, leader of the Liberals since 1898. He wished to contest Campbell-Bannerman's seat, but this was not possible. In the end, he was saddled with a hopeless constituency in Edinburgh, surprised everyone by his effectiveness at the hustings, and sliced a chunk off the Liberals' majority. Many believed that he would have won but for accusations that he was a Jesuit in disguise; someone had discovered his Catholic background.

Going into politics was a logical step. Doyle was forty-one, a figure of note, and politics brought him into contact with a new and refreshing set of people, far removed from ink-stained second-rate writers. Both winners and losers in the 1900 'khaki election' belonged to the same ruling clique. Lord Salisbury remained prime minister, but he gave way in 1902 to his nephew Arthur Balfour, because, declared J.L.Garvin of the *Observer*, 'it is desired by the ruling families that the minimum of change should be made'. Balfour was ten years older than Doyle. He regarded politics as a polite game, was vague and ethereal, and was known at school as 'Pretty Fanny'. He was an élitist and did not think the time right for democracy. Nor did Doyle. He disliked socialism, and the idea that women should get the vote shocked him.

Balfour was congenial to him, as he played golf at about the same level as Doyle, was modest, a good listener and hated cowardice. Balfour's political opponents were no less congenial to Doyle. Asquith also played golf, less well than Balfour, and was, wrote Doyle in his autobiography, 'a naturally sweet-tempered man, but under that gentleness there lay judgment and firmness ... He never said too much, but what he did say he lived up to.' Both Balfour and Asquith were far too subtle for thumbnail generalizations. Doyle remained on the periphery of their circle, far too honest and straightforward for the intricacies of party politics. In 1906 Doyle tried to get into Parliament again, fought an election at Hawick, and once again lost.

He made his appearance in *Punch*, as 'The Coneydoil or Shurla-combs'. 'This big friendly Creature is very shrood and saggacious. If he finds a footprint he can tell you what coloured hair it has and whether it is a libbral or a conservative – which is very clever I think. He plays all games and always makes a hundred. He likes to run through the 'Strand' with his tail in parts – all of them strong and healthy – then he collects it all together and it runs for a long time by itself.'

A friendly appreciation, and his failure in politics made no difference to his stature. Politics was merely an interlude, a form of therapy. It was time to return to fiction after the hard work on the Boer War, back to make-believe. A sequel to *The White Company*, with many of the same characters, was contemplated, but a meeting with Fletcher Robinson, whom Doyle had met in South Africa where Robinson was correspondent of the *Daily Express*, mercifully postponed another tale of medieval high jinks. They met again in March 1901 on a golfing holiday in Cromer, where Doyle was recuperating after a recurrence of mild fever caught in South Africa. Robinson told him of Dartmoor legends, especially one about a spectral hound. Spectral hounds are common in English folk lore, as the Black Dog of Lyme Regis or the Black Shuck of East Anglia, but the Dartmoor setting appealed to Doyle and he and Robinson spoke about a possible collaboration. Doyle wrote to his mother about the project, which would be 'a real Creeper!'

A visit with Robinson to Dartmoor soon followed. They stayed at Rowe's Duchy Hotel, Princetown. Princetown still has the quality of an American frontier town, totally untouched by the supermarket era, situated in one of the more inhospitable portions of the moor and catering for the prison and, haphazardly and unsystematically, for the summer tourists.

Perhaps fortunately Robinson did not go into writing partnership with Doyle. *The Hound of the Baskervilles* took rapid shape. Originally it was going to be, as Doyle said, a real creeper, perhaps on the lines of his 'The King of the Foxes', which came out in the *Windsor Magazine* in 1898, where a monstrous fox turned out to be a wolf escaped from a menagerie. Holmes was an afterthought, but as soon as his inclusion was contemplated the pieces fell into their pattern, with a prelude in the old rooms in Baker Street, an exciting middle section and a dénouement. Unlike *A Study in Scarlet* and *The Sign of Four* there is no flashback, except in the written account of the ghastly death of the first Baskerville.

There is little doubt that *The Hound of the Baskervilles* has proved to be the best known of the Holmes stories, and the only one of the Holmes novels that keeps the interest going throughout. The story sweeps forward, even though the murderer is known with fifty pages yet to go and Holmes is absent (supposedly back in London looking after other cases but really on the moors in disguise) for almost half the book. This supposed disadvantage actually turns out to be a stroke of genius, for the sudden reappearance of Holmes is unexpected yet exactly what the reader is waiting for, a *deus ex machina* to support poor blundering Watson.

Because of the absence of Holmes there is very little detective work done, though the detective interest is quickly established when Holmes gives a description of the mildly eccentric Dr Mortimer from the evidence of his walking stick. Holmes's second feat is not so impressive, except to Watson and Mortimer; from an inch or two of manuscript sticking out of Mortimer's pocket, Holmes deduces that it is of the early eighteenth century. 'It would be a poor expert who could not give the date of a document within a decade or so,' he says airily, basing his conclusion on the mixture of long and short 's's.

Doyle threw his readers a clever clue in the matter of the Missing

Boot. Unlike many of his competitors, he played fair. The first boot to be stolen from Sir Henry Baskerville is new, and is replaced. A boot from a second pair is stolen, and kept (to give the hound a scent). And soon Holmes sends Watson off to battle with the unknown, which may or may not be supernatural ('I have hitherto confined my investigations to this world,' says Holmes).

The suspects, it must be admitted, are very thin on the ground, and the two key ones are not very sharply differentiated. The red herring – the butler and his wife – is soon disposed of. This might seem to be a fault, a token of Doyle's indifference in not providing good villains, but it must be emphasized that a reader coming to the book for the first time is torn between looking for a murderer and a half-belief that Doyle is going to cross the border, as Poe did, into the supernatural, and that the spectral hound is really what it purports to be, a monster breathing fire and not a dog daubed with a preparation of phosphorus.

The success of the book lay not in the characterization or the detective work but in setting Holmes and Watson in a convincing and frightening environment. It does not matter that the women are vacuous and unconvincing, and that their motivations are very odd indeed. Sufficient that Holmes is back, as consistent and all of a piece as ever.

Doyle, with that instinct for the telling point that characterizes his Holmes stories, makes his Dartmoor outdo the genuine article. It is a Dartmoor that appeals to those who do not know it very well. In the first place, he makes Dartmoor much bigger than it really is; Dartmoor is shaped like a flat lozenge thirty miles by twenty. Yet Baskerville Hall is fourteen miles from Princetown. On the west, this would take it well past Tavistock, on the north to Okehampton, on the east into Bovey Tracey, and on the south to Ivybridge on the A38, a built-up area a few miles from Plymouth.

The reader's introduction to Dartmoor as Watson, Dr Mortimer and the new heir to the Baskerville estates travel down from London is graphic. 'There rose in the distance a grey, melancholy hill, with a strange jagged summit, dim and vague in the distance, like some fantastic landscape in a dream ... Our wagonette had topped a rise and in front of us rose the huge expanse of the moor, mottled with gnarled and craggy cairns and tors ... Suddenly we looked down into a cup-like depression patched with stunted oaks and firs which had been twisted and bent by the fury of years of storm.' This is fair enough, but Doyle adds to it by enumerating plants not found on Dartmoor, and everywhere describes granite as black, which it is not. There is nothing like the terrible Grimpen mire which adds so much to the novel's menace. Bogs there are, but they do not spell the instantaneous death of the Doyle version. Nor did they in 1901. These were minor matters, and there was high delight in the George Newnes empire, though nothing compared with the rapture of the *Strand* readers, a little older and greyer than when Holmes went to his doom.

But Doyle was stubborn on one point. *The Hound of the Baskervilles* dated back to pre-Reichenbach days, and he had no intention of resurrecting Holmes for the benefit of the idle readers of the *Strand*. More difficult to disappoint were American readers, and when an offer came from the United States of five thousand dollars for a short story Doyle could not resist. It was a blow to those who saw Doyle as incorruptible, as a potentially great novelist in the vein of Walter Scott who had unfortunately got bogged down in hack-work but had risen above it. It was the triumph of cynicism. Anyone, if the price was right, could be bought, and Conan Doyle, while not doing any-thing in the least disreputable, had admitted that he was human.

There were few writers of this period who were not tempted by wealth; King Edward VII had made the pursuit of riches respectable, and it was no disadvantage to be vulgar and ostentatious. The young Edgar Wallace, who had been a newspaper correspondent in South Africa during the Boer War, was working on the *Rand Daily Mail* at a salary of £2,000 a year, a very considerable sum of money when £300 a year was considered a good wage, on which one could keep a domestic servant. Wallace's pride in achievement was mirrored in his gold-headed cane, large hats and immaculate yellow gloves. When writers met, they talked contracts and money. 'I heard that Mrs Humphry Ward had £10,000 from *Harpers* for serial rights of "Lady Rose's Daughter" ', wrote Arnold Bennett in his diary in December 1903. It is difficult not to detect a note of envy. Writers who were not rich and did not mind admitting it were regarded as freaks. On 9 May 1904 Bennett dined with Lewis Hind, who had just relin-quished the editorship of the art magazine *The Academy* and was the author of popular guides to art such as *Days With Velasquez*. Hind told him that Max Beerbohm lived on the £5 a week he got from the *Saturday Review*. 'Strange, if true,' commented Bennett, aggra-vated that a man could be so lowly paid and yet be regarded as a writer of the first rank.

There was bitchiness between writers. On 27 May 1904 Bennett wrote: 'My new series begins to appear today in the *Windsor*. My name is not on the cover. Anthony Hope's stands there alone. And I am 37. Comment is needless.' In a decade or two Edgar Wallace and Arnold Bennett were to earn the same kind of money as Conan Doyle, Wallace by pot-boiling thrillers and Bennett by pot-boiling journalism. With his acceptance of the American offer, which made him the highest-paid writer of his age, Conan Doyle tacitly admitted that he, too, was pot-boiling, though the stew was of a superior flavour to the concoction of lesser writers. The revival of Sherlock Holmes was a key event in his life. It was a concession that he was an entertainment writer, a provider of what the public wanted.

The success of Wallace and Bennett was measured in conspicuous consumption. Doyle's expenditure was on a less ostentatious scale, but his life as a country squire demanded a considerable income. Some of it went in, as he admitted, ill-conceived ventures, in gold mines that yielded no gold, though he was also a director of the successful picture-postcard firm of Raphael Tuck and had interests in a firm of musical-instrument makers.

Doyle had to sustain a role during a period in which he was under intense stress. His wife Louise was still alive, while Jean Leckie hovered in the wings. His sister and his brother-in-law, the novelist E. W. Hornung (1866–1921), deplored the relationship between Doyle and Miss Leckie. To Hornung it made no difference whether it was platonic or not.

To his children, Mary and Kingsley, Doyle was remote and dangerous. Worst of all, he was unpredictable. At one time he had joined in their games, a Father Christmas at the right season, a nursery horse at other times, boisterous but not rough. There were flashes of geniality, as when he asked the children to carry his golf clubs on a Sunday when the routine was usually church, and they were allowed liberties other children might have envied; girls and boys in their teens were not often permitted to go on holiday by themselves as the Doyle children were, and middle-class parents would have considered it socially dangerous to let their offspring canter about barefoot. He encouraged them in any sports they set their mind to, and Mary took up rifle-shooting.

But they always kept an eye on him. If they failed to deliver a message he had committed to them they dreaded the wrath which may have fallen on them. If they spoke out of turn at the dinner table, there could be the frightening appearance of a stern Victorian pater-familias at their bedside.

As Doyle was worrying about the health of his wife, and about the ambiguous situation of Jean Leckie in her own particular limbo, he was also wondering whether the public would take to Holmes again.

Tastes had changed over the ten years since Holmes had hurtled over the cliff, and writers had more latitude over what were once forbidden subjects. Novelists were writing more honestly about sex, and what was once considered an advanced novel, Grant Allen's *The Woman Who Did*, was now laughably old-fashioned. H.G.Wells was beginning to make inroads with his accurately observed novels of lower-middle-class life, and adventure novels were fresher and livelier. The best seller of 1902 was A.E.W.Mason's *The Four Feathers*, which catered for much the same audience as Doyle's *The Tragedy of the Korosko*, only more successfully.

Although public library stocks doubled between 1901 and 1914, fewer books were being published, though the decline since 1897 had been arrested in 1902 with a total of 5,839 (to give this figure some kind of reality, the figure for 1975 was more than 35,000). Many of these were sixpenny reprints of Victorian novels the copyright of which had recently expired (this put *Tom Brown's Schooldays* into the charts). The most popular writers were those who wrote for the women's market, and the doyenne of these was Mrs M.E.Braddon (1837–1915), who had created a furore in 1862 with *Lady Audley's Secret*, which had sold more than a million copies, and who was still going strong. By the time she had finished, Mrs Braddon had written seventy sensational romances.

At the same time as the queens of the circulating and public libraries were captivating their readers, there was a trend for cheap reprints of the classics. The World's Classics, published by Grant Richards and later taken over by the Oxford University Press, date from 1901, and Collins' Classics from 1903. In 1906 came Everyman's Library. These splendidly produced books competed in the market place with new novels and achieved large sales. The reading public applauded such enterprises, but writers were depressed; for every novelist who made a living at his profession, ten suffered through the plethora of sixpenny reprints.

In a sense, Conan Doyle was fortunate. He was not competing with A.E.W.Mason and other best-selling novelists, but with magazine writers of a pretty low order, and his ace in the hole was Sherlock

Holmes. Although Holmes had apparently ceased to function for a decade, he was not forgotten. In 1893 a dramatist named Charles Rogers wrote a melodrama called *Sherlock Holmes*, a farrago of nonsense in which Watson had married the woman Holmes was in love with. Watson disappears, and Holmes is reproved by Mrs Watson for not finding him. Eventually Watson is discovered, deprived of his memory as the result of a blow on the head delivered by his kidnapper, a maniac named Wilton Hursher. To save Watson, Holmes injects him with a rare Indian drug that renders him lifeless, and is arrested for murder. He escapes and prevents an autopsy on his friend. Rogers was careful only to use the names of Holmes and Watson, and so avoided infringement of copyright.

More significant was a venture by the American actor William Gillette. Doyle had written a Sherlock Holmes play and had offered it to Herbert Beerbohm Tree, but Tree wanted his part rewritten to suit his own personality. As Doyle did not wish to do this the idea was dropped, but Doyle's agent retrieved the play and sent it to the American impresario Charles Frohman, who passed it on to Gillette. Gillette liked it, but sent a telegram to Doyle to ask if he could get Holmes married. Doyle told him that he could marry or murder him or do what he liked with him.

As soon as the play was completed, Gillette lost the text in a fire in San Francisco, but rewrote it, visited England to obtain Doyle's approval and have a 'copyright performance' played in London, and then returned to the United States to arrange a premiere. The story was based on 'A Scandal in Bohemia' and 'The Final Problem', with bits of dialogue filched from other stories. Holmes is eventually lured to a gas chamber in Stepney, but smashes the oil lamp on the table. The gang try to locate Holmes by the glow of his cigar, but Holmes has fixed the cigar to a window frame, and escapes through the door. The curtain falls with Holmes and the heroine embracing, and the villain, Professor Moriarty, captured.

The play opened in New York in November 1899, was a great success, and after an American tour Gillette and his company brought it to England, opening at the Lyceum in September 1901. It was a slick gadget-ridden show that brought a kind of Holmes to the London theatregoer. The *Westminster Gazette* thought that it was a burlesque, *The Stage* that it was a non-success, and *The Times* was austerely critical. Nevertheless, the play continued for more than six months at the Lyceum, and this was followed by tours; four companies took it around Britain, and translations of it were taken up on the Continent. Gillette played Sherlock Holmes until 1929, when he was seventy-six.

In 1900 *Sherlock Holmes Baffled* was put on as a film – all forty-nine seconds of it as a what-the-butler-saw type peepshow. It was the prelude to a mountain of films about Holmes, and, unimportant in itself, it reveals how well the name of Sherlock Holmes was known even to those who sought their entertainment at the end of piers and in the booths where cinema was born.

Although these spin-offs were deplored by the purists, they helped to keep Sherlock Holmes before the general public, and introduce him to those who thought that *The Strand* was a continuation of Fleet Street and nothing else. To his credit, Gillette did not devalue Holmes, though he was nothing like the character as visualized by Sidney Paget. He played the part in a grim still style, and managed to convey something of the quality of Doyle's creation. The subsidiary characters were less fortunate, though the preposterous introduction of Billy the Pageboy offered Charlie Chaplin his first stage role. Gillette and his Holmes were sufficiently celebrated to furnish a subject for the cartoon in *Vanity Fair*, as well as provide material for music-hall sketches such as *Sheerluck Jones or Why D'Gillette Him Off?* (1901) and *Surelock Holmes* (1902).

Doyle seems to have been gently amused by such ephemera, not appreciating that parody is the biggest tribute of all. A more worldly wise author would have subtly sponsored these feeble burlesques, as well as the hundreds of imitations of Sherlock Holmes who featured in their own series in the magazines. They have been called, for the purpose of a television series, the rivals of Sherlock Holmes. In reality they were so many cart-horses led into the starting gates alongside one thoroughbred. The thoroughbred had been out at stud, and while he had been gone a little languid betting had been carried out. When the thoroughbred returned, the cart-horses' lack of breeding was evident. Nobody backed them any more. It was, in every sense of the word, a one-horse race.

9
THE RIVALS OF
SHERLOCK HOLMES

Sherlock Holmes's competitors came from a wide variety of backgrounds. They were millionaires (Arnold Bennett's Cecil Thorold), literary agents (Clifford Ashdown's Romney Pringle), forensic experts (R. Austin Freeman's Doctor Thorndyke) or scruffy idlers (Baroness Orczy's Old Man in the Corner). They were mainly amateurs, and although a few of them ostensibly had jobs most of them were youngish men about town. A quantity of their adventures took place in Europe, to lend a cosmopolitan air and prevent a direct comparison with the very real world of Holmes's London.

Their creators were a mixed bunch, good writers looking for easy money and hacks using their hoary styles with a detective interest grafted on. To describe the stories as invariably clumsy would be to over-generalize, but a brisk trot through them gives the impression of haste and disinterest, and sheer incompetence. 'The Ripening Rubies' by Max Pemberton has the merest vestige of plot; an adventuress steals some rubies, conceals them in her dress, and is eventually apprehended by the hero. 'The Case of Laker, Absconded' by Arthur Morrison has some pretence of characterization, and deals with the appropriation of £15,000 by a bank clerk. The detective discovers that the clerk has been kidnapped, and the money taken by a substitute. The clue is in the form of a slip of paper that conveniently falls out of a folded umbrella. Guy Boothby's 'The Duchess of Wiltshire's Diamonds' is absurd nonsense, relying for any effect on a trick jewel box and without an atom of suspense or surprise. L. T. Meade and Robert Eustace wrote a story called 'Madame Sara' which was published in *The Strand* shortly before the return of Sherlock Holmes. It was a monstrous hotch-potch of nonsense, resting on the ability of

Madame Sara, a beautician, to kill two women so that her confederate could claim the proceeds of a will. She kills one, and nearly kills the other. Madame Sara is not only a beautician but a dentist – so the plot demands – and the customary deadly poison is secreted in a tooth of the heroine, who is saved from death by the quick action of Eric Vandeleur, 'no longer the man with the latest club story and the merry twinkle in his blue eyes' but 'the medical jurist, with a face like a mask, his lower jaw slightly protruding and features very fixed'. This Neanderthal-type creature did not need recourse to a surgery or even a pair of pliers. He 'examined the tooth long and carefully. There was a sudden rapid movement of his hand, and a sharp cry from Mrs Selby. With the deftness of long practice, and a powerful wrist, he had extracted the tooth with one wrench.'

Assumption often takes the place of deduction in the Holmes stories, but rarely did Doyle introduce the mind-boggling improbabilities inherent in the work of his imitators. The best of the lesser detectives are most interesting when they are cool and composed, and work on scientific lines, like Freeman's Doctor Thorndyke. Tales dealing with mysterious ciphers have to compete not only with 'The Dancing Men' but Poe's 'The Gold Bug', though Freeman put a neat twist in his 'The Moabite Cipher' by making the cipher (cracked by Thorndyke) meaningless when transcribed. The real message is revealed when the paper on which the code is written is soaked in water. Thorndyke finds this out by wondering why the code is written in Chinese ink (which is not soluble in water). Not that there was any need for a cipher as cover; the letter was an arrangement for a burglary, and burglaries are not usually arranged through an exchange of letters. But given this improbability, it is the kind of clue, presented to the reader, that Doyle would not have disdained.

The detective-story writers of the nineties and the Edwardian period made much of little. They were obliged by the rules of the game to run to three thousand words, and yet the story had to be sustained on one clue. Arnold Bennett's 'A Bracelet at Bruges' concerns the loss of a bracelet in a canal; the owner is showing it to an acquaintance, who drops it. The owner goes off to find a policeman, returning in a few seconds. The canal is dragged, but there is no trace of the bracelet. Fortunately, the millionaire detective Cecil is watching from Bruges belfry with binoculars. He later examines the railings by the canal, and discovers a silk thread attached to them. The solution is simple; the acquaintance is the usual adventuress, and the bracelet is hooked on to the end of a silk thread and then dropped. When the owner is away, the bracelet is hauled up. Freeman played fair with his reader by mentioning the Chinese ink; Bennett did not mention the thread.

In a sense, Arthur Morrison played too fair in the story monstrously entitled 'The Affair of the Avalanche Bicycle and Tyre Co., Limited', published in 1897. He hits the reader across the face with his single clue, and immediately destroys what little interest there is in his narrative. The story is about a fraudulent cycle firm and a cycle race to exploit the particular make of bicycle. The best cyclist rides a rival bicycle, and must be nobbled on a trial run. This is done by throwing an iron garden chair in front of his wheels as it is getting dark. Who threw the chair? No doubt about it to the reader, despite what the author might have thought. The villain is set up near the start of the story, a Mr Paul Mallows who 'had the large frame of a man of strong build who had had much hard bodily work, but there hung about it the heavier, softer flesh that told of a later period of ease and sloth'. Thus was he labelled. On his first appearance, Mallows cuts his finger on the handle of his carriage door. The detective has some black sticking plaster with him ('I always carry it – it's handier than ordinary sticking plaster'). After the cycle crash, the detective examines the iron chair, and from one of the nuts he 'secured some object – it may have been a hair – which he carefully transferred to his pocketbook'. No one in his right mind would have thought it was a hair; it was clearly a piece of black sticking plaster. The detective does not bring Mallows to justice, but blackmails him; Mallows does not like this, and tries to lock the detective in an enamelling vat.

Even an addict must have winced at the utter imbecility of such a story – but Morrison was a reputable writer whose effusions were not merely tolerated in the absence of anything better but welcomed. In his stories about the East End of London, Morrison (1863–1945) brought a sense of reality commensurate with his subject, but in his detective stories, which mainly featured Martin Hewitt, Investigator, he returned to the pot-boiling of his early gaudy tales of the supernatural. As a journalist he worked on the *National Observer* with J.M.Barrie, Stevenson and Rudyard Kipling. He was also a collector of Chinese and Japanese paintings, which he sold to the British Museum.

R. Austin Freeman (1862–1943) also wrote under the name of Clifford Ashdown, who created Romney Pringle for *Cassell's Magazine* in 1902. Freeman was bitterly ashamed of Clifford Ashdown, not without reason. Ashdown's 'The Assyrian Rejuvenator' is preposterous and tedious: Pringle reads a letter left in a restaurant and finds out that a Lieut.-Colonel Sandstream is trying to sue the maker of a 'rejuvenator' (price ten shillings and sixpence) and that the maker is being stubborn. In disguise (why he disguises himself is never clear) Pringle goes to the Assyrian Rejuvenator Co., returns in another disguise, helps himself to a batch of ten and sixpenny postal orders, interviews Colonel Sandstream (for no very clear reason), returns for more postal orders, and disappears into the night. There is no detective interest, no clues and no point.

Dr Thorndyke did not come on to the scene until 1907, and was one of the best substitutes for Holmes. Freeman had the requisite medical background to make his forensic science convincing, becoming a house physician at Middlesex Hospital in 1886 and later going on a medical expedition to West Africa. In 1912 he innovated by describing the crime first before letting Thorndyke loose on it, a successful experiment that was widely emulated.

Thorndyke did not have the personality that Doyle built into Holmes, and Freeman was more of a plot designer than a storyteller. In an age when forensic science was becoming known to the general public (and which created its own legendary figure in Sir Bernard Spilsbury) Thorndyke was a reasonably convincing figure. Writers who thought that the recipe for a successful detective story was to give the hero massive intellectual gifts could come to grief, as a mastermind can easily turn out to be an unctuous swot. Only one was convincing, Professor Van Dusen, created by Jacques Futrelle in 1907. Van Dusen was a weedy man with a big domed head who seemed to resemble Grumpy of *Snow White and the Seven Dwarfs* with a dash of Dopey in his 'perpetual, forbidding squint'. Be that as it may, Futrelle's Thinking Machine, as he is referred to throughout the stories that feature Van Dusen, was novel without being bizarre. In 'The Problem of Cell 13' Futrelle wrote a neat terse how-was-it-done story, showing Van Dusen breaking out of the death cell of a seemingly impregnable prison, just to prove his brilliance (making use of a disused pipe through which rats come and go, he unthreads lisle from his socks, uses a rat as a messenger by tying the thread to it, and links up with a reporter who sends in the materials for escape). After the sloppy inconsequence of most detective stories, Futrelle comes as a refreshing surprise and shows that Doyle could have had a rival, though sadly Futrelle died in the *Titanic*, still a young man.

Other detective-story writers were no competition. Max Pemberton (1863–1950) had served his apprenticeship as editor of the boys' magazine *Chums*, and was editor of *Cassell's Magazine* from 1896 to 1906. *Cassell's* was of a much older vintage than *Strand* and other newcomers, and although it tried to change with the times it was never as lively as its main competitors, though it did serve as a platform for Freeman and the editor himself. Guy Boothby (1867–1905) did not live long enough to find out what his true metier was, but turned out about fifty adventure stories, a few with a detective flavour, and some based on his Australian background. The awful story 'Madame Sara' was the product of Mrs L.T.Meade, who usually worked in collaboration with a doctor or someone with a scientific background and who died too soon (in 1914) to apply her talents to television doctor series, a task for which she was eminently suited. She also wrote a large quantity of stories for girls such as *Bashful Fifteen*, and contributed to most of the magazines of the time. Her most faithful collaborator was the mysterious Robert Eustace, eventually tracked down as Dr Eustace Robert Barton. He was going strong as late as 1930 when he was associated with Dorothy Sayers in her fine detective novel *The Documents in the Case*.

The detective stories of Baroness Orczy were subsidiary to her historical extravaganzas such as *The Scarlet Pimpernel*, while the stories of Maurice Leblanc – creator of Arsène Lupin – and E.W.Hornung – Doyle's brother-in-law and responsible for Raffles, gentleman-criminal – look backward to the police romances of Gaboriau and forward to the thriller. Hornung's Raffles tales eschew the straight morality of the now traditional detective stories, with right and wrong clearly defined. The crooked private detective, as represented by Romney Pringle, was smudging the edges, but the glorification of the villain and indifference to traditional values reached a minor peak in Hornung. Raffles was put out as a modern Robin Hood, but he was too second-rate a character for that, something of a suburban gigolo who resembles most Leslie Charteris's The Saint (though even inferior to him). However, it showed a new way for entertainment novels to go.

Perhaps the most unashamed replica of Sherlock Holmes was Sexton Blake, packaged for the boys' market. Max Pemberton was not the only detective-story writer involved in the juvenile field. Responsibility for the creation of Sexton Blake lies at the door of Hal Meredith, an otherwise unknown writer, and Sexton Blake first appeared in the boys' paper *The Halfpenny Marvel* in 1893. He 'belonged to the new order of detectives. He possessed a highly cultivated mind which helped to support his active courage. His refined, clean-shaven face readily lent itself to any disguise.' Like Holmes, he had 'a spare athletic figure and a lean and somewhat ascetic face', but unlike Holmes he had a 'quick spontaneous smile'. But that was in 1938. He may not have possessed the charisma of Holmes, but he was longer-lived.

The adolescent mind was not ready for the feats of Sexton Blake. *The Halfpenny Marvel* did not wax rich on him, and in 1894 Blake transferred to the more congenial *The Union Jack*, moving from New Inn Chambers to, naturally, Baker Street, acquiring an assistant, Tinker, a landlady and a bloodhound named Pedro. In 1915 he appeared in novelette form in the Sexton Blake Library, on film in *The Stolen Heirlooms* in the same year and continued to ply his busy microscope until 1963, by which time he had become an uneasy echo of James Bond.

Many of the writers of detective stories had no illusions about their work. They were professionals, and if the public wanted tales with a detective interest then they would provide them. Eden Phillpotts is now chiefly known by his stories of West Country life, but he was willing to make his contribution to the genre. In November 1898 he was discussing the possibilities of the serial with Arnold Bennett:

'I've written 12,000 words of it,' he said; 'started on Friday, and have done 3,000 words a day. It's disgustingly easy. I've no trouble with plots, you know, and the rest is mere writing.' He then explained the plot for me [Bennett] and it was decidedly a proper 'popular' plot.

'And what is the *dénouement*?' I asked.

'Haven't the least idea. But there's a brass ornament with mysterious signs on it that I expect will do great things towards the end.'

Later he said, 'I shall finish it in a month – 70,000 words. And if anyone would make it worth my while, I wouldn't mind betting that I could do twelve such serials a year – easily.'

Those writers who could appeal to the public made an immense amount of money. The only requirement was to be inventive. George R. Sims is today remembered through his 'Christmas Day in the Workhouse', but he was a prolific and versatile writer, churning out tales of low life and the obligatory detective stories (*Dorcas Dene, Detec-*

tive, 1897). His income was over £15,000 a year (a quarter of a million in today's money, almost tax-free). Sims did not have to be good, only prolific.

When the low quality of magazine fiction, detective and otherwise, is considered, perhaps it is not surprising that George Newnes was so anxious to re-enlist Sherlock Holmes. Even the weakest Holmes story seemed infinitely superior to the run-of-the-mill hackwork, and in 1903 Doctor Thorndyke was four years in the future, and G.K. Chesterton's Father Brown did not arrive on the scene for eight. Doyle wondered how the public would take to Holmes. There was the possibility that he would have difficulty in establishing Holmes in the nineteen-hundreds as comfortably as he had in the eighteen-nineties, if only because the very accoutrements that had helped to set Holmes so firmly in his environment had changed drastically. A Holmes who used the telephone, now accepted with enthusiasm, would have been incongruous, and how would Holmes take to the utilitarian tramcar (in 1903 the 8½-mile route from Westminster Bridge to Tooting was opened)? Would Holmes shop at Harrods, built in 1901, or dine at one of the new lavish gorgeous hotels, such as the Ritz?

Doyle ducked the problem. He set his new series of Holmes stories between 1894 and 1898. The first thing he had to do was to bring Holmes back from his watery grave in a convincing manner. The Holmes saga has been described as fairy-tales for grown-ups. The crowds who thronged round the station bookstalls in October 1903 would have accepted any solution. The day of the counterfeit was over.

'The Empty House' begins with a not particularly enthralling account by Watson of the murder of the Honourable Ronald Adair. While Watson is looking at the scene of the crime at 427 Park Lane he knocks against an elderly deformed man carrying several books. The man snarls with contempt, and Watson sees 'his curved back and white side-whiskers disappear among the throng'. Watson goes home, and the book-collector turns up to apologize for his gruff manner. It is Holmes in disguise, and Watson faints. It is time for Doyle to take a deep breath and explain. Holmes tells Watson how they tottered together upon the brink of the fall, but having some knowledge of 'baritsu, or the Japanese system of wrestling' Holmes slipped through Moriarty's grip, Moriarty lost his balance, and with a horrible scream went over. Recapitulating for the benefit of sceptical readers, Watson points out that two lots of tracks went down the path and none returned.

This is simply explained. Holmes, knowing that the rest of the Moriarty gang were after him, climbed the rocky wall above the path, which was not so sheer as Watson had formerly made out. Danger was not yet over, for one of Moriarty's gang had seen the result of the struggle and hurled down a boulder. Holmes escaped, travelled two years in Tibet, visiting the Head Lama (originally spelled llama, which is a South American mammal), passed through Persia, looked in at Mecca, and paid a short visit to the Khalifa at Khartoum. He had also investigated coal-tar derivatives in the south of France (and was thus a pioneer in modern plastics). It did not ring altogether true. It was not like the reader's mental picture of Holmes, the scurry from trouble and the cruel desertion of Watson.

If Holmes had dropped out of sight to escape the revenge of the Moriarty gang it argued that he was not the supreme being that he had been built up to be. However, readers reasoned that there must have been some more plausible motivation and that Holmes had been engaged in some highly secret machinations involving Very Important Persons that, regrettably, excluded Watson. Watson was not a babbler but he did have a penchant for writing everything down, with the collusion of the Literary Agent referred to by the sherlockians as D.

The Baker Street rooms had been retained through the agency of Holmes's brother Mycroft, and Holmes's belongings, files, furniture and fittings remained undisturbed. Watson had been living in Kensington, but for the purpose of the new series he had to be available as narrator. Doyle handled this with consummate ease: 'In some manner he had learned of my own sad bereavement, and his sympathy was shown in his manner rather than in his words. "Work is the best antidote to sorrow, my dear Watson," said he ...' ('The Empty House'). Doyle was sufficiently subtle not to specify the nature of the bereavement, leaving the reader to assume that it was the death of Watson's wife. Watson, it is tacitly understood, would have swapped a dozen wives for the companionship of Holmes, and 'It was indeed like old times when, at that hour, I found myself seated beside him in a hansom, my revolver in my pocket and the thrill of adventure in my heart.'

By setting the new series ten years back Doyle was able to capitalize on nostalgia for an age that seemed remote. The Boer War had done more than reveal the incapacity of the British Army to deal with a major threat. It had shown how many nations were unfriendly to Britain, and in particular demonstrated the hostility of Germany. Half a century before, Palmerston would have sent a gunboat up the Elbe had the Germans shown such impertinence. The nation was shaken and uneasy, apprehensive about the future. Germany had always been the traditional friend, and many resented the alignment with France, largely due to hatred of Germany by Queen Alexandra and the Francophilia of the new king. Now that Victoria was dead there were no proscriptions on the Entente Cordiale.

The nation looked back at the nineties, when everything was stable. A wave of escapism swept the country, epitomized by the success of Lehar's *The Merry Widow*. Sherlock Holmes was part of the reassuring past – upright, chivalrous, incorruptible, above the law when the law was unfair, and omniscient. In the cosy corners of their suburban homes the bank clerks and small tradesmen pored over the blue cover of the *Strand*, turning the pages for the latest Holmes case. It was, indeed, like old times. The reader could forget the rattle of the tramcar outside the front door, and listen instead to the clatter of hooves through late-Victorian fog.

The new adventures numbered thirteen, and were collected in 1905 and published as *The Return of Sherlock Holmes*. Some were better than others, and often the detail did not bear too close a scrutiny. In 'the Empty House' the most dangerous of Professor Moriarty's lieutenants, Colonel Moran, uses an air-gun with a revolver bullet to try to assassinate Holmes. Doyle, being knowledgeable about firearms and having his own range, should have known better. An air-gun can never be anything more than a sporting toy. In 'The Norwood Builder' the case centres around a will. It is a will that would have been thrown out of any solicitor's office with contempt as insufficiently witnessed. A pile of supposedly human bones turns out to be animal remains. 'Well, well, I dare say that a couple of rabbits would account both for the blood and for the charred ashes,' says Holmes airily. Not for any policeman with a head on his shoulders.

'The Dancing Men' gives Holmes the chance to practise his detective skills on Watson, and is a good old-fashioned cryptographic problem, but Doyle commits an appalling error in 'The Solitary Cyclist', in which a forced marriage is carried out in an unlicensed place by an unfrocked priest with the woman more than unwilling, in fact screaming and struggling. Bicycles also feature strongly in 'The Priory

School'. 'I am familiar with forty-two different impressions left by tyres,' comments Holmes, and his reading of cycle tracks is an interesting development of the time-honoured attention to footprints. The marks made by cows play a significant part in this story. 'It is a remarkable cow which walks, canters, and gallops,' says Holmes. Of the story 'Black Peter' the least said the better, and its successor 'Charles Augustus Milverton' is a charming muddle, noteworthy because of Holmes's near-seduction of a servant girl for the purpose of gaining information. 'The Six Napoleons' has the plot of the villain hiding something of value in an article of no consequence, in this case a fifteen-shilling plaster bust, and 'The Three Students' deals with mayhem at a university, unnamed, with the odds on Oxford. Holmes is pursuing researches in 'Early English Charters' and is called in by a college tutor to investigate examination paper leakages.

There are three suspects, and it is obvious to any reader of detective stories which one is guilty – the least probable, 'Gilchrist, a fine scholar and athlete; plays in the Rugby team and the cricket team for the college, and got his Blue for the hurdles and the long jump'. Too good to be true, and so it proves. When he is exposed he demonstrates that anyone who gets a Blue cannot, by the laws of fiction, be a rotter. 'I have determined not to go in for the examination. I have been offered a commission in the Rhodesian Police, and I am going to South Africa at once.'

In 'The Golden Pince-Nez' Holmes smokes himself silly so that he can drop tobacco ash on the floor and get footprints; 'The Missing Three-Quarter' is a rather trite university story, but 'The Abbey Grange' is Holmes at his best, harking back to 'The Speckled Band' with a plot involving a bell-pull. The last story of the batch was 'The Second Stain', somewhat humdrum. Watson reveals that Holmes has retired from London 'and betaken himself to study and bee-farming on the Sussex downs'.

Like the first two series, *The Return of Sherlock Holmes* has its ups and downs, but Doyle binds the stories together more cleverly by referring back to different cases and putting them in a chronological context. If there was criticism from readers, it was that there was not enough London material, and that Holmes was too fond of university towns and the country. There was not enough fog in Baker Street. And eventually *Strand* used up the stories. Doyle was busy on something else, on more Brigadier Gerard stories, and on *Sir Nigel*, which although it uses the same characters as *The White Company* goes back further in time. It was published in *Strand* between July 1905 and December 1906. It ran to 132,000 words, and it was, he wrote to his mother, 'my absolute top!' Rudyard Kipling liked it, but otherwise, as Doyle wrote later in his autobiography, 'it attracted no particular notice from critics or public'. It was well reviewed, but as a boyish adventure yarn.

In his reawakened enthusiasm for historical novels Doyle took care not to make the grand gesture of killing off Holmes again, but it was several years before Holmes appeared in the *Strand* again, in the serialized novel *The Valley of Fear*. It took him very little time to write. He estimated that it would run to 50,000 words, and by the first week of February 1914 he had done nearly 25,000. He anticipated the completion of the novel before the end of March. He told the editor of *Strand* that in the first part there would be one surprise which he hoped would be a 'real staggerer' to the reader. He also mentioned that in the 'long stretch' Holmes is abandoned. 'That is necessary,' he decided.

John Dickson Carr, master of the locked-room mystery novel, rated *The Valley of Fear* highly, and called the first part 'a very nearly perfect piece of detective-story writing'. It begins with the receipt of a coded message; the key does not arrive, and Holmes breaks the code. This is Doyle at his lively best, with Holmes good-humoured and pleasantly sarcastic ('Your native shrewdness, my dear Watson, that innate cunning which is the delight of your friends'). When the inspector calls to tell Holmes that the man referred to in the coded message has been murdered, there is a short dissertation on Professor Moriarty, who is behind the whole thing, and away they all go to Birlstone Manor in Sussex. The location of the first part of the book is based on Groombridge, not far from where Doyle lived.

Well-constructed as the section is, there is something lacking in atmosphere, and the drawbridge which is drawn up at night has no more impact than a theatrical prop. Darkest Sussex was different from the darkest Devon of *The Hound of the Baskervilles*. The plot revolves around the assumption by the police that the man found dead with his head blown off by a shotgun is the master of the house. All agree that this is so, not only his wife and friend but servants and outsiders who knew him. Is a face the only way one can tell one person from another? In fiction, yes, and the writing skates agreeably along, with false clues littered about and Doyle cleverly leading the reader along, describing the relevant true clues in a relaxed subtle manner that is his alone. It is all too relaxed. The action is restricted to the manor house, with the actors moving around, occasionally displaying emotion, searching a room or making pregnant remarks. It is all too much like a George du Maurier cartoon; there is no need for Watson's trusty revolver, and the killer in a yellow coat riding a bicycle has as much menace as Noddy.

Half the book goes by, the reader transfixed because Doyle is near his story-telling best if not quite at it, and then the mystery is solved. 'I wish you to journey back some twenty years in time,' requests the narrator, 'and westward some thousands of miles in space . . .' promising that at the end of it he and Holmes 'shall meet once more in those rooms in Baker Street'. So the book shifts to America, and the reader is flung into a savage mining community with its own laws, cliques and barbarities. This was necessary, Doyle had told the editor of Strand, but for whom? Hardly the reader, whisked into a melodramatic re-creation of primitive capitalism that flatters the bosses and points out the viciousness of organized labour. Perhaps Doyle felt that American sales depended on a large chunk of American legend. In addition there is a love interest of the kind popularized by Charlie Chaplin and later by B-Westerns, with the daughter of a lodging-house winning the hero's heart 'from the instant that he had set eyes upon her beauty and her grace'. There is a rival: 'It seems to me, mister, dat you are gettin' set on my Ettie. Ain't dat so, or am I wrong?'

How the readers must have waited patiently, instalment after instalment, for the promised return to Baker Street! Eventually they got it – all two and a half pages of it. It was Doyle's fourth and last Sherlock Holmes novel, and after the let-down there must have been many one-time fans who wished that the author was still the impecunious Doctor Doyle, recently of Southsea, and not a talking head who for some reason only known to himself had a rooted objection to giving value for money, and persisted in whisking Holmes out of sight as soon as the bait was taken.

Between the finish of the short stories in Strand and the start of the serialization of The Valley of Fear, there was work by Doyle available, but not the kind of material that appealed to his most faithful admirers. There was Through the Magic Door, a run-through of his literary enthusiasms with gentle pats on the head for the straightforward authors of the past and an appreciative nod to Poe. Lloyd George bought the book, thinking it was an adventure story. It was well received, and no doubt it cost Doyle very little time and trouble. He did not have to write to keep the wolf from the door, and there were distractions in plenty; it was said that he could write anywhere, in a roomful of people, and as he wrote he was able to take part in the conversation. From the evidence of his lesser books, and the dialogue in the second half of *The Valley of Fear*, one can well believe it.

It is natural for people from impecunious families to develop a taste for unusual luxuries when they have the opportunity. Success had to be seen to have its fruits, and Edwardian opulence encouraged the open display of riches. In accordance with his ideas that there was nothing better on God's earth than a crackshot, Doyle had a rifle range laid out in his grounds. There was also an electrically driven monorail, motor-cars, a motor-cycle and a motorized bicycle called an auto-wheel which anticipated the moped by half a century. When a star-studded bunch of French dignitaries came to see Doyle to pay their respects to the creator of Sherlock Holmes, Sir Arthur greeted them in style, the epitome of bourgeois grandeur.

In 1906 Lady Doyle, the modest and uncomplaining Louise, died. She was the last link with Dr Doyle of Southsea, the struggling G.P. with a talent for the pen. In 1907 Doyle married Jean Leckie.

10
FIGHTS
FOR JUSTICE

Many people applied to Conan Doyle hoping that he would help to solve their problems, but in most cases they were disappointed. He protested that he was not Sherlock Holmes. Occasionally he did play detective, and his two major cases were successes. In 1906 he was reading a paper called *The Umpire* and read about George Edalji, arrested more than three years before for cattle-maiming in the Black Country. Edalji's father was a Church of England clergyman, though a Hindu, but had managed to survive racial prejudice for eighteen years until 1888 when he was pestered with a series of anonymous letters. A servant admitted writing them, and the matter was forgotten. Between 1892 and 1895 more letters were sent to him, and others in the district, the work of a new hand. Some of the letters threatened death to Edalji.

Practical jokes were played on Edalji, bogus advertisements in his name were placed in newspapers, and postcards supposedly signed by Edalji were sent to other clergymen. One of them stated that the writer would expose the recipient for adultery and rape. Rubbish was strewn on the Edalji lawn, and a key from Walsall Grammar School was left on the doorstep. The chief constable thought that it was all the work of George Edalji, the clergyman's son, and he told the older Edalji so. In 1895 the persecution stopped.

In 1903 there was a series of outrages on animals; sixteen sheep, cattle and horses had their stomachs cut open, and anonymous letters accused George Edalji, who was in practice as a solicitor in Birmingham. The police arrested Edalji, and searched the Edalji house, finding four stained razors, a pair of muddy boots, blue-serge trousers, also with black mud on them, and a coat, damp and stained. A pony had been disembowelled in a field nearby, killed to put it out of its agony, and a strip of hide was packed into the parcel of clothes. When the police surgeon examined the coat he found hair on it, food stains and two spots of blood on one of the cuffs. When asked to account for his movements, Edalji said that he had been to see his boot-maker, and walked around for a while, so getting muddy. He con-fessed that he had been expecting the arrival of the police. A handwriting expert maintained that Edalji had written the letters accusing himself of the crime. Edalji was sent for trial, and imprisoned for seven years.

The Birmingham newspapers though that Edalji had been making sacrifices to strange gods in which cattle mutilation was part of the ritual. It was what one would expect from black men, nor did public opinion shift when the cattle injuries continued while Edalji was in prison. It was obvious to the police that Edalji had accomplices who were deliberately carrying on his wretched hobby so that doubters would begin to ponder on the justice of it all. A man did confess that he had disembowelled his own horse on the night in question, but he emigrated to South Africa and said that the confession had been forced from him by the police.

Not everyone was happy at the way in which Edalji had been treated, and solicitors and barristers signed a petition which was for-warded to the Home Office, though ostensibly no action was taken. But after three years Edalji was freed. Having lost his career, he set out to explain himself in the periodical *Truth*. Other papers took it up; whatever the facts, it was clear that the case had been a shambles, with the police changing their mind about the time of the crime, from early evening – when Edalji had his bootmaker as alibi – to the early hours of the next morning – when Edalji's father was the alibi, and by reason of his relationship not so convincing. The mud on Edalji's clothing was not that of the field in which the horse was attacked, which was a mixture of clay and sand. The horse-hairs on the coat were due to police incompetence in mixing all the evidence together. The stains on the razors were rust, the spots of blood on the cuff were of no importance, perhaps from gravy or underdone meat.

It was not a case that Inspector Lestrade would have put in front of Holmes. It savoured of victimization, and the easy option, the grab-bing of the nearest suspect. It indicated how irrelevances could be tormented into damning circumstantial evidence, and how even a solicitor could be landed with a barrister who could not fight a case.

'The conduct of the police still seems to me the worst part of the affair,' Barrie wrote to Doyle.

Doyle went deeply into the case, visiting the site of the crime, realizing that to commit the offence Edalji would have been obliged to cross railway lines, clamber over fences, and wade through muddy fields, which would have caused havoc to his clothing. Furthermore, Edalji was both myopic and squinted, which, wrote Doyle in *The Story of Mr George Edalji*, 'gave the sufferer a vacant, bulge-eyed, staring appearance, which, when taken with his dark skin, must assuredly have made him seem a very queer man to the eyes of an English village, and therefore to be naturally associated with any queer event'. Doyle set out to find the real culprit. He turned his attention to Walsall Grammar School, where Edalji had been a pupil. During the case a boy named Greatorex had been mentioned, and he had been at school with Edalji. And no one had explained why a key to Walsall Grammar School was placed on the Edaljis' doorstep. Suspicion fell on a boy named Royden Sharp, through the assistance of an ex-headmaster, and to confirm Doyle's suspicions he received an anonymous letter abusing the headmaster.

From the evidence of handwriting, Doyle deduced that there were two anonymous letter writers between 1892 and 1895, an educated man and a semi-literate boy. In 1895 Sharp left the neighbourhood, was apprenticed to a butcher, served in the merchant navy and was on a cattle-boat in 1902. He then returned to plague the Edalji family. Sharp was never brought to justice, and no one ever found out why he had built up such a hatred against George Edalji. It may have been nothing more than the detestation of a stupid working-class boy for a clever foreigner (though if Sharp was semi-literate it is surprising that he managed to get into a grammar school in an age when such education was restricted to boys of reasonable intelligence).

Doyle wanted a retrial for Edalji, but never got it. The scandal that arose from the affair played a big part in inaugurating the Court of Criminal Appeal. There was widespread sympathy for Edalji, and an appeal by the *Daily Telegraph* raised £300 for him. The Law Society re-admitted him to the roll of solicitors.

Doyle's second major case concerned Oscar Slater, a German Jew who lived on the fringes of the law and was a bad lot. On 21 December 1908 an elderly woman, Miss Gilchrist, was battered to death in her Glasgow flat and robbed of a diamond brooch in the form of a crescent. Her servant Helen Lambie was out for ten minutes buying a newspaper. The people in the flat below, the Adams family, heard noises, and Mr Adams investigated. They both saw a man leaving the Gilchrist flat. Adams had forgotten his glasses, and the man's face was indistinct, though in person he was 'gentlemanly and well-dressed'. Together, the servant and Adams found the body by the fireplace, her head on the fender, and her false teeth nearby.

Slater and a Frenchwoman with whom he was living had been in Glasgow for six weeks. Slater alleged that he was a diamond-cutter. The police circulated a description of the man they wanted to interview, and the next day a fourteen-year-old girl, Mary Barrowman, told the police that she had been walking past the building about the time when the murder took place, and had been bumped into by a man emerging from it. She offered a different description. Adams and Miss Lambie had opted for a man about five foot six, dark, with a light grey overcoat and a dark cap. Miss Barrowman thought him tall, young, wearing a fawn cloak and a 'round hat'.

Four days later Oscar Slater tried to sell a pawn-ticket for a diamond brooch, but this brooch had been put in pawn more than a month before the murder. Nevertheless, the police thought they had their man, and when it became known that Slater and his girl friend had sailed for New York in the *Lusitania* on Boxing Day 1908 the Glasgow police cabled their colleagues in America to arrest him. An extradition order was necessary, and could only be obtained if there was some reason to suspect Slater. The three witnesses were shown photographs of Slater; the two girls enthusiastically selected him as the murderer, but Mr Adams was less sure. On the strength of their evidence, the witnesses had a free trip to America. They were shown Slater in a corridor leading to the courtroom so that there would be no mistake.

A murder weapon had to be found to complete the police case, and a small upholsterer's hammer in Slater's possession was selected. The first hearing of the case was at Edinburgh on 3 May 1909, and the prosecution had found no less than a dozen witnesses who had seen Slater in the area of the Gilchrist flat. Slater, who had not opposed extradition, thinking that it was a simple matter to clear his name when the facts of the brooch were known and he had proved that the trip to America had been arranged weeks previously, began to have doubts. An identification parade was a charade; nine of the men in the line-up were plain-clothes policemen.

It was a classic frame-up. Slater's alibi – that he had been dining at home with his girl friend and their servant – was contemptuously dismissed. The Lord Advocate, Alexander Ure, was determined to have Slater found guilty. The jury was split; nine members found him guilty, five found the charge not proven, and one thought Slater not guilty. He was sentenced to be hanged on 27 May. A petition to save him was signed by 20,000 people, and two days before the execution the sentence was commuted to life imprisonment. Doyle was approached to somehow redress a self-evident wrong.

Edalji had a body of influential men behind him – the law profession; Slater was an unsympathetic character, destined to be behind bars at some time or other, and few tears were shed over his fate. Even those who felt uneasy about the actions of the police and their jumping to conclusions were not sure that Slater had nothing to do with the murder. Why had he embarked for New York using a false name? Although he claimed that this was to make a fresh start, there was no evidence that his past wrong-doings were sufficiently important to warrant a pseudonym – unless he was, indeed, in deep trouble. His contention that he was escaping from a troublesome wife was not treated seriously.

There was no sense of urgency about an inquiry into the Slater case, and months ran into years as different facts came to light. A grocer named MacBrayne declared that on the night of the crime he had seen Slater on his own doorstep, confirming Slater's alibi. This information had never been given to the defence counsel, and had been expunged from the records. A Glasgow detective named Trench had admitted that he did not believe in Miss Lambie's identification; Trench was persecuted by his fellows, and charged with concealment.

It was nearly sixteen years after the trial before anything was done. Slater sent a message to Doyle through a discharged convict, and Doyle tried to stir up interest. A Glasgow journalist, William Park, took the matter up, followed by other journalists. The two key witnesses, Lambie and Barrowman, were tracked down. They had been bribed to put the finger on Slater. Miss Lambie had been paid £40 and Miss Barrowman £100. Miss Lambie confessed that her employer sometimes received mysterious visitors, and it was accepted that she herself would be out of the way when they arrived. It was a scoop for the *Empire News* which published Lambie's statement, and a few days later Slater was released for 'good conduct', eighteen years after he had been sentenced. 'What a cesspool it all is!' wrote Doyle, despairing of 'wooden-headed officials'.

His involvement in the Edalji and Slater cases demonstrated to the world his love of justice and his championship of those who had no one to speak for them. It was not general altruism on behalf of the underdog; Doyle's social conscience, in so far as the poor, the unemployed and the aged were concerned, was no more active than that of his bloated pleasure-loving contemporaries. In 1906, standing as a Conservative, he was opposed to the party of progress, the Liberals, who did, whatever their motives, bring in unemployment benefits and the old age pension. Doyle's interest was in the victims of injustice, casualties arising from the clumsy machinery of the law.

These cases also showed how difficult it was fighting the system, and that when bureaucracy is threatened its components close ranks, whether they are civil servants, the armed forces or the police, and that all is sacrificed, including truth, for the purpose of self-preservation. This was difficult for anyone with the straightforward personality of Doyle to understand. Had he not interfered, he would have been able to preserve his illusions. Whatever their faults, the policemen in his fiction are a fine body of men, as committed to the finding and punishment of wrongdoers as Holmes. Few questioned the actual structure of the police force. In fact, it was very shaky, and the lack of coordination not only between the various forces but between departments made incompetence all too believable and corruption easy. A bad apple in a box was not always seen. The Metropolitan Police was 2,000 under strength, and the recording systems throughout Great Britain were in a mess – not until 1914 was the Criminal Record Office formed to centralize records. In an age when the telephone was widely accepted, when it had revolutionized business life, the police still resorted to the telegraph under the naïve belief that it was more secret than the telephone (where the operator could listen in). In 1903 a new broom arrived as chief of the Criminal Investigation Department, and he vowed to root out corruption wherever it might be. In 1904 a constable who had planted a knife and a hammer in the pockets of a suspected person was sentenced to five years' imprisonment for perjury. The actions taken by the police in the Edalji and Slater cases were no doubt exceptional, but how far did the evidence of malpractices bite into Doyle's certainties, building on his disillusionment?

Another event occurred which struck at his fundamental beliefs; it was concerned with sport. Throughout his life Doyle had been proud of his sporting achievements, and his versatility. The good man was a good sportsman, and the good sportsman was a good man; it was a self-evident proposition. The Olympic games muddied the issue, and in 1906 in Athens and 1908 in London there was an uneasy feeling that professionals were taking part under the guise of being amateurs. Doyle was contracted by the *Daily Mail* to cover the Marathon of 1908. The first man into the stadium was an Italian, Dorando, out on his feet, swaying and staggering. Although he was first through the tape he was disqualified as he had been helped over the final circuit round the track, and the gold medal went to an American. The Italian had competed in the Olympic tradition, running himself into the ground, and the victory of the American was resented, more so as the Americans had carried off the lion's share of the medals in the 1906 Athens Olympics. In 1906 the Oxford rowing coach had formally protested against professional American oarsmen being allowed to compete in British races, pretending that they were amateurs.

It was not sport as Doyle, or the majority of the British, thought of it. Participants were not taking part for the sake of the sport, but for personal aggrandizement and national prestige, and the Americans in particular were backed with huge funds while in the 1906 Olympics a paltry £150 was refused the British team, to help with expenses and in no way prize money. Sport was becoming big business. 'I am by no means assured that sport has that international effect for good which some people have claimed for it,' wrote Doyle in his autobiography, reflecting back on the 1908 Olympics and the Dunraven yacht race, which was also carried out in an unsportsmanlike spirit.

The readers of the *Daily Mail* shared Doyle's regret that the courageous little Italian was deprived of his medal by too eager bystanders, and he started a subscription for him in the *Daily Mail*, which realized £300 and enabled Dorando to start up as a baker in his own village. Virtue did get a reward, but unfairness could not always be alleviated by the payment of a small sum of money. Doyle's interest in sport was capitalized on in 1912, when Great Britain did badly in the Stockholm Olympics. Lord Northcliffe thought that Doyle could get the sporting men to rally round and sort out their differences in time for the Berlin Olympics. It was believed that the answer would be an appeal to the public for money. It was the lazy way out, and Doyle had in mind a figure of £10,000. He returned from his holidays and found that £100,000 had been asked for, and the organizers of the appeal were being accused of professionalism, the vice Doyle hated most in sport. In the event, only £7,000 was raised and the war prevented the Berlin Olympics. 'We were all playing another game by then,' recollected Doyle.

The enthusiastic reception that had been given to his pamphlet on the Boer War had persuaded Doyle that he was the right man to air national and international wrongs. There had been an ambiguity about the Boer War, and Doyle had been forced to play down material that did not fit in with his message. In 1909 Doyle became involved in African affairs again.

In 1876 King Leopold II of the Belgians summoned a conference at Brussels of geographical experts to promote the International Association for the Exploration and Civilization of Africa. The carve-up of Africa was to be made genteel. Leopold was particularly interested in the Congo region, and invited the great explorer· H. M. Stanley to Brussels. The result was the formation of the International Association of the Congo, with Stanley as agent. Stanley spent four years in the area and by 1884 had founded twenty-two stations. Leopold was providing most of the funds, and it was gradually realized that the International Association of the Congo was less international than its title suggested, and that Belgium wanted to have a slice of the Africa cake.

Portugal put in a claim for territory at the mouth of the Congo, as it had been discovered by Portuguese explorers centuries earlier; the French began prowling round, and M. de Brazza founded Brazzaville. A congress in Berlin in 1884 recognized the International Association as a sovereign state, with the Americans the first to agree. The Congo Free State was born. It was specified that 'the trade of all nations shall enjoy complete freedom'. The European population of this vast area of 900,000 square miles was 254, of whom 46 were Belgians.

It was said of the Holy Roman Empire that it was neither holy nor Roman, and it can be said of the Congo Free State that it was neither free nor a state. It was not Belgian, and it was not international; it was the private preserve of King Leopold, acknowledged by the Belgian parliament in 1885 which authorized Leopold to be the 'chief of the state' and which declared that 'the union between Belgium and the new state of the Congo shall be exclusively personal'. Amiable agreements with Portugal and France were made about boundaries. It was not an easy task for Leopold, as the Arab slave-traders resented the interference in their affairs and their power was not destroyed until 1892. Belgium poured money into the Congo on the understanding that after ten years it would have the option of annexing the state. Occasionally discussions took place in the Belgian parliament about the Congo. Accusations of mismanagement were levelled, and remained unrefuted. Matters were even worse than the Belgian parliament thought.

The treasure of the Congo Free State lay in ivory and rubber. In 1885 it was decreed that the state should have the monopoly of ivory and rubber in what was euphemistically called the 'vacant lands'. It transpired that there was little that was not vacant land; natives had to get a special permit to leave their villages. The white traders protested against interference in their own affairs, and they were accommodated. But the natives were not; one lot of slavers had been replaced by another.

Parts of the state were leased to concession companies; it was capitalism at its most naked, and French, British and American money was invested in these concession companies, the best known of which was the Anglo-Belgian India-rubber and Exploration Co. An area of 112,000 square miles, called the Domaine de la couranne, was the private property of Leopold; this remained secret until 1902. In 1896 Joseph Chamberlain admitted that natives from Sierra Leone employed in the Congo to construct a railway had been ill-treated. Instructions were given that no more natives from British colonies should be recruited for work in the Congo.

Roger Casement, British consul at Boma, protested against the condition of the natives engaged in the rubber trade, and drew the attention of the British Government to ill-treatment and mutilation of men, women and children who had already been deprived of their land. He joined with E. D. Morel, agent of a shipping line, and they founded the Congo Reform Association, circulating influential writers including Doyle. In 1903 the matter was discussed in the House of Commons; without division, it was agreed that something should be done 'to abate the evils prevalent in that state'. His Majesty's government would 'be glad to receive any suggestions'. Only Turkey, which hardly had a history of enlightened rule over subject peoples, responded.

Leopold, although no doubt aware that the great nations were not overanxious to interfere in the Congo, appointed a commission to look into Casement's allegations. It was hand-picked by him, and nothing came of it. In 1908 he handed the administration for the Congo Free

State over to the Belgian Government, which did not want the responsibility. In 1909, Doyle began stirring up trouble. *The Crime of the Congo*, 45,000 words, was written in eight days. He thought it was a record.

He also wrote to President Theodore Roosevelt whom he much admired, and circulated sixty American newspapers with the facts. Roosevelt was cautious. 'Never draw unless you intend to shoot' was his maxim, he explained to Doyle. Mark Twain, the venerable American reporter of a vanished age, was no help when he was approached. Regarding the Congo, 'any intimate consideration of it excites and distresses him to a degree which we think dangerous'. It was easy to chicken out on the Congo; it was a long way away. Easiest most of all for the Americans, who had no territorial commitments in Africa.

Unlike the Boer War, there was no 'other side' to the argument. Healthy indignation could run rampant – provided that it did not lead to armed intervention. German East Africa had a border with the Congo Free State across Lake Tanganyika, and German warships were on the lake (*vide* the film *The African Queen*). A colonial adventure was the worst thing that could happen, with perhaps three nations, France, Britain and Germany, wading in for the spoils.

Rudyard Kipling, writing to Doyle on 29 August 1909, advised caution. 'If Belgium chooses to tell us to mind our own affairs (with a few nasty remarks about India thrown in), what can we do?' he asked sagely. Parallels could easily be drawn with the East India Company, and with the treatment of the natives in the British West Indies. And behind the manœuvres of governments was the disinclination to interfere with the concession companies, which were doing very nicely.

The Congo Free State was tyranny, but tyranny on a shoe-string. As late as 1908 the European population numbered a mere 2,943, 1,713 of whom were Belgians. There was no massive colonizing force as there was in India. This worked to the advantage of individuals, who could operate without scruples and carry out secret deals of which a government, with the best will in the world, could never hear. The Belgians never got the empire-building habit, but the greed and ambition of Leopold II left a lasting legacy.

Once again, as in the cases of Edalji and Slater, Doyle was applauded for his work in publicizing the predicament of the downtrodden and the cruelly treated. It may be that his appeal to the Americans did something to curb the more blatant examples of savage exploitation, but in a slightly different climate – if for example his appeal had gone out after the Spanish-American War when the Americans were openly empire-building – his blunt uncompromising behaviour might have been interpreted as rashness, encouraging the Americans to take the initiative in the Congo, using as an excuse the desire to protect their own nationals, if any, who were engaged in business there. There were no direct economic reasons for U.S. involvement in the Congo, as there were regarding Cuba during the Spanish-American War – to save the sugar industry, largely American financed. There was enough rubber for all from Central and South American, and it was more accessible and easier to farm.

It would have been a rash man who told Sir Arthur Conan Doyle what books he should write and what subjects he should stay clear of. He was the embodiment of the British conscience, more particularly to himself. He epitomized old-fashioned virtues, and also old-fashioned prejudices. He has been summed up with marvellous precision by Eric Partridge. Doyle was 'an engaging fellow and much more versatile, I mean *capably* versatile, than he's been credited with being. His aberrations resulted from his genial, simple (in the very best sense) trust in the sincerity and ability of others – so many of them silky self-seekers or self-deluders – or both.'

Who were these silky self-seekers and self-deluders? There were, of course, the politicians of the Asquith and Balfour period who wished for the perquisites of government without responsibility and who were always looking for the easy way out of any difficulty. There were journalists and general purpose do-gooders, such as W.T.Stead, for whom any cause was enough if it reflected well upon them. There were writers who were propagandists first and craftsmen afterwards, and who fastened themselves on to Doyle like leeches. And there were the celebrated, the men and women who were well known because they were well known, who found Doyle easy to work on and that Good Causes made them more celebrated than ever.

The old-fashioned virtues included courtesy, kindness and contempt for pointless cruelty. He was at one with the gentry in his advocacy of the stiff upper lip, and in matters of etiquette he was punctilious, resenting acquaintances who called him, uninvited, by his Christian name. In 1904 he took the *Daily Express* to task for terming the Japenese 'Japs'. In World War One some of the reluctance to award the unpopular nicknames disappeared, and Doyle was not backward in using the term 'Boche' for the Germans.

He believed in a settled order and in a hierarchy; he believed in institutions that made for a settled order, whether it was the family or the British Empire, an uncorrupt legal system or an efficient police force. He disliked people or movements that threatened stability. The paradoxes of Shaw infuriated him; it was immoral to make fun of serious matters, for who knows how unthinking impressionable people would respond?

He reacted in a genial simple way to national events. When covering the funeral of Queen Victoria for the *New York World* he described her reverently as 'the dead saint'. Whatever her qualities, saintliness was hardly one of them. Doyle was merely reflecting the emotional attitude of most Englishmen at the time. Victoria was the mother of the nation, and anyone who argued about it was a cad. A decade later Doyle wrote up the funeral of King Edward VII for the *Daily Mail*, referring to the 'troop of kings who escorted their dead peer, with the noble Kaiser riding at their head. England has lost something of her old kindliness if she does not take him back into her heart today'. The article was later issued as a pamphlet, and when Doyle came across a copy after the Kaiser had become a nastier version of Satan he placed a full stop after peer and crossed the panegyric through.

He epitomized middle-class prejudice in his attitude towards anything out of the ordinary in the arts. In his notebook for July 1912 he commented: 'One of the singular characteristics of the present age is a wave of artistic and intellectual insanity breaking out in various forms in various places.' He drew a distinction between queerness and madness, between Wagner's operas and Strauss's *Electra*, between the Pre-Raphaelite painters and the Post-Impressionists, and between the French Symbolists and the Italian Futurists. Although *Electra* could be seen as a logical development of Wagnerian music drama, which was now established and almost old-fashioned (and had been since 1898 when Shaw wrote *The Perfect Wagnerite*), the other pairings are rather odd and French Symbolism can in no way be linked with Futurism. Doyle continued: 'Nietzsche's philosophy in a purely mental way is symptomatic of what I mean. It is openly founded in lunacy for the poor fellow died raving. One should put one's shoulder to the door and keep out insanity all one can.'

There speaks the voice of Victorian reaction, the assembled chorus of fuddy-duddydom which deplored all artistic manifestations that were unfamiliar and novel. Doyle's ignorance about art and music occasionally flaws the Sherlock Holmes stories. In 'The Mazarin

Stone', published in *The Case-Book*, Holmes tells the villainous Count Sylvius that he will 'try over the Hoffmann Barcarolle upon my violin'. No musician, or person who knew anything at all about music, would refer to the barcarolle from Offenbach's *Tales of Hoffmann* in such a manner. On another occasion, to draw attention to Professor Moriarty's wealth, Holmes mentions the picture that Moriarty owns. Not by Velasquez, Botticelli or Gainsborough, but Greuze (1725–1805), a painter of trivial pretty pictures for the French court in its decadence and long rejected as an important painter. A man who puts his money into Greuze is not a man to be highly regarded, except by unscrupulous picture dealers looking for an easy mark.

Doyle's attack on the Post-Impressionists as mad was symptomatic of the choleric-colonel approach to art. In 1910 an exhibition of paintings by Cézanne, Gauguin, Matisse and other French artists was organized at the Grafton Gallery. Doyle was at one with *The Queen*, which thought the paintings jejune, barbarous and imbecilic, and the *Daily Telegraph* which preferred the terms weird, uncouth and tortuous. The *Morning Post* considered that these 'hysterical daubs' would be for art students 'a justification of their own worst endeavours'. Robert Ross talked about 'pavement art'. Considering the nature of the animal, it would not be fair to expect Doyle to recognize the merits of the Post-Impressionists. He was among the mob in deploring them, indignant that such proof of arrant decadence should disgrace the walls of a gallery. And he was the voice of the mob; the public trusted him, whereas politicians were regarded as shifty. If Sir Arthur said the Post-Impressionists were rogues and charlatans, a practical joke played on an affable British public, then there was no doubt that he was right.

He was unquestionably better at righting wrongs than being an arbiter of taste. He may not have been able to differentiate between Matisse and a hole in the wall, but he knew what was right and what was wrong. It was, for example, wrong for women to get the vote. He had made his position clear in 1900 when he first tried to get into Parliament, though he made a reservation for women tax-payers, and he never wavered in his convictions. He was a hard-liner, and when the suffragettes went out on to the streets smashing West End shop windows, digging up lawns, painting house doors and slashing pictures, he was in no frame of mind to advise conciliation. He made his views known in the *New York American* in May 1914, maintaining that the best way to oppose woman suffrage was to back the militants, of whom the general public had had more than enough.

He would have agreed with H.G.Wells that 'a large part of the woman's suffrage movement was animated less by the desire for freedom and fullness of life than by a passionate jealousy and hatred of the relative liberties of men'. The sex war reached unparalleled heights, and whereas Doyle had stoutly castigated the police on account of their behaviour in the Edalji affair he kept silent when evidence of police brutality to the suffragettes was confirmed. On the day that was known as 'Black Friday', when 115 women were arrested, policemen struck women with their fists, kicked them when on the ground, twisted arms, rubbed faces against the railings of Parliament Square and pinched their breasts. The more lively and rebellious women were marched down side streets and beaten.

There never was a more urgent case for Doyle to make a stand, in the cause not of right or wrong but of sanity. The 1914–18 war brought women the vote, painlessly and undemonstratively. But it was no thanks to Doyle. His genuine concern for the underdog, as evidenced in the Edalji case, could be blocked by his prejudices. In this he was no more than human; but more, perhaps selfishly, was expected of him. It is interesting to compare his attitude with that of John Galsworthy, newly come to fame with *The Man of Property*, the first book of the Forsyte saga. Realizing the inevitability of woman suffrage and unfairness in keeping the vote from women, Galsworthy donated autographed copies of his books to help the cause.

Doyle suffered from his avowed detestation of suffragettes. Vitriol was poured into the letter-box of his house at Crowborough. Mindless reaction resulted in mindless violence and idiocy. But on other matters Doyle worked hard to change the law when it seemed to work against the underprivileged. This was particularly noteworthy in his efforts to reform the divorce law.

In theory, divorce had been covered in 1857, but the law favoured the men. A man could get a divorce merely on the grounds of the unfaithfulness of a wife, but for a woman to obtain legal satisfaction adultery had to be coupled with something else, preferably brutality. Brutality was an ambiguous phrase; men were allowed to 'chastise' their wives for shortcomings, real or imagined. Even when there were grounds, women were reluctant to go to law, for the cost of a divorce was rarely less than £700 (£10,000 in present-day money). For fifty years after the passing of the act there were never more than a thousand divorces a year.

In 1906 a number of prominent men, including the classical scholar Gilbert Murray and Thomas Hardy, as well as well-known jurists, formed a society for the reform of the divorce law. The cause for divorce should be the same for men and women, and the grounds should be extended to cover madness, chronic drunkenness and the imprisonment for a lengthy period of a spouse. Doyle was appointed president of the society, and threw himself into the controversy with enthusiasm, sometimes embarrassing his colleagues, as when he denounced judicial separation, which could be a sensible solution to a problem and not, as Doyle maintained, a wretched attempt at compromise.

Nevertheless, Doyle's *Divorce Law Reform* was a cogent well-reasoned homily, and had a part to play in encouraging the setting-up of a Royal Commission, the recommendations of which were published in 1912. With the suffragettes in full flow and their disturbances in the House of Commons a recent painful memory, it was not a tactful time to pursue any attempt at sexual equality, and the Church of England was adamant that matters were perfectly satisfactory as they stood. Marriage, to the clergy, was still a religious undertaking and not, as it was gradually being realized, a social compact. Doyle came into conflict with the Church authorities, and his hostility towards organized religion was never dispelled, surfacing in a virulent form when he espoused the cause of spiritualism, to which many clergymen adopted the same posture as they had towards divorce reform.

The Church won, and once again Doyle realized how difficult it was to fight the Establishment. Doyle was dead before the recommendations of the Royal Commission became law and the parity of the sexes was finally established.

In 1912 Doyle rushed in again, to put right another instance of gross injustice. Unfortunately it was not to rail at the Church, crooked policemen or a greedy unscrupulous monarch, but to protect the memory of the captain and crew of the *Titanic*, which sank in April after hitting an iceberg on its maiden voyage. The newspapers found a lot of mileage in the disaster, applauding the resolute behaviour of the captain who went down with his ship, and inventing detail when there was none. High marks were awarded to the ship's band, which played ragtime while the ship went down. One of the leading men in the principal communication medium – newspapers – was Kennedy

Jones of the *Daily Mail*. His personal motto was 'Nothing really matters' and he was willing to wring his readers' hearts on any pretext if he could increase circulation.

Bernard Shaw countered in the *Daily News* on 14 May, and accused the journalists of an 'explosion of outrageous romantic lying'. The first demand of the shipwreck situation is women and children first, but 'how the boat is to be navigated and rowed by babies and women occupied in holding the babies is not mentioned'. The second demand is that all the men, except foreigners who must be shot by stern British officers, must be heroes, and the captain a super-hero. So Captain Smith was treated like Nelson. Bernard Shaw hammered home the basic undeniable fact: 'The one thing positively known was that Captain Smith had lost his ship by deliberately and knowingly steaming into an ice field at the highest speed he had coal for. He paid the penalty; so did most of those for whose lives he was responsible. Had he brought them and the ship safely to land, nobody would have taken the smallest notice of him.' As for the band playing on, this was reassurance to the passengers, especially the third class. There were never enough lifeboats, and by the time they realized what was going on the boats were gone. 'I ask,' went on Shaw relentlessly, 'what is the use of all this ghastly, blasphemous, inhuman, braggartly lying? Here is a calamity which might well make the proudest man humble, and the wildest joker serious. It makes us vainglorious, insolent and mendacious.' He concluded by commenting that no other nation would have behaved as absurdly.

On 20 May, Conan Doyle rolled up his sleeves to castigate Shaw. The Irish buffoon, he believed, had met his master. But Shaw was the most devastating intelligence of his age, a master of language. Doyle lumbered up to him like a punch-drunk pugilist who had the added disadvantage of having iron balls attached to his feet. He was a talented story-teller, not a debater, and every step he took made defence of Captain Smith ('an old and honoured sailor who has made one terrible mistake, and who deliberately gave his life in reparation') more sentimental. Doyle was right in praising 'the beautiful incident of the band'. The musicians were heroic. But Doyle, with his over-sell, managed to make them into maudlin martyrs.

Shaw answered two days later. 'I hope to persuade my friend Sir Arthur Conan Doyle, now that he has got his romantic and warm-hearted protest off his chest, to read my article again three or four times, and give you his second thoughts on the matter; for it is really not possible for any sane man to disagree with a single word that I have written.' And Shaw reiterates his argument, each paragraph bitingly rational: 'But if vociferous journalists will persist in glorifying the barrister whose clients are hanged, the physician whose patients die, the general who loses battles, and the captain whose ship goes to the bottom, such false coin must be nailed to the counter at any cost.' Captains who brought their ships through ice-fields by doing their duty received no mention. There were captains who actually knew what the capacity of their lifeboats was, who crewed them; there were captains who even organized lifeboat drill among the passengers.

Shaw picked out a plum, and held it up. 'The captain of the *Titanic* did not, as Sir Arthur thinks, make a "terrible mistake". He made no mistake. He knew perfectly well that ice is the only risk that is considered really deadly in his line of work, and, knowing it, he chanced it and lost the hazard. Sentimental idiots, with a break in the voice, tell me that "he went down to the depths": I tell them, with the impatient contempt they deserve, that so did the cat.'

Rarely did Doyle cross swords with a master. He kept to his own set. Controversy, like war, is something one wins. It was game, set and match to Shaw, and Doyle did not challenge him, or others of his breed, again. When he did dispute, he arranged for it to take place on his own ground and he made the rules.

11
INTO
THE UNKNOWN

In 1912 Doyle produced another hero in the person of Professor Challenger. If Sherlock Holmes was the hero of a young writer, Challenger was that of a middle-aged one, and as soon as the reader encounters him he realizes that Doyle has produced a winner, a fully-rounded character, consistent and believable and far removed from the bellicose and cardboard Gerard or the pageant figures of *Sir Nigel*. If there is something of Doyle in Sherlock Holmes, there is even more in Challenger, though he owed his genesis to recollections of the physiologist William Rutherford, who had taught at Edinburgh during Doyle's time there as a medical student.

Like Doyle, Challenger is a big strapping man, contemptuous of weaklings. Challenger is also a bully who takes great pleasure in throwing journalists out of his house, and to hell with the aftermath. He is the key man in a well-contrasted quartet: the peppery sardonic Summerlee, the white hunter Lord John Roxton with quaint Woosterish vocabulary, Challenger himself, and the narrator, a neatly characterized journalist, brave, naïve and eager to hero-worship in the same way as Watson.

The background of *The Lost World* is scientific, zoological, geographical. For once, Doyle did not have to delve into history to get his facts right, and make certain that the data were injected into the stories to prove that he had done his homework. The scientific material had been thoroughly assimilated long before, perhaps as early as his student days, and he presents it in a convincing manner, not trying to impress the reader. He was naturally interested, and it shows, whereas in certain of the Holmes stories Doyle has to pretend that Holmes is well up in, for example, music and other matters with which he himself is not intimate, and thus overplays his hand. The scene in which Challenger is putting the journalist Malone to the test, throwing nonsense questions at him, is masterly. Although the questions are nonsensical, they are not so much so as to be foolish: 'I suppose you are aware that the cranial index is a constant factor ... and that the germ plasm is different from the parthenogenetic egg ... and that telegony is still *sub judice*?' The average reader would pass these by, at one with the unfortunate Malone, and would be shocked when Challenger roars that Malone is an imposter, 'a vile, crawling journalist, who has no more science than he has decency in his compostion!'

The Lost World is not only of interest because Doyle has taken his pen with a verve and a delight, but because Doyle, for almost the first time since his domestic tale *A Duet*, has succeeded in drawing a portrait of a flesh-and-blood woman. Gladys, whom Malone loves, is only in the story for a page or two, but the characterization is so deft that Malone's impetuosity in going with Challenger on his expedition to prove himself is seen as necessary and not an absurd romantic gesture: 'That delicately bronzed skin, almost Oriental in its colouring, that raven hair, the large liquid eyes, the full but exquisite lips – all the stigmata of passion were there. But I was sadly conscious that up to now I have never found the secret of drawing it forth.'

Gladys is the kind of chirpy New Woman, thoroughly emancipated and sure of herself, made fashionable by H.G. Wells, the kind of girl that Doyle and his generation resolutely refused to allow the vote. After the stereotyped women of *The Valley of Fear*, Gladys is refreshing. When Malone becomes too romantic Gladys quashes him amiably and sweetly: 'You've spoiled everything, Ned,' she said. 'It's all so beautiful and natural until this kind of thing comes in. It is such a pity. Why can't you control yourself?' Gladys's ideal is of a 'harder, sterner man, not so ready to adapt himself to a silly girl's whim ... a man of great deeds and strange experiences'. So, in accord with the plot, Malone goes off. But the action is not arbitrary and Gladys a mere convenience to get him on his way.

There is more straightforward description in *The Lost World* than is usual in Doyle in his lighter vein, a dangerous process in magazine serials where the reader is tempted to skip over long sections with no dialogue. But Doyle manages it because he makes the description interesting, interesting because he was fascinated by the great rain forests of the Amazon as they existed in his imagination. He could stretch his reader, because his audience would have no means of knowing whether Doyle was accurate, and by drawing ever so lightly on its capacity for suspended judgement he could fill in the various prehistoric animals on the unexplored plateau.

The Brazil that Doyle pictured was a fantasy land that had ceased to exist more than half a century earlier, and he had probably got his information from his boyhood reading (*The Naturalist on the River Amazons* by H.W.Bates had been published in 1863, and was widely known, reissued in the Everyman Library in the 1900s). The Amazon of 1912 was not the awesome neglected wilderness of Bates, and Manaos was a metropolis of 40,000 people, with a magnificent opera house, hotels that rivalled Paris in splendour, and was fully lit by electric. Yet Doyle saw it as a picturesque village; so much we can gather from his brief reference to it, and the comment by the narrator that 'here we were rescued from the limited attractions of the local inn', as though it was some Sussex village with five hundred inhabitants.

Prehistoric animals living on top of a plateau in company with apemen and Indians was a pretty fancy, but although Doyle explicitly tries to deal with the improbability of it, especially the question of supplying enough food for the vast creatures, he is not altogether convincing. He speculated that the prehistoric creatures survived by eating each other. It takes six days for the party to circle the base of the plateau, so the area of the lost world is not very great. When the four travellers arrive on top of the plateau, the beasts are very busy breaking down huge trees; and they have been presumably breaking down trees throughout the hundreds of thousands of years they have been stuck up there. Their section of tropical forest would not have lasted very long at that rate.

When Doyle was enthusiastic about a subject it did not have to make sense, and he did not bother to follow it through and weld a story into a logically coherent whole. In a sense, he is the precursor of the children's serials of the 1930s cinema, in which each episode ends on a question mark. How the problem is resolved is of no consequence, provided that it is; he was a victim of the serial-writing habit in which impetus is all. Doyle has provided a good deal of source material to the cinema; a version of *The Lost World* was filmed in 1925, and later it formed a basis for *King Kong*.

The Lost World is an important book, not only in the context of Doyle's literary career but as an indication of his preoccupation with the unknown. It harks back to Jules Verne and to certain stories of Edgar Allan Poe such as 'Voyage to the Moon'. Verne and Doyle had much in common: both were utterly bourgeois, delighting in the luxuries that success had brought them, and both admired the same writers, Sir Walter Scott, Robert Louis Stevenson and Fenimore Cooper, author of *The Last of the Mohicans* (1826), a boyhood favourite of Doyle's.

Verne was entirely of his age – he died in 1905 – and although he was the first major writer to be involved in science fiction, a considerable number of science-fiction novels were published in the nineteenth century, most of them anonymous. These included *A Fantastical Excursion into the Planets* (1839), *History of a Voyage to the Moon* (1864) and *Politics and Life in Mars* (1883). They all had in common the unlikelihood of being ridiculed by experienced travellers.

The Poison Belt followed *The Lost World*, with the same quartet, and Doyle's deftness in handling a contrasting group of people probably owes something to his growing theatrical experience. Compared with the higher peaks of Edwardian drama, such as Shaw or Granville Barker, Doyle's drama is unimportant, though it did appeal to the West End audience whereas Shaw's plays died the death when they moved from the tiny Royal Court in Sloane Square. The Edwardian theatregoing public was ultra-conventional, enjoyed costume romance and heavy character acting, and Doyle supplied these happily enough, whether it was in *Waterloo* or the adaptation of the pugilistic novel *Rodney Stone*, which had a novelty value in its boxing bout on stage.

The Poison Belt was Doyle's second novel of the 'what would happen if ...?' type and was one of many to reflect a mood of apprehension arising from the probability of European war. The threat was cosmic rather than localized, as with William le Queux's novel, serialized in the *Daily Mail*, dealing with the 'horrid and thrilling invasion' of London by the Germans. With *The Lost World*, Doyle had in mind a mixed readership of children and adults, very clear from his dedication:

> I have wrought my simple plan,
> If I bring one hour of joy,
> To the boy who's half a man
> Or the man who's half a boy.

Presumably *The Poison Belt* had the same audience in mind. The world passes through a noxious gas, and all living things die. The first symptoms are personality disorders, with men and women acting out of character, and Challenger, by means of spectrum analysis, anticipates the disaster; he and his friends hole up in an airtight room in his house, supplied with oxygen. Eventually the oxygen runs out, and, philosophically, they unseal the room to meet their death. But the poison belt has passed on, leaving the planet clear. They motor to London through scenes of disaster, meeting one old lady who has oxygen to keep her alive, but otherwise everyone is dead. Intensely depressed, they return to Challenger's home in the country, but suddenly a carthorse begins to move, golfers continue golfing, children continue playing, and the chauffeur rubs his eyes and carries on hosing the car, oblivious of the time that has elapsed. Death was a form of catalepsy.

This theme has furnished material for innumerable science-fiction stories and films. Doyle was at his best when describing the scenes of disaster, fires burning, trains crashing, and he succeeds in evoking the claustrophobic feeling of the airtight room, with the occupants aware that their oxygen supply is running out. One of the most interesting episodes concerns the quartet's facing of death, and for the first time in his novels Doyle's inner preoccupation with life after death comes to the fore as propaganda. The mouthpiece is Challenger, and for the purpose he goes into a dreamy monotone that is decidedly out of character: 'Nature may build a beautiful door and hang it with many a gauzy and shimmering curtain to make an entrance to the new life for our wondering souls.' He addresses the sceptical Summerlee, claiming that he was 'too great a thing to end in mere physical constituents, a packet of salts and three bucketfuls of water'. In case the reader has failed to get the message, Challenger returns to it soon afterwards:

As to the body, we do not mourn over the parings of our nails nor the cut locks of our hair, though they were once part of ourselves. Neither does a one-legged man yearn sentimentally over his missing member. The physical body has rather been a source of pain and fatigue to us. It is the constant index of our limitations. Why then should we worry about its detachment from our psychical selves?

Challenger did not brook any argument. He did not speculate, he stated. If people did not like what he said, he was either intolerably rude or he knocked them down. Despite the more sensational theme, the tone of *The Poison Belt* is cooler than that of *The Lost World*, where Doyle tries to make the reader's skin creep. The narrator Malone has gone off on a reconnaissance by moonlight, and finds himself in a nightmare country: 'I remembered again the blood-slobbered face which we had seen in the glare of Lord John's torch, like some horrible vision from the deepest circle of Dante's hell.' An unknown creature approaches. There came 'that low throaty croaking, far louder and closer than before. There could no longer be a doubt. Something was on my trail, and was closing in upon me every minute ... Then, suddenly, I saw it.' The creature is something of a let-down, a mere flesh-eating dinosaur with a face like a toad.

As a general purpose fiction writer for the magazines Doyle had done his share of horror stories, some of which were collected in 1922 for a gimcrack anthology entitled *Tales of Twilight and the Unseen*. He was well apprenticed in the excessive use of adverb and adjective, and was well acquainted with the past literature of supernatural horror. In his biography of Doyle – refuting which Adrian, Doyle's son of the second marriage, wrote a booklet – Hesketh Pearson drew attention to a little-regarded side of Doyle: the preoccupation with the weird and the hideous, stable-mates to his intense interest in the gory side of war.

Doyle shared the tastes of the man in the street, what Pearson called a mixture of strange desires, domestic sentiment, cruelty, kindness and morbidity. The interest in sadism could result from suppressed sexuality, and it must be remembered that between the illness of his first wife and his remarriage, Doyle lived a tense unsatisfied life, celibate because his code of conduct demanded it. If strange fantasies lurked and sidled out through the medium of fiction it was not remarkable; it would have been odd had his conflicts not been apparent in some way.

This tendency was deplored by Doyle's contemporaries, as if there was something immoral about it, but the point to consider is that the fantasies surfaced and Doyle did not bother to apologize for them. His lack of guile and his openness was in sharp contrast to the inner guilt and prevarication of men, and women, who epitomized the spirit of respectability, and whose own preoccupations with the sadistic, the masochistic and the morbid were never expressed, or, if they were, in diaries and letters not for public consumption. A man as free from opprobrium as Charles Kingsley gave vent to his innermost feelings in obscene drawings, while John Ruskin's unhealthy thoughts bubbled forth in his diaries. A parallel can be drawn between Doyle and Aubrey Beardsley, whose interests in the perverse found open expression in his drawings, and between Doyle and the artist Sidney Sime, whose quaint original style did not disguise the sado-masochistic content of the subjects which he had selected, and in particular the preoccupation with necrophilia, a topic of interest to Doyle and the Decadents, M.R.James and Algernon Blackwood, as well as, more allusively, Charles Dickens and the great novelists of the early and mid-nineteenth century.

The audience for the occult was often the same as that for the Sherlock Holmes stories, and many magazines permutated horror and detective stories in response to the demand. There was not only *Strand* but *Tinsley's Magazine, Temple Bar, Belgravia, Blackwood's, Argosy*, the *English Illustrated Magazine*, as well as the more unlikely 'churchy' *Family Herald Supplement* and *Young Ladies' Journal*. In his occult stories, Doyle was apt to indulge his penchant for over-kill, and whereas in his Sherlock Holmes stories he was competing with nobodies he had some formidable rivals in the occult field, such as Algernon Blackwood and the best of them all, M.R.James. The latter in particular knew the value of restraint.

Most of Doyle's horror stories were soon forgotten, many of them unrevived until television found them an easily worked vein. Often they were macabre and unnecessarily nasty, but they lacked the feeling to do what the best horror stories did – in the words of Thomas Gray after reading Walpole's *Castle of Otranto*: 'It makes some of us cry a little, and all in general afraid to go to bed o' nights.' The biggest defect was that Doyle had not quite made up his mind whether he believed in what he was writing, and if the ghosts who pass through his stories were viable. When asked if she believed in ghosts, Madame du Deffand (1697–1780), correspondent of Horace Walpole, replied: 'No, but I am afraid of them.' Doyle was not afraid of anything.

Sado-masochism and the screaming horrors mix uneasily in Doyle's popular output. One of the most unpleasant non-occult nasties concerns the insanely jealous Turk who persuades his wife's lover, a famous surgeon, to remove her lower lip while she is drugged and her features hidden under her yashmak. Another has the leading figure infected by leprosy. The detective-story writer Max Pemberton was disgusted by this side of Doyle, who had, he said, a 'bias towards the horrific' and who 'spoke of fire and torture in terms which caused the blood to freeze'. 'The Curse of Eve' was too strong for Jerome K. Jerome, the editor of *The Idler*, and Doyle was obliged to tone it down. Another writer would have realized the repulsiveness of the theme and hastily destroyed the manuscript, but not Doyle. The original text deals with childbirth. The mother dies, but the baby survives, and the father tries to kill the child, shouting at it 'You little beast, you've murdered your mother!' Doyle was sufficiently pleased with the story to read it to a gathering at the Authors' Club, but when it appeared in print it was, as requested, toned down and mother and child live happily ever after.

Of greater interest was 'Playing with Fire', which deals with the evocation at a seance of a unicorn. It illustrates the least spiritualistic aspect of Victorian spiritualism, the glory in sensation, and the man who could write the fervent description of the materialization was not the cool observer that the Dr Doyle of the 1890s made himself out to be:

The luminous fog drifted slowly off the table, and wavered and flickered across the room. There in the farther and darkest corner it gathered and glowed, hardening down into a shining core – a strange, shifty, luminous, and yet non-illuminating patch of radiance, bright itself, but throwing no rays into the darkness. It had changed from a greenish-yellow to a dusky sullen red. Then round this centre there coiled a dark, smoky substance, thickening, hardening, growing denser and blacker. And then the light went out, smothered in that which had grown round it.

There is an interesting and crisp description of table-rapping, though this type of phenomenon, with which spiritualism in Britain had started, was now considered passé: 'The table was throbbing with a mighty pulse. It swayed steadily, rhythmically, with an easy swooping, scooping motion under our fingers. Sharp little raps and cracks came from its substance, file-firing, volley-firing, the sounds of a fagot [sic] burning briskly on a frosty night.'

Not surprisingly Egyptology was a spur to many occult writers, particularly to Doyle who was fascinated by death and dissolution. In 'The Ring of Thoth' an ancient Egyptian has found the secret of everlasting life, and seeks to be reunited with his loved one, long mummified. An amateur Egyptologist is locked in the museum, where the Egyptian has obtained a job as attendant, and sees it all. The attendant unwraps the mummy, and the watcher sees a cascade of long black glossy hair, a white forehead, delicately arched eyebrows, bright, deeply fringed eyes, a straight well-cut nose, a sweet, full, sensitive mouth and a beautifully curved chin. The attendant spots the Egyptologist, refrains from killing him and they converse. In the meantime 'the action of the air had already undone all the art of the embalmer. The skin had fallen away, the eyes had sunk inwards, the discoloured lips had writhed away from the yellow teeth ...'

There is a curious connection with a scene in *A Duet* where Frank and Maud visit the tomb of Pepys. Pepys was one of Doyle's favourite writers and perhaps the incident was based on experience. The pair talk with the 'clerk', probably the verger, and he describes how he saw the corpse of Pepys: 'When we first looked in I saw 'im lying quite plain – a short, thick figure of a man – with 'is 'ands across 'is chest. And then, just as we looked at 'im, 'e crumbled in, as you might say, across 'is breast bone, an' just quietly settled down into a 'uddle of dust.'

The surroundings, the skulls flanking the grave of Pepys's wife, lead Frank to introspection. As he looks at the stone bust of Mrs Pepys and then at his 'sweet, girlish bride, with those sinister skulls between, there came over him, like a wave, a realization of the horror which lies in things, the grim close of the passing pageant, the black gloom, which swallows up the never-ending stream of life. Will the spirit wear better than the body ...' Both stories, 'The Ring of Thoth' and the domestic novel, are concerned with the certainty of mortality, but in attitude they might be by totally different authors, the one full of cheap sensationalism and the other sober and cogent.

Many authors have lacked the ability for self-criticism, but few had the sense of certainty that Conan Doyle possessed, the certainty that what he did was good of its type. His willingness to reissue his early ephemera was always in evidence, whereas authors with more discrimination, such as Bernard Shaw, deeply regretted their early work, and took pains to either disown it or repress it. The lurid themes of some of the occult short stories and the gloating over deformity and the macabre show in Doyle if not an absence of sensibility at least confusion. As a story-teller working at top speed it is not to be expected that rank bad taste would bother him – at the time. But it did not bother him in retrospect, either.

The glaring faults of his weird stories, what he himself termed 'real Creepers', appear to a lesser extent in his Sherlock Holmes tales. Many of them are due to a lack of imagination; instead of imagination he had fancy. And what in another man would be a sterling quality weighed against him as a writer of weird and supernatural stories – his personal bravery. There is no instance of Doyle being scared of anything. The oldest and strongest emotion of mankind is fear, and the oldest and strongest fear is fear of the unknown. The unknown, whether it was the Egyptian mummy or a spirit form materializing in a corner of the room, had for him a prurient fascination. What has been called by H.P.Lovecraft 'the thrill of the chimney-corner whisper or the lonely wood' was outside his experience, but not outside his knowledge. He tried to diagnose what a typical horror-story reader was like, and often failed.

So we get genuinely horrific stories by men and women without a fraction of Doyle's writing ability simply because they shared the readers' attitudes towards the unknown. A typical example is one of the most frightening of stories, 'The Yellow Wall Paper' by Charlotte Gilman, who happened to be a social worker and who is now completely forgotten. She intuitively understood the psychology of fear, the breathless inexplicable dread that can attack the most mundane and level-headed of men and women. Doyle was good at the suggestion of the supernatural (as in *The Hound of the Baskervilles*) but when he entered the terrain cultivated by Edgar Allan Poe he was lost, a clumping fifteen-stone doctor with a piercing eye, daring anything to frighten him.

12
WAR

For a man who often voiced the opinion of the man in the street, Doyle was slow in appreciating the German threat. As he admitted in his autobiography, 'for a long time I never seriously believed in the German menace'. This was despite the efforts of the media. When he bought *The Times* Lord Northcliffe stated: 'I shall leave the Editor unrestricted control unless he should – which is quite impossible – fail to warn the British People of the coming German peril.' As early as 1902 newspapers were gleefully promising Germany what she feared most – encirclement. In 1906 Lord Grey was anticipating a German attack on France in the following spring.

Doyle's sanguine attitude was based on the premise that he 'knew it to be impossible that we should attack Germany save in the face of monstrous provocation'. The public would not permit an irresponsible government to do it (he had greater faith in democracy than was warranted). 'On the other hand,' Doyle continued, 'it seemed to be equally unthinkable that Germany should attack us.' He had not considered an attack on France, or on Britain being brought into a war through treaty obligations. In 1911 he realized the dangers, and in 1913 wrote an article in the *Fortnightly Review* called 'Great Britain and the Next War'. He considered that insufficient attention had been given to two novel threats – the submarine and the airship, though he thought the airship chiefly of use for gaining information. He did not think the aeroplane sufficiently advanced to be of use in a war.

He saw the submarine as a threat to food supplies, and that measures to encourage home-grown food should forge ahead. Then there was the probability that a submarine force would affect military operations should an army be sent to France or Belgium. There was a way out – a Channel Tunnel, which could be constructed within three years. Failing that, there should be a merchant fleet of food-carrying submarines. To give his opinions about submarines a wider airing, Doyle wrote a short story called 'Danger', published in the *Strand*, in which Britain is at war with a small imaginary country named Norland, which has a squadron of eight submarines. By an almost supernatural series of successes, these eight submarines sink sufficient ships to cause famine in Great Britain.

Neither the article nor the short story received much commendation, and were roundly attacked by naval and military experts. The common-sense advice of the article was countered by the cautionary tale propaganda of the story, the logistics of which were insane. Irrespective of neutral ships bringing in food, there were more than 8,400 ships flying the British flag, which meant that every submarine would have to sink 1,000 ships to bring Britain to its knees.

Doyle was not the first to point out the potential of the submarine; he was one of the last. As early as 1900 the Admiralty ordered five submarine boats from Vickers, Sons and Maxim of Barrow, using American designs; Great Britain was therefore ahead of the Germans (the U1 was launched in 1906). When Doyle was writing there were more than seventy-five submarines in the Royal Navy. Most were of small tonnage, but a thousand tonner was being built, and, as Winston Churchill wrote in a 1913 paper, 'the development of submarines of ocean-going capacity may be expected to modify [the] situation in our favour'. Although Doyle did foresee unrestricted submarine attacks against merchant vessels, allies and neutrals alike, his naïvety in conveying the message as a ludicrous adventure yarn may have helped prevent the danger being taken seriously.

He was also behind the times in his stricture on Britain's poor state of defence against submarine or surface vessel attacks on the fleet. 'It is a most singular thing that our Navy, with so many practical and clever men in it, with a genius like Winston Churchill at the head, and another genius like Lord Fisher in continual touch, did not realize, until faced with actual results, some of the most important and surely most obvious points in connection with naval warfare. It came, I suppose, from the iron bonds of tradition ...' He went on to speak of the vulnerability of naval anchorages such as Scapa Flow and Cromarty, and of slackness in providing them with coastal guns or anti-submarine nets. What Doyle should have realized – and it illustrates how thin his research could be when he was pursuing one of his enthusiasms – was that coast defence had nothing to do with the First Lord of the Admiralty or the First Sea Lord, but was in the province of the War Office, which was more interested in financing the army. Realizing the dangers to Scapa Flow and Cromarty, Churchill 'undertook in desperation to fortify Cromarty ourselves, arm it with naval guns and man it with marines. And this was the only new work completed when the war broke out.' Churchill and Doyle were at one in their appreciation of the vulnerability of the Scottish naval anchorages, but Churchill had the sense to keep it quiet while Doyle was only too pleased to shout out his findings to the world. The voice of the national conscience could be a raucous foghorn.

Many, who found Doyle's prognostications embarrassing and dangerous, were glad when he went to Canada in 1914, the guest of the Canadian Government, staying in New York en route where he saw a baseball game and marvelled at the wages the players were paid, £1,000 to £1,500 a season, which he thought was professionalism run mad. He visited the New York prisons, The Tombs and Sing Sing, and at the latter he arrived in time for a prisoners' treat, a music-hall troupe. 'Poor devils, all the forced, vulgar gaiety of the songs and antics of half-clad women must have provoked a terrible reaction in their minds!' Doyle was locked up in one of the cells, and sat in the electric chair, 'a very ordinary, stout, cane-bottomed seat, with a good many sinister wires dangling round it'. His reaction to Canada was banal and stereotyped, and his most curious comment was reserved for a shipload of Sikhs at Vancouver, demanding to be admitted to the country. Noting how grotesque it was ('for why should sun-loving Hindoos force themselves upon Canada?'), he asserted that 'there can be no doubt that it was German money that chartered that ship'. Having come off the fence and joined the anti-German lobby, nothing that the Germans did was too cunning and sly.

He returned to Britain in time for the war, which he assessed, with devastating honesty, as 'the physical climax of my life as it must be of the life of every living man and woman'. This is his description of the four-year holocaust that destroyed a civilization. If this had been said by a butcher from Balham or a pugilist from Hoxton one would have felt sorry for him. That it should have been spoken by Sir Arthur Conan Doyle comes as a shock. The war was an adventure, in which the hunting-shooting men would show what they were made of, and the courage of a nation would be tested. 'Each', Doyle continued, 'was caught as a separate chip and swept into that fearsome whirlpool, where we all gyrated for four years, some sinking for ever, some washed up all twisted and bent, and all of us showing in our souls and bodies some mark of the terrible forces which had controlled us so long.' It was the language of *The Hound of the Baskervilles* and fearful unnamed horrors, the message of a man who was watching a melodrama that excited and who, by a word or a deed, imagined that he could change the plot halfway through.

Not that the sentiment was rare; it is traditional to look on the outbreak of World War One as an occasion for gloom and despondency. But it was not so. The death wish was gripping Britain. War came, in Winston Churchill's graphic phrase, with 'soft, quiet voices purring, courteous, grave, exactly measured phrases in large peaceful rooms', with George v timid and incapable of the decisive action of his father Edward vii, the foreign secretary procrastinating and Asquith waiting to see. It was all very civilized, like, Churchill commented, waiting for the results of an election. Not so for the man in the street. Euphoria gripped him. He and his fellows gathered 30,000 strong outside Buckingham Palace and smashed the windows of the German Embassy (and the windows of any shops that bore German names). It was a time for adventure.

Throughout the war Doyle never ceased to prod the authorities with ideas, and some of them were taken up. He thought that the menace of submarine mines could be tamed by using something like a giant toasting-fork threshing the water, but the Admiralty preferred the paravane, which was towed by warships at various depths regulated by fins and cut the wires of the mines. More useful was his suggestion of life-jackets and collapsible india-rubber boats to help save seamen. So that the idea would not be automatically turned down by the Admiralty, he agitated for their introduction in the daily papers, and within a few days there was an order for a quarter of a million life-saving collars in the pipeline. He also demanded more lifeboats on board ship, and if, as naval authorities maintained, these were a nuisance in battle, Doyle thought it would be a good plan to tow them when there was likelihood of action.

He was also concerned with the vulnerability of troops. When the war opened, soldiers were equipped with the flat caps as used by bus conductors. Steel helmets were later introduced, but the body armour suggested by Doyle was only used for specific duties.

At the outbreak of war Doyle organized a home defence unit which he called the Civilian Reserve, and although this was disbanded by order of the War Office, others applied pressure and a volunteer force was formed. Doyle's body became the Crowborough Company of the Sixth Royal Sussex Volunteer Regiment, with Doyle himself as a common private. He enjoyed mixing with the farm labourers and other locals, and nothing delighted him more than to be patronized by some inspecting officer, and have the impertinent fellow cast down by the news that among the unprepossessing yokels was Sir Arthur Conan Doyle.

Keeping the sceptred isle safe for English womanhood was not enough for Doyle. In a time of enthusiastic pamphleteering it was not surprising that Doyle wished to contribute something. The result was a thirty-two-page penny pamphlet called *To Arms!* with a preface by F.E.Smith, Earl of Birkenhead. It was an essay in rabble-rousing. 'All our lives have been but a preparation for this supreme moment,' Doyle wrote, and sneered at the able-bodied men who were playing football and cricket, leaving the fighting to someone else.

As is often shown, the most recent converts are the most fervent and bigoted. Doyle maintained that for years Germany had regarded the British Empire, with 'eyes of jealousy and hatred ... a most bitter hatred, a hatred which long antedates the days when we were compelled to take a definite stand against them. In all sorts of ways this hatred showed itself, in the diatribes of "Professors", in the pages of books, in the columns of the press. Usually it was a sullen, silent dislike.' Germany thought Britain weak, decadent, 'a nation of decadent poltroons'. Britain would show her, 'the narrow bureaucracy and swaggering Junkerdom of Prussia, the most artificial and ossified sham that ever our days have seen'.

Doyle admits that not many inhabitants of Great Britain were concerned with the events in Serbia that sparked off the war. As he put it allusively, 'What was it to us if a Slav or a Teuton collected the harbour dues of Salonica!' The invasion of Belgium was a different matter. To refuse to act would have been cowardly, treacherous, dishonourable and humiliating. 'To Hell with Serbia!' Horatio Bottomley had roared in the pages of his tabloid. But no one said: 'To Hell with Belgium!' Doyle penned in the history of the Belgian commitment, a guarantee of neutrality signed in 1839, confirmed by Bismarck in 1870, and a treaty guaranteed by Britain 'and Britain could be relied upon'. Doyle was not to know that by secret agreement

Britain and France had arranged, if necessary, to invade Belgium themselves and regard the treaty as 'a scrap of paper'.

As for British war aims, she did not want to gain more colonies or possessions of any kind (though eventually she did). She merely wanted to make Germany 'a peaceful and harmless State' by breaking her naval power. The money then spent by Britain on her own navy could be diverted towards social ends. Britain was really fighting for the old Germany, the Germany of Goethe and Schiller, against the Germany of blood and of iron, of 'scolding Professors with their final reckonings, their *Weltpolitik*, and their Godless theories of the Superman who stands above morality'. Doyle seems to have had a particular objection to scolding Professors.

Doyle was not alone in putting his pen at the service of the state, and wilder and crazier diatribes poured from the presses. The Parliamentary Recruiting Committee of 12 Downing Street declared that 'we are fighting to destroy for ever the Robber Power of Germany'. Frederic Harrison saw the war as 'a world struggle of Civilization against Reaction'. Christabel Pankhurst considered that Germany was the chief threat to Women's Rights ('that country in which women's position is lowest and most hopeless is Germany'). Doyle's object in writing his pamphlet was to appeal to the British sense of honour and indignation; others found it better to frighten their readers with clairvoyance. The atrocities against civilians in Belgium would be repeated if or when the Germans occupied Britain. And atrocity stories there were in abundance to fan the flames of hate – rape, burying alive, cutting off legs, hanging upside down and lancing by the Uhlans.

To Arms! was followed by *The British Campaign in France and Flanders*, published volume by volume, using information provided by contacts in France, including some of the leading commanders in the field. Sir John French was not cooperative, no doubt being too busy leaking secret information to his mistress. After the war Doyle compressed the book into one volume. This was a massive project, and Doyle was meticulous in his research, though he was inclined to a boyish enthusiasm that sometimes clashed with the theme; he cut through muddle and confusion to present a clear picture where there was no clear picture, and by discreet editing he occasionally falsified the situation. As he declared to one of his contributors, Smith-Dorrien, 'an historian, in my judgement, is not bound to say all he knows'.

Of all the campaigns of World War One, perhaps the Somme has received the most attention. On the first day of the battle, 1 July 1916, 21,392 British soldiers were killed and 35,493 wounded. It took seven days and fifty-eight packed ambulance trains to clear the wounded. It was the most horrific day in the annals of the British Army, bedevilled by miscalculation, stubbornness, and indifference to casualties on the part of the generals. For front-line soldiers who knew more about the situation than officers in the rear, and who had patrolled and found that the German defences had not been demolished by a week-long artillery barrage, military policemen were situated at strategic positions so that they could shoot those reluctant to go over the top.

Doyle's handling of the tragedy of the Somme was typical of his attitude throughout the book. 'There was universal joy that the long stagnant trench life should be at an end, and that the days of action, even if they should prove to be days of death, should at last have come ... The preparations were enormous and meticulous, yet everything ran like a well-oiled piston-rod.' Throughout his account, Doyle often used the phrase 'heroic disaster', yet he could still speak of 'the stupendous achievement of the British', and the 'fiery ordeal' of the Somme was equated with some tin-pot battle in one of his historical novels. The General Staff was whitewashed; British leadership 'was admirable in its perseverance and in its general conception'. There was a mild reproof. It had, 'it must be admitted, not yet attained that skill in the avoidance of losses'. Doyle, in his history of trench warfare, was bland and unprovocative. He was, to the man in the street, the official historian, the man to be believed, the man who was trusted, the man who was not in the pocket of the politicians. If Doyle saw the Battle of the Somme as a stupendous achievement, then so it must be.

As a volunteer in the citizens' army, Doyle did his share of marching and drilling, as well as guarding German prisoners-of-war, whom he found 'excellent workers ... and civil, tractable fellows as well'. But such mundane duties could not keep him from the scene of battle, and when he was asked to report on the conduct of the Italian allies he agreed, provided that he was permitted to visit the Western Front first. As his uniform, he wore 'a wondrous khaki garb' with roses on the shoulder-straps instead of pips or crowns, and although he was not granted army rank he was happy with the title he presented himself under, a deputy-lieutenant of Surrey, an antique sinecure he had been given years earlier. General Robertson, with whom Doyle had corresponded and to whom the history of the Western Front campaigns was dedicated, offered him transport on a destroyer. The crossing was uneventful, and Doyle made his way towards the front, expressing his admiration of army confidence, and the 'extraordinary efficiency in organization, administration, material and personnel'. It was not a view shared by all civilian visitors to the front, and those who were determined to make trouble were kept well away. The officer, Colonel Wilson, detailed to deal with newspaper men was 'dark, quiet, affable', affable because in Doyle he had the perfect tourist, flash uniform and all.

Everywhere Doyle went he found cheerful bravery, even among the conscientious objectors. So far as he was concerned, conscientious objectors were outside the pale. They were 'half-mad cranks whose absurd consciences prevented them from barring the way to the devil'. But even these low creatures, having not been vouchsafed the privilege of being tied to wooden crosses in No-Man's-Land as a punishment for their unBritish attitude, were working with a will by the roadside, no small achievement for these 'neurotic and largely bespectacled' pacifists. The bully-boy side of Doyle came to the fore. War was the grand adventure, and conscientious objectors doing forced labour should have had no part of it. There were no conchies in *The White Company* or *Sir Nigel*.

Doyle's attitude towards conscientious objectors tells us more than that he had wholeheartedly adopted the conventional attitude to the war. It shows his gradual inflexibility over the years. Where was the understanding Dr Doyle of the Southsea days? There were no longer two sides to a question. Perhaps he would once have bothered to discuss their beliefs with the objectors, but now they were neurotic and bespectacled nobodies. It is a strange man who uses 'bespectacled' in a pejorative sense. And Doyle was not writing in the heat of the moment, but looking back in tranquillity when writing his autobiography.

A conscientious objector, Robert Mennell, looked back too. 'It was right at the beginning that I learnt that the only people from whom I was to expect sympathy were the soldiers, and not the civilians.' Mennell was put in a guard-room, and five soldiers were bundled in, under arrest for being absent without leave. They asked him what he was in for. 'Well, you see, I am a Quaker, and I refused to join the army, because I think war is murder.' There was silence in the guard-room, and one of the men whispered: 'Murder? Murder? It's *bloody* murder!' Mennell then concluded that they were friends. These anonymous soldiers had a common humanity that was lacking in Doyle; he was a cyclist who had got stuck in a tram-line and could not get out until he reached the terminus. He was more concerned in showing off his custom-made uniform, in meeting generals and influencing them, than in finding out how it was. He thought in terms of a self-flattering scenario and not a transcript.

Despite his loathing for conscientious objectors, Doyle did go out of his way to try to save Sir Roger Casement, who had been a hero in 1903 when he had spoken up against the Congo tragedy and had denounced atrocities in Brazil when consul there later. Shortly before the outbreak of war Casement had been in New York, and took the side of Germany. He travelled to Berlin and spoke to prisoners-of-war, trying to get them to take arms against their former comrades, but he only recruited fifty, and when his homosexual activities became too prominent for them to be overlooked the Germans were only too happy for him to go to Ireland to take part in the rising in Dublin on Easter Sunday 1916. He was landed by submarine, but was challenged by a policeman and arrested, charged with treason, and executed in August. Despite the petitions he organized, Doyle did not succeed in staying the execution.

There were many people who were in favour of the action of the British Government, including H.G.Wells, and there was a strong prejudice against Casement on account of his homosexuality. This, to Doyle, was less important than suborning soldiers. Before the war there had been growing leniency towards homosexuality, and it was gradually being recognized as a predisposition and not a heinous crime. The climate was turning from the witch-hunt atmosphere of 1895 and the Oscar Wilde trials. In his autobiography Doyle referred, in guarded terms, to Wilde's homosexuality: 'I thought at the time, and still think, that the monstrous development which ruined him was pathological, and that a hospital rather than a police court was the place for his consideration.' Kindly as this was intended, it illustrates how out of touch Doyle was with intelligent opinion and the efforts of Havelock Ellis and others to treat sexual inversion with compassion and objectivity.

Doyle had been strongly influenced by atrocity propaganda, and as the war moved on nothing could be too low for the Germans, though there were men, such as G.Lowes Dickinson, who tried in vain to keep a sense of perspective and cited evidence that racial hatred was not one-sided. He drew attention to an article in the *Saturday Review* of 11 September 1897, which stated: 'If Germany were extinguished to-morrow, the day after to-morrow there is not an Englishman in the world who would not be the richer. Nations have fought for years over a city or a right of succession: must they not fight for two hundred and fifty million pounds of yearly commerce?' Which, of course, is what the First World War was all about.

On 13 April 1915, Doyle wrote a letter to *The Times* about the German treatment of prisoners-of-war. On 9 May 1915 he published a penny pamphlet under the auspices of the Central Committee for National Patriotic Organization. The full-blooded patriotism and flag-waving of *To Arms!* gave way to bitter rancour of a kind that was to become increasingly common as the war progressed: 'Never again in our time will a German visitor be welcome in our country. Never again should our students of music flock to Dresden, of art to Leipsig and Munich, or our invalids to the overrated spas of the Fatherland. A deep fissure will divide the two races ...' No longer was the war being fought for the benefit of the German people against the Junkers.

The war methods of the Germans were 'systematic murder'. This covered Zeppelin attacks, submarine warfare and the bombardment of the east coast by warships. A delicate distinction was drawn between ports which had defences, such as West Hartlepool, where bombardment was in order, and places like Whitby, which had none. The reasoning behind the pamphlet was rather sick. Soldiers who read the pamphlet would learn of the torture of prisoners-of-war, and the truth 'may warm their hearts in the day of battle, and teach them that it is better to die on the field than fall into the cruel hands of German gaolers'.

There is no question that atrocity stories were manufactured by order of the various governments to give backbone to the wavering. Prisoners-of-war could be treated badly, on both sides. In the early years of war, when trench warfare had not yet made a war of movement obsolete, ill-treatment was often due to incompetence and logistic foul-ups and not deliberate brutality. British officers expected to be treated better than they were; for one officer cruelty was construed as having his greatcoat taken away from him. For another, cruelty was not having a batman. It was considered dastardly for the Germans to supply wooden clogs when prisoners' boots wore out. 'As sure as there is a God of Justice,' declared Doyle, 'these things shall be answered for. We bide our time and the end is not yet.'

The horrors of war were regarded as a personal affront. They were expected, but when they came they were not anticipated. In 1911 John Galsworthy tried to get agreement to stop the use of aircraft in war. G.K.Chesterton and George Bernard Shaw refused his appeal, Chesterton declaring that 'to stop aeroplanes would simply be to help the Prussians against the French, who have the best aeroplanes; and who surely require the sympathies of all who care for freedom and civilization as against a solemn barbarism'.

Shaw wrote that 'We know perfectly well that aerial warfare will *not* be ruled out, any more than (virtually) explosive bullets have been ruled out, no matter what pious wishes we express. It may be horrible; but horror is the whole point of war; the newspapers will be really jolly when showers of shells alternate with showers of mangled aeronauts on crowded cities.' It was the business of the *Titanic* again, reason versus sentiment, the very embodiment of which was Doyle. He did not lead the crowd or follow the crowd; he was in the crowd. He enthusiastically adopted the term 'Boche' and notwithstanding his horror at the bombardment of the east coast and the bombing of British cities he called for reprisal raids on German cities. He would have had his wish had it been possible, but the air force had not gone in for airships and although a four-engined Handley-Page bomber was built to raid Berlin the scheme was forestalled by the signing of the Armistice.

The authorities appreciated Doyle's wholehearted attitude to the war, and he was approached to see if he would head a propaganda department. However, Doyle preferred to remain freelance.

During the war, nevertheless, Doyle produced a book that was to have more lasting value than his history of trench warfare or his attempts to create permanent race hatred between the British and the Germans. This was another eagerly awaited collection of Sherlock Holmes short stories, *His Last Bow*. The title story is one of the few not narrated by Watson, and was written in response to the war. Holmes pretends to be an informer for a German spy and enters as 'a tall, gaunt man of sixty, with clear-cut features and a small goatee beard gave him a general resemblance to the caricatures of Uncle Sam'. Rather carelessly, the spy gives him the combination of the safe, and, with the possible exception of 'The Dying Detective' in the same volume, it is perhaps the weakest story of the canon.

These stories were unashamedly gathered together to make a book. 'The Cardboard Box' was first published in *Strand* in 1893, but not included in the hardback collection. A section of 'The Cardboard Box', a thought-reading episode by Holmes, was transferred bodily to 'The Resident Patient', presumably in the expectation that the reader would not remember what he had already read. 'The Cardboard Box' is a neat story dealing with the despatch of two severed human ears; 'The Adventure of Wisteria Lodge' is of 'The Red-Headed League' type, in which an unsuspecting man is persuaded to go somewhere for an ulterior reason, in this case to supply an alibi, for which purpose clocks are altered (it being assumed that the dupe does not have a watch with him). 'The Red Circle' is a rather laborious story dealing with one of Doyle's beloved secret societies, this time apparently the Mafia. The plot concerns the abstruse and long-winded manner in which a man on the run from the society keeps in touch with his wife, who is holed-up in a house.

'The Adventure of the Bruce-Partington Plans' is set in 1895, at a time when Holmes is investigating music of the Middle Ages, while the fog drifts outside the Baker Street ménage in a 'greasy, heavy brown swirl'. Despite the unconvincing security arrangements of the Woolwich Arsenal, from which secret submarine plans have been abstracted, the story rattles along at a fine pace, which is more than can be said of 'The Dying Detective'. Watson is called to the bedside of a dying Holmes, but Holmes refuses to let Watson treat him, preferring the services of the unpleasant Culverton Smith (no good can be thought of a man with 'a great yellow face, coarse-grained and greasy, with heavy, double-chin, [curious punctuation and hyphenation] and two sullen, menacing grey eyes'). Of course Holmes is not dying at all, and his 'illness' is a trap to get Culverton Smith to confess. With 'The Devil's Foot' Holmes is back in the gloomy menacing terrain of *The Hound of the Baskervilles*, with odd mind-bending vegetation. 'The Disappearance of Lady Frances Carfax' is a substitution story with the chloroform-soaked victim rescued before she can be buried alive.

Except for 'His Last Bow', the stories were sheer escapism. Real life was keeping the war effort going, meeting generals and attending medal ceremonies. As Doyle put it in his poem 'Victrix':

> How was it then with England?
> Her faith was true to her plighted word,

> Her strong hand closed on her blunted sword,
> Her heart rose high to the foeman's hate.

He liked generals, especially those who got on with the job:

> Haig is moving!
>   Three plain words are all that matter,
> Mid the gossip and the chatter,
> Hopes in speeches, fears in papers,
> Pessimistic froth and vapours—
>   Haig is moving!

Most of the generals he saw in France were well behind the front. They gave him the official line. Occasionally Doyle could get off on his own, as he did when he visited the ruined Ypres with his brother Innes, recently promoted colonel and eventually to make general. After France, Doyle went to the Italian front, but neither the Italians nor the Austrians they were fighting had much charisma, unlike the Australians, whom Doyle visited in September 1918. The Australians were rough, valiant, sporting but rude-handed, with a penchant for looting. He saw German prisoners being brought in, weary, shuffling, hang-dog creatures, and thought them 'uniformed bumpkins ... heavy-jawed, beetle-browed, uncouth louts', not so dissimilar from the nasty Culverton Smith who received his due deserts at the hands of Sherlock Holmes.

No one could accuse Doyle of lack of physical courage; when he was with the Australians he was under heavy bombardment, and did not flinch. However, the noise and clatter of shells was a discordant swan-song. In a few weeks peace came, and revenge was taken on the Germans, as Doyle wished. By and large, they had not played the game.

13
SPIRITS FROM THE VASTY DEEP

The poor accepted death philosophically. In the Victorian age the life expectation of men varied between forty in 1838 and forty-two in 1880, and working men who passed the age of forty were reckoned very fortunate. The middle and upper classes were cushioned against an early death by adequate food and a reasonable standard of hygiene, while they benefited from what medical skill there was available.

World War One saw the upper- and middle-class young men, the officer class, decimated on the Western Front. The life expectation for a newly arrived officer was hardly more than a fortnight. The consequence was a boom in spiritualism, with the bereaved seeking consolation and only too willing to believe that their menfolk had not died but only passed over. Fraudulent mediums exploited the situation to the utmost, cashing in on grief.

Typical of the young men who died in action was Raymond Lodge, trained as an engineer, commissioned in the 3rd South Lancashires soon after the outbreak of war, and sent to the front in early 1915. He served in the trenches near Ypres, and was later attached to a machine-gun section. He was killed by a shell fragment on 14 September 1915. In a memoir of him, his brother wrote: 'Let us think of him then, not as lying near Ypres with all his work ended, but rather, after due rest and refreshment, continuing his noble and useful career in more peaceful surroundings, and quietly calling us his family from paralysing grief to resolute and high endeavour.'

Raymond Lodge was only one officer among thousands, and only exceptional in that his father was Sir Oliver Lodge, a famous physicist who had specialized in the study of the ether, and who had become acquainted with psychical research in the mid-1870s, meeting Edmund Gurney, a founder member of the Society for Psychical Research. Gurney was collecting material for his massive book *Phantasms of the Living*, which struck Lodge at first as 'a meaningless collection of ghost-stories'. Gurney's energy and seriousness impressed Lodge, and through Gurney he met Myers. In 1883 a performer called Irving Bishop carried out sensational thought-reading stunts in Liverpool where Lodge was working, and this encouraged some girls working in a drapery to try it out, the results being sufficiently startling for the newly formed Society of Psychical Research to investigate. Lodge was involved in these examinations, and sent a paper to the scientific journal *Nature*, which was published in June 1884.

Lodge therefore became involved in psychical research about the same time as Doyle, but their approach afterwards diverged, Doyle being interested in the emotional inspirational side while Lodge tackled the matter as a scientist and with an objectivity lacking among many of his colleagues. In 1889 Lodge was asked to sit with the famous Boston medium Mrs Piper, with Myers taking notes. Lodge considered that there was a *prima facie* case for the genuineness of Mrs Piper, since he had received messages from dead relatives the content of which could not have been known to Mrs Piper. To satisfy researchers that Mrs Piper was not a fraud, gathering information to use at seances, one of the most assiduous of investigators, Richard Hodgson, went to Boston and employed an American detective agency to put her under constant surveillance.

Doyle and Lodge were knighted on the same day in 1902, and continued to have contact. Doyle looked up to Lodge, who was only eight years older but in almost every way a more mature person, without the schoolboyishness that occasionally perplexed admirers of the younger man. Lodge had found out what he was looking for, without allowing his beliefs to intrude into his scientific work, whereas Doyle had signally failed to organize his feelings and his knowledge.

Shortly before the death of his son Raymond, Lodge had had a message, supposedly from Myers who had died in 1901, through Mrs Piper, to anticipate some calamity which Myers said he would take steps to ease. Lodge had news of his son's death on 17 September 1915, and on 25 September his wife received at a sitting with the medium Mrs Leonard a message purporting to come from Raymond: 'Tell Father I have met some friends of his.' Asked for the name of one of these friends, the answer came that it was Myers, and two days later Lodge went to London to see Mrs Leonard. Many messages followed, containing a profusion of evidential detail, including reference to a photograph that no one knew existed and which only came to light later.

In 1916 Lodge wrote his book *Raymond or Life and Death* 'with examples of the evidence for survival of memory and affection after death'. It is a model of how such a book should be presented, with background material, Raymond's letters from the front and a serious non-sensational section dealing with the interaction of mind and matter, life and consciousness, and the relation between mind and brain. It was unquestionably the most important book dealing with a spiritualistic subject to come out of World War One, and it had a profound effect on Doyle, who added Lodge to Crookes and Flammarion in his pantheon, as another supermind who thought the same way as he did, if more coherently. Lodge had taken the precept of Thomas Huxley to heart: 'Sit down before fact as a little child, be prepared to give up every preconceived notion, follow humbly wherever and to whatsoever abysses Nature leads.' Unfortunately, Thomas Huxley was not on Doyle's list of the best minds. He had looked briefly at spiritualism, and given it the thumbs down.

The tone of Lodge was cool, even detached: 'People often feel a notable difficulty in believing in the reality of continued existence. Very likely it is difficult to believe or to realize existence in what is sometimes called "the next world"; but then, when we come to think of it, it is difficult to believe in existence in this world too; it is difficult to believe in existence at all.'

This is the kind of studied sentence that Doyle could never write. There is the cunning turning of the reader's attention from a hereafter which is unlikely to reality. The reader *knows* that he exists in an everyday world, but the persuasive tone used by Lodge compels him to think about it, and perhaps consider the possibility that it is difficult to believe in existence at all. If Lodge, who has studied the question, says it is difficult to believe in existence then perhaps, for he writes as if there is no question about doubt, he is right.

Raymond is a big book of more than four hundred pages, leading the uncommitted reader through a strange maze, without antagonizing anyone or stepping aside to lambaste some unfortunate. By the time it appeared, Doyle was ready to come out, colours flying. He had voiced his accretions of opinions through other mouths, in particular Professor Challenger in *The Poison Belt*, but, following the deaths of his son Kingsley and brother Innes, he produced in rapid succession two books, *The New Revelation* (1918) and *The Vital Message* (1919).

He made his position clear:

When the War came it brought earnestness into all our souls and made us look more closely at our own beliefs and reassess their values. In the presence of an agonized world, hearing every day of the deaths of the flower of our race in the first promise of their unfulfilled youth, seeing around one the wives and mothers who had no clear conception whither their loved one had gone to, I seemed suddenly to see that this subject with which I had so long dallied was not merely a study of a force outside the rules of science, but that it was really something tremendous, a breaking down of the walls between two worlds, a direct undeniable message from beyond, a call of hope and of guidance to the human race at the time of its deepest affliction.

It was emotional stuff, belonging to that class of literature known as inspirational, and there must have been a sinking of the heart when Doyle went on to write: 'The objective side of it ceased to interest, for having made up one's mind that it was true there was an end of the matter.' Doyle affirmed, he did not argue. He knew he was always in the right. Having made up his mind that he was a religious leader, he threw himself into his mission: 'Rouse yourselves! Stand by! Be at attention! Here are signs for you. They will lead up to the message which God wishes to send.'

The New Revelation is apocalyptic. Christianity, run for so long by good if misguided men, 'must change or must perish'. It was clear to Doyle that there was no fall of men, and therefore there cannot be atonement. Too much stress was placed on the death of Christ, and not enough on the life. The Christians had misunderstood the message.

Regarding the future life, there seemed to Doyle to be remarkable resemblances between all spiritualistic accounts. The spirit body is an exact counterpart of the old one, save that all disease, weakness or deformity has disappeared. At death, the spirit body stands or floats beside the old body, aware of it and the surroundings. It, he or she, cannot communicate with those left behind, because living organs are 'only attuned to coarser stumuli'. The spirit body finds itself among those who have gone before, is welcomed, and then has a sleep which varies from a few days to several months, depending largely on how much trouble it had in life.

The spirit comes to, and finds itself in its suitable sphere,

probationary for the less fortunate, a hospital for weakly souls. Higher
spirits can go up and down, but slower spirits have to work to move
up out of their sphere. Spirit life is predominantly of the mind, with
no food, money, lust or pain, but with music, the arts, intellectual
and spiritual knowledge going strong. Spirits are clothed, and live
in communities, nations being roughly divided from each other,
though language is no barrier as thought is the medium of conversation. All religions are equal, but bigots suffer because they cannot
believe what is happening to them.

There were transcendental chemists who could even make alcohol
and tobacco for unregenerate spirits (Doyle takes this from Lodge's
Raymond). These were no doubt the nuisances who sent down false
or jokey messages. As for advice to readers, they should read all the
literature on the subject, broaden and spiritualize their thoughts, and
be unselfish.

There was nothing at all recondite or obscure about *The New Revelation;* it was written for the typical Doyle reader, the subscriber to
Strand. It was treated cautiously by the critics, the *Daily Chronicle* considering it 'very frank, very courageous and very resolute' while the
Daily News thought it demanded respect and would reach a public
not interested in 'the long reports of the Society for Psychical Research'. The *Daily Telegraph* said that it disarmed criticism by its
frankness and its modesty. The spiritualists were taken unawares,
wondering what they had in their midst, and many of them were
alarmed by Doyle's full-blooded approach. They were even more
troubled by *The Vital Message*.

Doyle had gone back to his Bible, and found that Armageddon,
clearly the Great War, had been followed by the Second Coming.
This was evidently figurative, meaning that there would be 'an ascent
of our material plane to the spiritual, and a blending of the two phases
of existence'. And now that the war had been over for a year, he saw
its importance and its necessity. 'Can we not understand that it was
needful to shake mankind loose from gossip and pink teas, and sword-
worship, and Saturday night drunks, and self-seeking politics and
theological quibbles ...' However heinous a pink tea was, or is, or
whatever it is or was, it seems a poor excuse to initiate a world war.

Almost immediately Doyle launches into a swingeing attack on the
Bible, where the living and the dead are bound together, and the dead
have tainted the living. 'A mummy and an angel are in most unnatural partnership.' The mummy was the Old Testament, 'a docu-

ment which advocates massacre, condones polygamy, accepts slavery
and orders the burning of so-called witches'. There is a brief history
of spiritualism, much of it already contained in *The New Revelation*,
with praise of Mrs de Morgan's *From Matter to Spirit* (1863), one of
the first English books on spiritualism and one of the most uninten-
tionally funny books ever written. 'It is a question' ponders Doyle,
'whether anyone has shown greater brain power in treating the subject.'

In *The Vital Message* Doyle tackled the problem of the spirit body.
He used the concept of 'bound ether', and explained what this did.
If all that is visible of [the human body] were removed, there would
still remain a complete and absolute mould of the body, formed in
bound ether which would be different from the ether around it.' This
could be photographed. Regarding spirit photography, Doyle had no
doubt of its validity.

A good deal of the material is a re-running of *The New Revelation*,
with William James, somewhat surprisingly, included for the first time
among the heroes. William James, the founder of the philosophical
system called pragmatism, was never less than pragmatical when
dealing with spiritualism. Lodge is picked out as 'probably the leading
intellectual force in Europe', though Doyle is somewhat patronizing
about Lodge's extremely lucid style. 'Sir Oliver has not always the
art of writing so as to be understanded [sic] of the people,' he maintained, and suggested that Lodge cut out his own cackle and re-issue
Raymond for the cheap trade.

One of the problems facing the unlearned was the assurance that
the spirit body was a facsimile of the earth body, with deformities
removed, and the reconciliation of this with the equally authoritative
statement that 'no woman [need] mourn her lost beauty, and no man
his lost strength or weakening brain'. Who or what would decide when
a woman was at her peak, as a pretty teenager or a mature forty,
and who could say at what age a man loses his strength or has a
weakening brain? Then there were children. 'The child grows up to
the normal, so that the mother, who lost a babe of two years old and
dies herself twenty years later, finds a grown-up daughter of twenty-
two awaiting her coming.' Glib sentimentalities such as these robbed
Doyle of any kudos he obtained by joining the spiritualist ranks, and
his vision of the afterlife was that of the suburban husband who spends
his Sunday morning washing his car: 'Beautiful gardens, lovely
flowers, green woods, pleasant lakes, domestic pets – all of these things

are fully described in the messages of the pioneer travellers who have at last got news back to those who loiter in the old dingy homes.'

Cosiness and sincerity do not perform miracles, and although Doyle took the message to the plain man he did not succeed in inspiring a nation; a popular journalist, Hannen Swaffer, did more to capture the hearts and minds when he preached his brand of spiritualism. However, Swaffer was a chairbound prophet. Doyle stomped the country as a missionary, charting his journeys on a map, then took the message overseas, to Australia and New Zealand in 1920–21 and to the United States in 1922.

He was preceded in America by Lodge, who did not think his own visit worth mentioning at all in his autobiography. The Americans had become cynical about spiritualism, as frauds and exposures multiplied, and in the 1920s it was considered to be desperately old-fashioned and passé, and far inferior to Theosophy and Christian Science, the founder of which, Mrs Mary Eddy (1821–1910), had opposed spiritualism. Spiritualism suffered from the disadvantage of having no central commanding figure, unlike Christian Science or Theosophy, which had Madame Blavatsky, and as soon as a suitable candidate arrived he or she would be sure to have his credentials ruined by an ill-concealed trick.

The American tour of 1922 provided Doyle with the material for his *Our American Adventure*, and despite his enthusiasm he was aware of the pitfalls. 'No subject can be more easily made humorous than this,' he admitted, and waited with some trepidation for the arrival on the ship of the American reporters. He was surprised, for their questions 'were so clear-cut and intelligent that I saw signs of organized preparation'. In other words, the reporters had read his books.

They had plenty to bite on. Doyle was asked if the spirits ate. 'Any nutrition', he told them, 'is of a very light and delicate order, corresponding to the delicate etheric body which requires it.' He was asked, not too delicately, about sex in the hereafter. This had been a stumbling block to Victorian writers on spiritualism, who had performed linguistic miracles to evade both the subject and the question. Only one man had firmly faced up to the problem, William Holcombe, whose *The Sexes: Here and Hereafter* was published in 1869.

'A woman who closes her eyes in this world and opens them in another', he wrote, 'has lost nothing of her feminine character. She is not a man, nor a hermaphrodite, nor a nondescript, nor a spiritual

vapour floating in the mystic ether or universal thought. She is a living, breathing, sensitive woman; and, if regenerate, she has every
womanly quality intensified for a higher and better life. Woman is
woman still. Every muscle there, as here, is a feminine muscle; every
bone is a female bone. From her delicate and *spirituelle* features beam
forth the softness and beauty of the feminine soul, and on the elliptical
curves of her graceful form accumulates, as in this world, the charm
and magnetism of life.'

The body had tissues and organs corresponding to those of 'the
natural body'. With reservations. As poisons were not absorbed
through the human habit of eating, the use of the lavatory was not
necessary. 'The sexuality of man and woman consists really in the
sexual difference between their souls, which are thence anatomically
represented in their bodies.' There was marriage in the hereafter,
but no sex. Marriage, said Holcombe, was a good thing. Even monks
and nuns would find out their mistake, and find their conjugal mates.
Unhappy marriages on earth, marriages for 'external and selfish
motives', would be cancelled out. The poet Coventry Patmore in his
Religio Poetae echoed Holcombe's views. Sexual life on earth bore 'the
clearest marks of being nothing other than the rehearsal of a com-
munion of a higher nature'.

Doyle had not thought the matter through. He dismissed the whole
matter briefly and succinctly. 'As there is no sexual relation, as we
understand it,' he told the reporters, 'this problem is not very complex
and is naturally decided by soul affinity.' Very much the Holcombe
and Patmore view, though the problem was more complex than he
thought. Although spirit woman was living, breathing and sensitive,
and had organs, muscles, bones and tissues 'corresponding' to those
on earth, it was somewhat arbitary to reject those attributes that were
indelicate. The sexual and excretory organs, after all, helped to produce the 'elliptical curves of her graceful form' and the less elliptical
unnamed shapes of man.

Reporters also probed about Doyle's rash speculations that spirits
smoked cigars and drank hard liquor in the hereafter, the latter being
of intense topical interest as prohibition had been declared in the
United States. Doyle managed to survive the inquisition. On the way
to his hotel he noticed that the members of the police were clear-cut
athletic young men, where formerly they had been 'fat, inefficient
and corrupt'. He contrasted the hotels of England with those of
America, commending the cleanliness and additional facilities of the

American hotels, especially the cupboard space in hotel rooms and the provision of ice. He was less enthusiastic about hotel dining-rooms, where the service left much to be desired.

He had arrived in time for a crime wave. This he assigned to the 'after-effects of the war, and the habits of unrest which soldiery, or even economic disturbance, engenders'. After all, he reminded English readers, the Americans had their rationing as well, and bravely faced up to their meatless days. But all these were unimportant compared with his mission, to take the good news to the natives in the wake of Sir Oliver Lodge.

At his first lecture in New York there was an audience of 3,500. 'Evidently it was a crowd which had its dead,' commented the *New York World*. The audience listened, 'with most profound respect. Nobody doubts all that he said except a very ignorant person.' Doyle, and his agent, were very pleased with the reception, and success followed at other venues. In Boston there was a message from Myers, who had long passed over. 'You have gone a step farther than I,' commented Myers.

There were reporters who were not so pleasant as those of the *New York World*, reporters who prefaced their stories with 'Do Spooks Marry?' or 'High Jinks in the Beyond', and there were cities where the seeds fell on barren ground, such as Chicago, where there was a marked lack of enthusiasm. Doyle thought Chicago noisy and expensive, and found the press impertinent. He had taken his wife and family with him, and the papers in Chicago reported that 'the young Doyles are bored stiff with their parents' Spiritualism, but want more yarns from him'.

The lack of response in some places was due to the expectation of seeing and hearing the creator of Sherlock Holmes, but instead having to suffer the exhortations and homilies of an elderly man with, there were no two ways about it, a bee in his bonnet. In Toronto, there was actual hostility, and a Canon Cody mourned that there was a falling-off from the days when Doyle used to write detective stories. Doyle wished that his wife would take a fuller part in the business, instead of looking at the trip as an occasion for sightseeing. 'If she could let her burning feelings have full play, and voice her deep womanly desire to bring comfort to the stricken, she would be a world-force.' But Lady Conan Doyle kept in the background.

There were compensations that made Doyle forget the occasional obtuse newspaperman (though by and large he preferred the American reporters to the English who, he claimed, were ignorant and insolent). There were interesting people to meet – an ex-gangster named Morrell who, after spending some time in solitary confinement in a strait jacket, found that he had the ability to leave his body and assume extra-corporeal form, and Marconi, who had intercepted wireless waves of a length of 30,000 metres and had speculated that perhaps they were messages from Mars. Doyle considered that it was more likely that they were experimental attempts at contact from the dead. There was also Major Schroeder who, although he did not contribute very much to spiritualistic theory, had had an experience that might well at some future date be tied in with the canon. In 1920 Schroeder had beaten the altitude record in his aircraft, reaching 37,000 feet. At 12,000 feet he had seen snow-white birds like robins and, more oddly, spider webs with spiders still on them.

When he was at Harvard, Doyle found the opportunity to consult the university's stock of alchemical books 'which seem to allude directly to ectoplasm, showing that these medieval philosophers were really a good deal ahead of us in some phases of psychic knowledge'. Like many ignorant laymen, Doyle refused to believe that the main aim of alchemy was to make gold. This, he thought, was a cover to prevent the Church persecuting alchemy, conveniently forgetting, or, more likely, not knowing, that throughout much of the history of alchemy the Church actively encouraged this entertaining hobby. In alluding to mercury, Doyle decided that the alchemists meant ectoplasm. 'There cannot be the least doubt,' he asserted.

When he wanted, Doyle could still pen a vivid simile, as when he and the family visited Niagara Falls and stood on the rock underneath it staring up through the water at the sun. The water seemed to him like alabaster. He also attended a baseball game, and, heresy indeed, prophesied that it would eventually supersede cricket as a British national sport on the grounds that 'life is too serious now for games that last days on end'. He died a quarter of a century too soon to see the introduction of the one-day cricket match that would have satisfied his requirements.

While he was in America he frequented numbers of mediums, but found few of them impressive. The more spectacular materialization mediums had retired when their exposure ratio reached danger point, and he was irritated by the prevalence of Indian guides. 'Why Indians should be specially interested with these powers, and be the janitors of the great gates, I cannot imagine,' he wrote. He could not ignore the number of fake mediums who had been found out. They were, he said, 'human hyenas'.

Doyle's agent pronounced the tour a financial success, and he returned to the United States and Canada the following year, travelling altogether fifty thousand miles and addressing nearly a quarter of a million people, feted in Hollywood and receiving up to three hundred letters a day. Throughout the rest of his life he was always on the move, presiding at a spiritualist congress in 1925, visiting South Africa, Kenya and Rhodesia in 1928, and later taking in Scandinavia and Holland. It was a tribute to his constitution, and his belief in the great cause.

He continued to write books, some of them published at his own expense and sold at a psychic bookshop he opened in the shadow of Westminster Abbey. Emulating Lodge's *Raymond*, Doyle published in 1927 *Pheneas Speaks*, 'Direct Spirit Communications in the Family Circle', on the title page of which was blazoned 'No Copyright (U.S.A. Excepted)', so that those who wished could extract sections. This book was the result of Jean Conan Doyle's discovery in 1921 that she was able to trance-write, leading in 1924 to trance-speaking. The Pheneas of the title was a guide who appeared for the first time in December 1922.

Pheneas Speaks represents the triumph of wish-fulfilment, with sceptical friends who had died coming back to recant and offer help to the Doyles and to assure them that they were especially privileged to be where they were when they were: 'England is to be the centre to which all humanity will turn. She is to be the beacon of light in this dark, dark world.' Pheneas later said that 'Things are already working, but the human eye cannot see it. In a storm you only hear a far-off rumble at first, and then it comes on and on till it is roaring overhead.' The guide had a few things to say about international events: 'I want to tell you something else. There is not going to be much trouble about the League of Nations. They will automatically fall into the position of a jury, representing the spirit of God's love, sympathy and tender anxiety for mankind. In the new world, that is.'

Hannen Swaffer is brought into the dialogue. Swaffer had written lengthily on the return of Lord Northcliffe. Northcliffe had died in 1922, and apparently was no longer the autocratic and ruthless press baron but a diligent worker for the cause. Doyle's mother came through, and said there would be coming changes in which God would speak to Fleet Street, and that the psychic bookshop would be 'like a great flare in a peasoup mist'. There were negative forces at work, but the power of light would defeat them. Doyle's future biographer, Dr Lamond, was praised as a 'great vibrant soul ... tell him from me [Pheneas] that the long lane is near its turning'.

His literary friends and acquaintances were baffled by Doyle's preoccupations, and spiritualists remained uneasy, though they were aware that Doyle was spending his considerable income on their behalf and that royalties from his spiritualistic books went into the movement. It has been said that he spent a quarter of a million pounds on spiritualism. Psychical researchers were nonplussed by his multitudinous activities, and irritated at his espousing of mediums who had been found out in fraud. Eventually he resigned from the Society for Psychical Research when it refused to endorse one of his favourite mediums.

A note of acidity even crept into a letter Lodge wrote to his friend J. Arthur Hill in August 1923: 'I rather regret Doyle's decision – if it is a decision – to set up a Spiritualistic Church in London. But that I suppose is a natural outcome of his missionary activity. I suppose he regards himself as a sort of Wesley or Whitefield [George Whitefield, one of the founders of Methodism].'

As at Southsea in the 1880s, Doyle was in the 1920s a strong committee man, president of the London Spiritualist Alliance, president of the British College of Psychic Science, president of the Spiritualist Community, and associated with the Marylebone Spiritualist Association. From his psychic bookshop he ran a small museum containing the religious relics of the movement. He backed Sunday meetings at the Aeolian Hall, and later at the Queen's Hall, and the Marylebone Association engaged the Albert Hall for every Armistice Day morning. Doyle was the target of many abusive letters from cranks of all persuasions. A letter addressed to 'The Devil' reached him, and he was frequently accused of blasphemy.

Because of his standing and reputation for integrity, Doyle was largely spared personal attack in the press of the kind directed at Hannen Swaffer, who had featured in a cartoon showing him surrounded by goblins who were throwing tambourines and other psychic objects at him with the caption: 'The spirits throw things at him – and they're right.' Edgar Wallace was one of his chief tormenters. Wallace's attitude was shared by many journalists, scepticism mingled with discomfort. In an article 'Why not leave the dead alone?' in *London Opinion*, he attacked the movement in no uncertain terms:

I do not believe that anyone by falling into an epileptic fit, or a good imitation of one, secures the mysterious power of bringing themselves into touch with these personalities which have no longer habitation in the human frame ... why should spirits blow horns and tin trumpets, and pick up tambourines and shake them? When we depart this mortal life do the sanest of us become clowns? Why is all this dreary nonsense necessary if it is not that it is tricks which are easily performed by an unscrupulous medium? ... As I have said before, charlatanism reigns in this peculiar sphere.

Notwithstanding Wallace's candid opinion, this did not prevent Doyle making overtures to him not as a mere convert but as a possible leader of the spiritualist movement. Doyle recognized Wallace as a masterly story-teller who appealed to the same kind of public as himself. To some degree, Wallace recanted after a curious occurrence in which Hannen Swaffer's dead sister-in-law appeared in a corner of his study, told him that he ought to be ashamed of himself, and offered her condolences on his heavy losses at Newmarket. 'There it is,' said Wallace, 'and, to use a commonplace, you can't get away from it. The only change of attitude it will make, so far as I am concerned, is that I shall no longer sneer at spirits.'

Despite the brave face of Doyle and his supporters and his confidence that a new dawn was approaching, the 1920s saw a decline in spiritualism. There were several reasons for this, one of them being the antipathy of the age to seriousness, the love of novelty for its own sake, and the frenzied pursuit of frivolity. Another reason was the mundane fact that time cures all things, and as the war receded the bereaved were less bereaved and the dead heroes, if not forgotten, were mourned less strenuously. Among ordinary folk contact with the dead was no longer so pressing, especially as it was not so easy to get into communication – explained by spiritualism as the natural progression of the spirit away from its earth-bound environment. Seances were no longer a source of comfort, but a disappointment.

As if aware that he had been preaching a false dawn, Doyle turned to warning the nation of the consequences of ignoring spiritualism and all it stood for, and predicted calamity, mostly of an unnamed type. He was following the traditional line of messiahs – if persuasion failed, then bring on damnation and hell-fire. One of Doyle's pamphlets incurred the displeasure of Lodge: 'Of course he says some true things, but I rather regret his saying them. It might be proper enough for a man who has studied Literature and Theology to say some of them; but everyone knows he has not studied them, and if he had he would have expressed himself differently.'

This was in 1928. Doyle had still not got his ideas in order, and had resorted to exhortation and proclamation. In a shouting match he had few equals, but that was not what was needed. He had been much cleverer earlier when he presented the search for spirit guidance as an adventure story in his *The Land of Mist* (1926), which sold 38,000 copies in five years. It was reprinted in Hutchinson's Universal Library, selling at a shilling a volume, rubbing shoulders in the series with the works of Ethel M.Dell, Edgar Wallace, and less exalted figures such as 'Rita' and Mabel Barnes-Grundy.

The Land of Mist uses the characters of *The Lost World* and *The Poison Belt*, and has something for everyone; the main plot concerns the speedy conversion of the narrator Malone and the slower conversion of Professor Challenger. A curious feature of the book is the overlooking of Challenger's dicta on the future life laid down in *The Poison Belt*, where he proclaims that he is more than buckets of salt and water. In almost exactly the same words in *The Land of Mist* he states that that was all he was.

The book is almost as autobiographical as *The Stark Munro Letters*. In the foreword Doyle states that 'there is no incident in this volume which has not come within the immediate personal ken of the writer, or else has happened to those in whom he has full confidence ... Accuracy of statement has been cultivated throughout, and some of the seance-room conversations are absolute transcriptions of stenographic reports.'

Unlike the non-fiction books on spiritualism, the novel has a clear narrative, with the hero and heroine taking in one aspect or other of the occult at a time, first a spiritualist church, where the congregation was 'not distinguished nor intellectual, but it was undeniably healthy, honest, and sane. Small trades-folk, male and female shopwalkers, better-class artisans, lower-middle-class women worn with household cares, occasional young folk in search of a sensation ...' It was all very comfortable and old-fashioned, and Doyle was harmlessly patronizing, though with his skill at thumbnail sketches unimpaired. He includes a bore who talks about Atlantis, to inform his readers that not all spiritualists are commendable. The best spiritualist are those who have done well in the world, such as Mailey the barrister, or are converted after some traumatic experience. Lord John Roxton is compelled to change his tune after a session in a haunted house, an episode in which Doyle was in his element: 'They only knew that the black shadows at the top of the staircase had thickened, had coalesced, had taken a definite, batlike shape. Great God! They were moving! They were rushing swiftly and noiselessly downwards! Black, black as night, huge, ill-defined, semi-human and altogether evil and damnable.'

The story of the haunted house was taken from an account by Lord St Audries of a haunted house near Torquay, published in the *Weekly Despatch* in December 1921, and compared with it the tales of nice honest mediums and their persecution by the law, the quaint utterances of the Chinese guide Chang, or the melodramatic conversion of Professor Challenger are anti-climactic. It was clear that the fascination of the eerie and the weird side of the supernatural was still as impelling to Doyle as it had been thirty years earlier, and that when he was writing on such matters he could hold a reader spellbound, even a reader tuned to the rapid-paced thrillers of Edgar Wallace or to the new hero figure, Sapper's Bulldog Drummond.

14
THE COMING
OF THE FAIRIES

The espousing of spiritualism lost Doyle many friends, and his old acquaintances, such as James Barrie, were inclined to fight shy of him, becoming cautious and careful in his company and taking care not to involve themselves in controversy, much as newspaper reviewers did when they were handed his later books. In his book *Moral Courage* (1962), Compton Mackenzie praised Doyle's bravery in throwing in his lot with the spiritualists, but other writers were resentful. In his 1920 book *All and Sundry*, E.T.Raymond complained: 'He wants to have the best of all possible and impossible worlds, to be at ease both in Zion and Valhalla, as well as in a scientific lecture room. It is all very human and natural.'

It was easy in 1920, with Doyle's public conversion to the cause only two years in the past, to look upon it all as a passing aberration, akin to dabbling in historical novels, while not a few cynics saw it as a cunning publicity stunt to reawaken interest in the author as a prelude to another batch of Sherlock Holmes stories.

There was resentment, incomprehension, and there was malice. In 1920 a curious book was published in Hamburg by Ferdinand Hansen, an American of German extraction. It was called *The Unrepentant Northcliffe*, and its only interest is that Hansen had written to Doyle and Doyle had replied. The book is a vicious attack on Lord Northcliffe and Doyle for their anti-German sentiments during the war, though there is no question that Doyle did overstep the mark and become inflamed by his own rhetoric. Hansen referred slightingly to the 'all-red-eyed patriotism of Sir Arthur Conan Doyle', and the 'utterances of this blustering Termagentes'. 'During the war he saw nothing but German devils – just as now he has taken to spook chasing and table rapping.' In a letter directed to Doyle Hansen wrote: 'I think the real trouble with you is psychological, perhaps even pathological. You are suffering from the "inferiority complex". As an ultra-patriotic Briton of the old school, you simply cannot forgive the German for having proved himself in so many ways the moral, mental and physical superior of the Briton during the war.'

There were Englishmen who thought that Doyle's trouble was psychological, even pathological, but did not dare to say it. Doyle was a figure of mark, though less so as the years went by and his influence on the sporting breed became insignificant. But even those who kept an open mind about spiritualism and Doyle's involvement in it were driven to speculation about Doyle's mental state when in 1920 he became the prime propagandist in the cause of fairy folk. Doyle's interest in every aspect of supernature drove him to the edge, and beyond, of the ludicrous, and the Singular Case of the Fairies is as curious, and as discomfiting to his supporters, as a bad Sherlock Holmes story such as 'The Creeping Man'.

In May 1920 Doyle was in conversation with Mr Gow, the editor of the spiritualist periodical *Light*, and learned that alleged photographs of fairies had been taken. Gow had not seen them, but referred Doyle to a Miss Scatcherd, who in turn referred him to Miss Gardner. Her brother Edward was a fervent Theosophist, who, as their sister told Doyle, believed in fairies, pixies and goblins, and had been in touch with a family in Bradford where the little girl, Elsie, and her cousin, Frances, went into the woods and played with the fairies.

Elsie wished to photograph them, and after a time the sceptical father lent her his camera. The two girls went into the woods near a waterfall, and as Frances enticed three fairies and a pixie, Elsie stood ready with the camera. Some time later the plate was developed, and to the father's 'utter amazement' the 'four sweet little figures came out beautifully!' Gardner obtained the negative, and took it to a professional photographer who pronounced it genuine, and offered £100 for it.

Intensely interested, Doyle followed the matter up, and was brought into communication with Gardner's cousin, a Miss Blomfield, who had two fairy photographs taken by the girls, and soon Doyle had the opportunity to examine them. One was of a dancing goblin, and the other was of wood elves in a ring. A few days later, Doyle received a letter from May Bowley, an artist who had examined the photographs with a magnifying glass. Miss Bowley commented that the hands did not look like human hands, and that 'the beard in the little gnome seems to me to be some sort of insect-like appendage'. She also mentioned that 'the whiteness of the fairies may be due to their lack of shadow, which may also explain their somewhat artificial-looking flatness'.

At this stage, Doyle was brought into direct contact with Gardner, who had been lecturing on the fairies at the Theosophical Society hall in Mortimer Square, London. Gardner told him that he had shown the photographs to two experts, one in Leeds and one in London, and although the latter had been instrumental in exposing fake spiritualist photographs he had been convinced by the fairy photographs. Gardner was not interested in any money that could be made out of it, though his cousin, Miss Blomfield, had mentioned to Doyle that Gardner was enquiring into the question of copyright. A meeting between Doyle and Gardner satisfied Doyle that the Theosophist was no wild-eyed visionary, and it was arranged that Gardner should meet the girls while Doyle showed the photographs around his circle, including Lodge.

Lodge was no credulous fool, and his initial response to the photographs, shown to him in the hall of the Athenaeum Club, was that photographs of the fashionable Californian classical dancers had been taken and superimposed upon a rural English background. Doyle was annoyed by this; he was already determined to believe in the genuineness of the photographs.

Nor were spiritualists in general more enthusiastic than Lodge, even those who were most indignant when it was suggested that the hundreds of spirit photographs being circulated among them were fakes. They were interested in photographs of their dead ones returned to a half-life, but not in fairy folk, as they would add a further complication to the problems of spiritualism. Fairies might be fitted into the Theosophical theory (and as 'elementals' they were basic to the system), but not into spiritualism.

The spiritualists used their own weapons of clairvoyance and spirit guides to downgrade the photographs. One man was informed by his spirit guide that they were taken by a short fair man with his hair brushed back, who did it to please the girl Frances. The photographer was not English, but lived where 'the houses, instead of being in straight lines, are dropped about all over the place'. The spiritualist, a 'Mr Lancaster', thought, for some arcane reason, that the photographer came from either Denmark or Los Angeles. Nevertheless, 'Mr

Lancaster' (a pseudonym invented by Doyle) made one very shrewd comment:

I should very much like the lens which would take persons in rapid motion with the clarity of the photo in question, it must work at F/4.5 and cost fifty guineas if a penny, and not the sort of lens one would imagine the children in an artisan's household would possess in a hand camera. And yet with the speed with which it was taken the waterfall in the background is blurred sufficiently to justify a one second's exposure at least.

Doyle told Gardner of this message, and was somewhat disconcerted to learn that the spirit guide had described one of the photographers who had examined the negatives, a Mr Snelling. Gardner went back to Snelling, to find out more about him. Snelling had worked for the Autotype Company for thirty years, and had recently set up on his own in Harrow. He assured Gardner that there was no question of double exposure, and that the figures, despite appearances, *had* moved during the exposure, which was 'instantaneous'. Not being a photographer, Gardner took this seriously, though instantaneous is meaningless. By 1920 cameras were quite sophisticated, and the term instantaneous could refer to 1/25th of a second or 1/100th of a second, or even 1/1000th of a second. As it happened, the exposure proved to be 1/50th of a second.

This being so, the movement of the waterfall in the background of the photograph examined by 'Mr Lancaster' should have been 'frozen'. But even though out of focus, it is not.

Doyle went to the Kodak offices in Kingsway, and two experts of the company could find no evidence of superimposition though they assured Doyle that they themselves could produce such pictures if they were called upon. This irritated Doyle. He would have liked the Kodak certificate of genuineness and a confession that even with the techniques at their disposal the Kodak experts would be unable to recreate such delightful pictures. It savoured, declared Doyle, of 'the old discredited anti-spiritualist argument that because a trained conjurer can produce certain effects under his own conditions, therefore some woman or child who gets similar effects must get them by conjuring'.

It was time to make a direct approach to the girls, but when he sent a book to Elsie it was the father who replied. Mr Gardner went north. In the Christmas number of *Strand*, Doyle brought the world of the fairies into the hearths of the middle classes, introducing them to Elsie Wright and her cousin Frances who, three years earlier, had taken such amazing photographs. The father, an electrician, had developed the plates himself. 'Oh, the fairies are on the plate – they are on the plate!' one of the girls called out as the image began to appear.

In his account, Doyle did not stick strictly to the facts. He acknowledged that Kodak Ltd had refused to testify to the genuineness of them, but assigned the reason to their fear of some possible trap, though he did mention the assessment of another photographic company, 'which it would be cruel to name', that the background consisted of theatrical properties. Doyle appended a report by Gardner after his visit to the Wrights. Sketching in the background, Gardner put his encounter with the photographer Snelling into a dramatic form to add zest to the narrative. The Wrights, parents and children, impressed Gardner; they all possessed 'transparent honesty and simplicity'. The girls, who were now working, told him more about the fairies, gnomes and goblins, their colouring (pale green, pink, mauve), particularly marked in the wings, the bodies being pale. When there was not much rustling in the woods they could hear the fairy pipes. One of the girls pointed out a fairy pipe on one of the photographs, supposed by the uninitiated to be wing-markings.

Doyle examined this pipe with a lens. 'There is an ornamental rim to the pipe of the elves which shows that the graces of art are not unknown among them.' He appreciated the abandon of the fairy folk as they let themselves go in a dance. 'They may', he decided, 'have their shadows and trials as we have, but at least there is a great gladness manifest in this demonstration of their life.' The elf was a compound of the human and the butterfly; the gnome was more moth. Could they be thought forms? He did not pursue this. It was enough that fairies were alive and well and living in Yorkshire, and that 'the thought of them, even when unseen, will add a charm to every brook and valley and give romantic interest to every country walk'. They would jolt twentieth-century materialists out of the mud.

Although he was then in Australia propounding the spiritualist cause, Doyle waited for the reaction to the article in *Strand*. It signally failed to create the furore for which Doyle had hoped, and the main response was embarrassment and puzzlement that such a steady magazine as *Strand* had published it. But Doyle and the Sherlock Holmes stories had made *Strand* the periodical it was, and it was the least that the proprietors could do, letting Doyle pursue his latest hobby-horse. *Punch* failed to pick up the story and its humorous possibilities, contenting itself with the small change of twenties humour with 'Ode to a Haggis' and arch definitions ('A sceptic is a man who counts the legs of a centipede').

The magazine *Truth*, once a hard-hitting exposé journal, was contemptuous, asking that Elsie finish her fun and explain how it was all done. The *Westminster Gazette* cautiously did a follow-up, sent a 'special commissioner' to Yorkshire, and told its readers precisely where the fairies were, whereas Doyle had been ambiguous – Cottingley, two or three miles from Bingley. The Wrights lived at 31 Lynwood Crescent; cousin Frances at Dean Road, Scarborough. Mrs Wright appeared a straightforward woman, but as the reporter probed more facts came to light, the most interesting one being that when Elsie Wright left school she worked a few months for a Bradford photographer. Mr Wright was less forthcoming; he was 'fed up' with the whole business, though his account agreed with that of his wife and the girls.

Elsie Wright was now working at Sharpe's Christmas Card Manufactory, and at first refused to see the reporter, but later relented. Miss Wright was tall, slim, red-haired, 'fed-up' with the whole thing, but she affirmed that she had really seen the fairies, and had been doing so since 1915. When pressed for further details she withdrew into her shell. It was no surprise to her that no one else in the village had seen the fairies – she and her cousin were privileged. They only appeared in bright sunny weather, and recently they were more transparent than they had been in 1916 and 1917, and were 'rather hard'. 'You see,' she said, 'we were young then.'

Fairy-believers and fairy-watchers continued to come forth. They include Halliwell Sutcliffe, a fifty-year-old novelist who lived nearby in Skipton and wrote *A Man of the Moors*, *Priscilla of the Good Intent* and similar yarns of moorland life. He had never actually seen fairies himself, but a schoolmaster acquaintance had seen and played with them in the meadows. Another novelist, William Riley, also believed in them, but like Sutcliffe had not seen any.

The literary weekly *John O'London's* did a one-page précis of the *Strand* article without comment, and shortly afterwards Maurice Hewlett took Doyle to task in its pages. Hewlett, a poet and novelist, speculated that Doyle had a 'hospitable mind' and that the girls had been pulling his illustrious leg. He was not happy about the photographs, declaring that they were in 'picture flight', not photographic flight. 'They are in the approved pictorial, or plastic, convention of dancing. They are not well rendered by any means. They are stiff compared with, let us say, the whirling gnomes on the outside wrapper of *Punch*.' Those very gnomes that Richard Doyle had designed.

A very cogent objection to the genuineness of the photographs came from Major Hall-Edwards, an authority on radium. He thought there were two ways the pictures could be faked, by sticking the pictures of fairies on cardboard, carefully cutting them out, and placing them close to the girl, or by sticking figures of fairies cut from a magazine or book on to a photograph of the girl sitting in a field, and re-photographing the tampered photograph. An anonymous artist, writing to *John O'London's*, was certain that the former method was used, and produced as possible models the illustrations to Lang's fairy books, drawn by H.J.Ford: 'The photographs are genuine enough, but the "fairies" are not rounded natural objects, taking natural light and shade, but are flat and little more than outlined. Had they been rounded objects, such as statuettes or real figures of any kind, there would have been that elusive "lost and found" quality of outline inseparable from the play of light and shade, as seen in the girl's face and hair.'

A month after the *Strand* article appeared, a very formidable adversary appeared, the 'fiction factory', Edgar Wallace. Wallace was just setting out on a series of detective novels that owe much to Sherlock Holmes, culminating in *The Mind of Mr J.G.Reeder* (1925), and he attacked the photographs from a new angle: 'Why must Conan Doyle's fairies be by Clarkson and wear the kit sacred to provincial pantomime? And why, oh, why, must they be trained by John Tiller of Manchester? For that they are Tiller fairies nobody with a knowledge of the stage will question. Note how they point their toes in the approved ballet-dancing style. Any of the sixteen Palace girls could have told Sir Arthur the name of the step they are performing, and had the photograph borne enlargement they could have recognized the faces of the fairies.'

J.E.Wheelwright put the controversy into verse:

If you, Sir Conan Doyle, believe in fairies,
  Must *I* believe in Mister Sherlock Holmes?
If *you* believe that round us all the air is
  Just thick with elves and little men and gnomes,
Then I must now believe in Doctor Watson
  And speckled bands and things. Oh, no! My hat!
Though all the t's are crossed and i's have dots on,
  I simply can't, Sir Conan. So that's that!

This tone of rather contemptuous good humour would have caused most people to think again, but Doyle was inured to ridicule and the more his critics sneered the more convinced was he that the fairies were real and that the general public was blind to the possibilities of establishing communication with an alien race, a race not inconveniently on Mars but in the hedgerow. He and Gardner decided to encourage the girls to produce more photographs. Gardner left them with a camera and in due course three more prints were provided 'altogether beyond the possibility of fake'.

The public did not deserve them. Doyle's soul was 'filled with a cold contempt for the muddle-headed indifference and the moral cowardice' which he saw around him. Only Gardner was not failing him. His enthusiasm made up for the boorish attitude of the masses, even when it extended to the bobbed hair and up-to-date fashions of the new batch of fairies. The flying fairies were 'super-Pavlovas in miniature' and Gardner was wildly excited by the first photographs ever of a fairies' bower. 'Seated on the upper left-hand edge with wing well displayed is an undraped fairy apparently considering whether it is time to get up. An earlier riser of more mature age is seen on the right possessing abundant hair and wonderful wings.' The photograph of the bower also featured a mischievous smiling elf wearing a close-fitting cap.

In August 1921 the girls were brought together again for a third series, and a stereoscopic camera and a movie camera were provided. But the weather was against the girls, and a seam of coal had been found nearby; the fairy glen was polluted by human magnetism. So there were no stereoscopic photographs or movie film, though an amenable clairvoyant accompanied the girls and saw all that they saw. The place was swarming with elemental life, including the rare breed, undine, which was entirely nude and of a dazzling rosy whiteness. The wood elves were dressed in a tight-fitting one-piece skin which shone as if wet, and had disproportionately large hands and feet. They had no teeth, but wide mouths, and were surrounded by a greenish light. A brownie was taller than most of his companions, eight inches high, dressed in brown, with bag-shaped cap, knee-breeches and large pointed feet. The fairies themselves had long semi-transparent skirts, and floated slowly accompanied by tinkling music.

They were not all jolly creatures, and some of the fairies leered maliciously. Frances had the privilege of seeing a life-sized fairy, clothed in tights. There were also unnamed elemental creatures which acted in lieu of horses for the pixies and gnomes, but they, alas, were to remain unphotographed and largely unbelieved in, except by Doyle and Gardner and a few of the hardier enthusiasts.

The fairies were hardly more than a nine-day wonder, though Doyle continued to receive letters from devotees long after the whole business had been forgotten by most and Miss Wright and her cousin Frances had disappeared from view, no doubt passing through a suspended adolescence into adulthood. Many of the letters were written by men and women who would see anything that was in vogue. A Mr Matthews writing from San Antonio, Texas, declared that his three daughters could see fairies prior to puberty, but never afterwards. The fairies explained that 'We are not of the human evolution. Very few humans have ever visited us. Only old souls well advanced in evolution or in a state of sex innocence can come to us.' The fairies taught these three girls dancing.

The Rev. Arnold Holmes was brought up in the Isle of Man, where belief in the little folk was especially strong, and when out riding he saw 'a small army of indistinct figures – very small, clad in gossamer garments'. A Mrs Hardy, writing from New Zealand, professed to have seen 'eight or ten tiny figures on tiny ponies like dwarf Shetlands'. They wore close-fitting suits. A Canadian lady sent Doyle a photograph of fairies taken by her eleven-year-old daughter, which even Doyle thought ambiguous and maybe nothing more than an interesting arrangement of leaves and shadows.

A Miss Winter of Blarney, County Cork, received 'communications from a fairy named Bebel several times, one of them lasting nearly an hour'. Fairies found it easy to talk to rabbits, but were averse to dogs, which chased them. Fairies rode on the backs of hens, but did not care for them as the hens jeered at them. Miss Hall of Bristol had seen a fairy when she was six or seven, but had not mentioned it to anyone before for fear of ridicule. He was a funny little man playing hide-and-seek among the flowers, sage-green in colour, with limbs like geranium stalks. The creature was about three inches high, and nude. A water diviner, J.Foot Young, had seen bare-legged short-skirted fairies dancing on the slopes of Oxeford Hill in Dorset, and Mrs Ethel Wilson of Worthing had seen them playing in the sea, and riding on the waves, 'like little dolls, quite small, with beautiful bright hair'. Mrs Rose of Southend-on-Sea had always seen fairies, in the shrubbery and under trees, always playing, occasionally indulging in gymnastics. She noted various types, and had seen gnomes arranging a moss bed for the fairies.

Doyle considered such cases significant, though one wonders what Sherlock Holmes would have made of them, these largely uncorroborated musings of, mainly, imaginative women. Not that history is without its staunch believers. In 1838 the folklorist, collector of ghost stories, folk-song collector, hymn-writer and clergyman-schoolmaster Sabine Baring-Gould saw a legion of two-foot dwarfs. His wife also saw a little green man with beady black eyes a foot or fifteen inches high, and, not to be outdone, so did his son, whose description was more elaborate – a little man wearing a red cap, a green jacket and brown knee-breeches.

Dr Vanstone attempted to find a rationale. 'I have been distinctly aware', he wrote, 'of minute intelligent beings in connection with the evolution of plant forces, particularly in certain localities; for instance, in Ecclesbourne Glen [near Hastings]. Pond life yields to me the largest and best sense of fairy life, and not the floral world. I may be only clothing my subjective consciousness with unreal objective imaginations, but they are real to me as sentient, intelligent beings, able to communicate with us in varying distinctness. I am inclined to think that elemental beings are engaged, like factory hands, in facilitating the operation of Nature's laws.' There is muddle here, though Doyle accepted it without demur. How can 'they' be sentient intelligent beings if they are admitted products of the 'subjective consciousness' which must mean, if it means anything, the unconscious mind of the narrator?

In what can only be described as frantic efforts to believe in the existence of fairies, as creatures in space that could be photographed, Doyle was willing to overlook all the objections. It was his role to believe, and once again his clinical training as a doctor clashed with native credulity – native in the sense that his family came from Ireland, where the belief in the little folk was sufficiently widespread as to be unremarkable. No doubt Doyle was aware of the literature of fairyland, though he did not parade it when involved with Elsie and Frances, of the nymphs of Homer, of the Rev. Mr Kirk's *The Secret Commonwealth of Elves, Fauns and Fairies*, written in the seventeenth century and published by Sir Walter Scott in 1815, and of the Arabic fairies, the *geni*, who feature in *The Arabian Nights*.

It is interesting that the preoccupation with fairies was shared by his father and his uncle. Richard Doyle drew innumerable fairies, illustrating the book *In Fairy Land* in 1870, and his few easel paintings have fairy themes. These include *The Witch's Home* and *Wood Elves Watching a Lady* in the Victoria and Albert Museum, and *The Triumphant Entry – a Fairy-tale Pageant*, a large detailed work containing several hundred figures in the National Gallery of Ireland. Conan Doyle's father was even more obsessed, and his mythical monsters, fairy scenes and dream subjects must have seemed outlandish to the stolid Edinburgh citizens of his time.

As if to announce his commitment to fairy-folk Doyle organized an exhibition of his father's work in 1924 under the heading of 'The Humorous and the Terrible'. *The Times* reviewed it whimsically: 'The terrible did not terrify us. The more deliberately humorous did not amuse us. But nearly everything charmed us.' The pictures were 'engaging in their amiable fancy', though the critic noted that there was 'little mastery of drawing', a fault that could never be laid at the door of brother Richard. Doyle's father had not been good at anything, at supporting a large family, at giving guidance to his children, or in inculcating the doctrines of the Catholic Church into his brood.

It may be that Doyle as a boy had absorbed so much fairy culture that in his sixties the scepticism that greeted the fairy photographs seemed an attack on all that he held most dear – the appeal of the borderland and the supernatural. These had been a solace to his father, condemned to a life of languid drudgery at the Edinburgh Office of Works, and they had been a spur and inspiration to him. The fairy photographs could be seen as proof that his father had not been a failure, that the hours and years he had spent painting the unseen creatures of his mind had been worthwhile, that Charles Doyle had not been wasting his time but had been vouchsafed a glimpse of another co-existent life.

In no way did Conan Doyle commit these considerations to paper. He never explained why he was so committed to the belief in fairies, and why, when he tried to discuss the matter rationally, bias took over. The objections raised by Edgar Wallace and Major Hall-Edwards he brushed away angrily, as if they were impertinences. He stood on his dignity, alongside his improbable colleague, Mr Gardner.

As with the girls Elsie and Frances, Gardner slid into the anonymity of the mediocre when the fairies lost their interest. As a Theosophist he had a vested interest in fairies and the like as elementals, though his thinking on the Yorkshire fairies would have received short shrift from the founder of Theosophy, the formidable Madam Blavatsky.

He reckoned that they were 'allied to the *lepidoptera*, or butterly genus, of our familier acquaintance rather than to the mammalian line'. They had little or no mentality, simply an irresponsible joyousness of life. They were in human form because of 'the powerful influence of human thought'. If fairies were real creatures akin to the butterfly, this would surely imply that human thought has the power to transmute or amend species? Elsewhere Gardner changed his tack. Fairies were nature spirits, responsible for plant growth. Without their help 'the three factors of sun, seed and soil would never take place'. Normally fairies have no defined shape, as they work inside the plant, some above the ground, some in the roots. Some are delegated to 'paint' the flowers. If startled, they change back to a 'magnetic cloud'.

Gardner believed that the elaborate Red Indian head-dresses were inspired by fairy wings. There was no birth or death, and propagation was carried out by fission. Despite their admitted mindlessness fairies are able to perform on flute and pipe. Gardner hoped for future co-operation between mankind and the fairies. This hope was not widely shared; no one except the staunch band of fairy-watchers was greatly interested.

15
THE
LAST PHASE

Between 1921 and 1927 Doyle wrote another dozen Sherlock Holmes stories for *Strand*, and if they did not come up to the standard of those of the first period they do show glimpses of his story-telling talent. There are some nasties among them, a fascination with deformity and disease, that hark back to the pot-boiling occult yarns. There is the leprosy afflicting Godfrey Emsworth in 'The Blanched Soldier' which turns out to be 'a well-marked case of pseudo-leprosy or ichthyosis, a scale-like affection of the skin, unsightly, obstinate, but possibly curable'. There is the professor in 'The Creeping Man', who creeps because of his self-experimentation with monkey glands. And there is the woman in the incomparably dull 'The Veiled Lodger' who has her face mangled by a lion.

Two of the stories are allegedly from the pen of Holmes himself, and stalwarts have winced at the self-indulgence and girlishness shown by the great detective when he chose to write up his own cases. In 'The Mazarin Stone' Doyle recounted the story in the third person in a very lack-lustre manner, and it is precisely this characteristic that permeates so many of this last dozen. It is evident that he was not very interested, and this is shown not only by his customary carelessness but, more damaging, by his loss of an ear for dialogue, the quality that carried through the less interesting cases of the halcyon years. The clients have become stereotypes, symbols of goodness, badness or duplicity. Instead of irony Holmes purveys facetiousness, seen at its most intrusive in 'The Three Gables', in which he not only exchanges excruciating badinage with the pretended maid Susan but exposes himself as a racialist in his dealings with Steve, a Negro petty criminal.

Everywhere there is evidence that Doyle has lost touch with the way people think and behave, and the motivations behind the various murders and mayhem are often ludicrous. There is a preponderance of powerful evil men outside the reach of the law. In 'The Illustrious Client' the villain gets his just deserts, and has vitriol thrown into his face by a discarded mistress, but the law is 'human and elastic' and the sentence is the lowest possible for such an offence. The main objections to Baron Gruner are that he keeps a 'lust diary' and has mesmerized a sweet innocent girl into falling in love with him. The high regard Doyle had for titles is seen in 'Shoscombe Old Place', where Watson maintains that it is 'out of the question' and 'a monstrous supposition' to imagine that Sir Robert Norberton killed his sister. After all, Sir Robert is a boxer, an athlete, a plunger on the Turf and a lover of fair ladies. It does not matter that he is 'so far down Queer Street that he may never find his way back again'.

Watson is right. Sir Robert did not kill his sister, only concealed the body in the family crypt after the sister had died of natural causes. By not announcing her death (the plot demands) Sir Robert's creditors would not pounce on him before he had won enough money on the Derby to repay them. Being a gentleman, Sir Robert receives a 'mild censure for the delay in registering the lady's decease' and looks likely to have an 'honoured old age'. Had he been a commonor or a foreigner his lot would not have been as fortunate.

Holmes has lost his admirable consistency and pragmatism, and shows a tendency to drop into Americanese. Throughout his writing life Doyle had kept a weather eye on the American market, and this now affected the speech of Holmes. There was also a tendency for Holmes to over-use criminal argot, and philosophize in a manner that can only be described as half-baked. In the last story of the canon, 'The Retired Colourman', he muses on life to Watson: 'Is not all life pathetic and futile? Is not his story a microcosm of the whole? We reach. We grasp. And what is left in our hands at the end? A shadow. Or worse than a shadow – misery.' One of the qualities that endeared Holmes to his readers was his self-confidence and assurance. Even these were going as Holmes's creator passed into old age. And yet among this last clutch there are stories that are fit to stand with those of the golden years, such as 'Thor Bridge', a brilliant how-was-it-done rather than who-done-it, and 'The Three Garridebs', in which Doyle puts a new gloss on an old theme – the fixing-up of a dupe with a curious job to get him out of the way. Instead of copying out the *Ency-*

clopaedia Britannica the amiable and eccentric Nathan Garrideb is lured to Birmingham to give the villain access to the counterfeit money hidden in Garrideb's cellar.

In his preface to the collection Doyle is at pains to put Holmes in his place: 'That pale, clear-cut face and loose-limbed figure was taking up an undue share of my imagination ... Had Holmes never existed I could not have done more, though he may perhaps have stood a little in the way of the recognition of my more serious literary work.' So that even as late as 1927 Doyle never realized his role and limitations. 'And so, reader, farewell to Sherlock Holmes!' he concludes breezily, trusting that the detective has proved a distraction from the worries of life as he inhabited 'the fairy kingdom of romance'. This must have seemed to veteran enthusiasts the height of impertinence. What was the man Doyle thinking of? The fairy kingdom of romance?

Reviewing *The Case-Book of Sherlock Holmes*, *Punch* went into verse:

> What though these last adventures show
>   No weakening of the magic vigour
> Which centuries (it seems) ago
>   Informed that fascinating figure,
> How can we measure them or urge
>   Our stricken souls to jubilation
> When every phrase is like a dirge,
>   Each tale a funeral oration?

The same year saw the publication of S.S. Van Dine's *The Canary Murder Case*, with Philo Vance as the logical successor to Sherlock Holmes. Philo Vance, as *Punch* had it,

> Is art-collector, *viveur*, wit,
>   Profound psychologist, logician,
> And merely for the love of it
>   Helps the police-force in their mission.

Notwithstanding the continuing loyalty towards Holmes, many were obliged to recognize that he was old-fashioned, and that the current crop of fictional detectives was a more formidable body than the crude imitators of twenty and thirty years before. G.K. Chesterton's Father Brown was in his element, and so was Inspector French. H.G. Bailey's Reggie Fortune had first appeared in 1920, the year Agatha Christie had established new guidelines for detective stories with *The Mysterious Affair at Styles*; she was to produce the classic *The*

Murder of Roger Ackroyd in 1926, with the narrator as murderer. Doyle was no longer competing with hacks, and American writers, such as Van Dine, were entering the lists, showing that detective stories could have pace and vividness.

The reader was no longer prepared to bother with a client narrating his problem, and he was more critical, wanting genuine deduction and not presumption. If there was a timetable and maps dotted about the text, so much the better. There was also competition from easier roads, such as the thriller. 1927 also saw Edgar Wallace's *Traitor's Gate*, while 'Sapper' was in full flow with his Bulldog Drummond books. Entertainment literature was following a new path along which Doyle was temperamentally unable to go.

Doyle still felt that he had something to offer to the reader of fiction. Holmes was played out, but there were other characters who could be manipulated to fit into his new preoccupations with the occult, the off-beat and the odd. To Doyle's eternal credit, Holmes remained bogey-proof to the very end.

Doyle's interest in the weird reached a peak towards the end of his life when he published *The Maracot Deep and Other Stories*, and they form a strange parallel to his spiritualistic writings of the period, with a strong vein of allegory and hints of the depression he felt in the failure of spiritualism to take the world by storm. *The Maracot Deep* is a logical successor to *The Lost World*, and although the characters have changed, there is still the well-contrasted group, with an unspeakable American taking the place of Roxton. Roxton's dialogue was terrible, but Scanlan's is worse, a debased Brooklynese that could have been derived from B-feature gangster movies had they been in existence then.

Instead of exploring life on a South American plateau, Doyle now dealt with life at the bottom of the Atlantic, reached in a diving-bell which breaks its cable and sinks into a chasm several miles deep, settling on 'thick elastic ooze'. The explorers are rescued by the descendants of the original occupants of the lost world of Atlantis, and take up their abode in an underground city inhabited by two races, small Negroes and large whites. It is an advanced civilization, with synthetic food and drink and a form of television that works by telepathy, so that the inhabitants can relate their history to the new-comers, and vice versa. Radio has not been discovered, but Professor Maracot and his associates rig one up and somewhat surprisingly receive programmes from the world above.

Maracot is not a Professor Challenger with a new name. There is no question of the personage he most resembles: 'The long, thin, aggressive nose, the two small gleaming grey eyes set closely together under a thatch of eyebrows, the thin-lipped, compressed mouth, the cheeks worn into hollows by constant thought and ascetic life, are all uncompanionable. He lives on some mental mountain-top, out of reach of ordinary mortals.' He is clearly Sherlock Holmes, older and wiser, but with powers that Holmes never acquired, revealed near the end of the book when the group is confronted by the Lord of the Dark Face, who lives in a part of Atlantis shunned by the friendlier natives. The building in which he dwells is decorated with statues and ornaments, 'carved with the highest perfection of art, but horrible and revolting in their subjects. All that the most depraved human mind could conceive of Sadic cruelty and bestial lust was reproduced upon the walls.'

The Lord of the Dark Face is a perfect athlete seven feet tall and clad in black leather. He resembles Holmes, too, with his 'extraordinarily clear-cut and aquiline' face, and he talks like him. He tells the intrepid trio that he is about to destroy the undersea world, but Maracot prays and reduces the Lord of the Dark Face, in the manner of Poe, to a 'semi-liquid heap of black and horrible putrescence'.

Throughout the story there are various threats posed by strange underwater creatures, often electric, usually toad-like and somewhat amorphous, but perhaps the most interesting section of the book deals with the history of Atlantis as shown to the visitors on the television screen – a thin disguise for Doyle's musing on present times, with 'people who were restless and shallow, rushing from one pursuit to another, grasping ever at pleasure, for ever missing it, and yet imagining always that in some more complex and unnatural form it might still be found'.

This might at first be a modern re-interpretation of the decline and fall of the Roman Empire, but Doyle is clearly talking about the contemporary scene when he refers to 'the reformers at work who were trying to turn the nation from its evil ways, and to direct it back into those higher paths which it had forsaken. We saw them, grave and earnest men, reasoning and pleading with the people.' All to no avail. Doyle turns to his hobby-horse, the failure of the Church and its deliberate antagonism towards 'the reformers': 'We could see that it was the priests of Baal, priests who had gradually allowed forms and show and outward ceremonies to take the place of unselfish spiritual development, who led the opposition to the reformers. But the latter were not to be bullied or browbeaten. They contined to try for the salvation of the people.' Some took note, but others 'turned away laughing and plunged ever deeper into their morass of sin. There came a time at last when the reformers turned away also as men who could do no more, and left this degenerate people to its fate.'

There was one reformer, 'a man of singular strength of mind and body, who gave a lead to all the others. He had wealth and influence and powers, which latter seemed to be not entirely of this earth. We saw him in what seemed to be a trance, communing with higher spirits ...' Although the subsequent building of an ark might seem to indicate that the man referred to is Noah, the tone, reverent and hushed, might lead to speculation that Doyle was speaking of himself. There is also a curious section in which Doyle speculates about reincarnation, an optional extra for the spiritualist movement which rather resented the concept being taken over by Theosophy.

The Maracot Deep was not strong enough to exist on more than one level. It was another adventure yarn, with allegory as a side issue, lively science fiction in the tradition of Verne, and desperately old-fashioned compared with Aldous Huxley's *Brave New World*, which followed only four years later. The other three stories in the collection are minor. Two of them have Professor Challenger back in form as regulation Sixth Form bully, an intellectual Flashman who bristles if he is not regarded as the greatest, cleverest man in the world. His conversion to spiritualism had clearly been misguided and a waste of Malone's time, though Malone is the muddied oaf of *The Lost World*, still a journalist who gets the odd jobs.

The Disintegration Machine is on the level of a boys' magazine story, and it concerns a thoroughly nasty character named Theodore Nemor who invents 'a machine of a most extraordinary character which is capable of disintegrating any object placed within its sphere of influence. Matter dissolves and returns to its molecular or atomic condition. By reversing the process it can be reassembled.' Nemor is a combination of villainous attributes, short, thick, a hunchback without a hump, a face like a dumpling with pimples and blotches, eyes like a cat, a long thin moustache, and a loose, wet, slobbering mouth. It is unusual for Doyle to write in a character so fully. Naturally Nemor has yellow fangs, a velvety voice with a trace of a foreign accent, and a massive head which, in the shorthand of adventure stories, means he is clever. Briefly, the story is about how Challenger sits in a chair and is disintegrated, and brought back again. In the first instance, as a joke, Nemor brings him back without his beard or hair – the machine can be adjusted to do this. When Challenger persuades Nemor to be disintegrated, the inventor reluctantly agrees. Challenger, of course, is the saviour of mankind; he leaves Nemor disintegrated, and civilization is saved.

When the World Screamed is an odd one indeed. Challenger speculates that the earth is a living organism, spends a fortune drilling an immensely deep hole, and finds that beneath the rock is 'a greyish material, glazed and shiny, which rose and fell in slow palpitation'. An engineer, accompanied by Malone, harpoons it, and the earth emits a terrible scream. 'Through every vent and every volcano she voiced her indignation. Hecla bellowed until the Icelanders feared a cataclysm. Vesuvius blew its head off ...'

If Doyle's missionary zeal perplexed his old friends, there was just as much speculation about these stories and why a man of nearly seventy should waste his time on this ranting nonsense. They did demonstrate that Doyle's basic interests had not changed for nearly fifty years. Neither had his style and approach. But generalizations fit Doyle as little as they fit Dickens, for the 1920s saw the publication not only of the sensationalist rubbish but of perhaps his best non-fictional work, his two-volume *History of Spiritualism* (1926). Despite some credulous moments, this is an admirable and very readable run-through of spiritualism from its earliest days in America, and it shows how authoritative Doyle could be when he took the trouble and had the material at his fingertips.

The care and attention he devoted to *History of Spiritualism* was unquestionably in anticipation of the type of reader who would buy such a book. Unlike his previous books on spiritualism, there is little exhortation or crude propaganda. This is not a book written expressly for the typical reader of *Strand*, who happened to have a few spare shillings jangling in pocket or purse.

Although Doyle did not face the key issue of sex in the hereafter, with which Holcombe had had such a problem in *The Sexes: Here and Hereafter* in 1869, he did not dodge any other subject, especially the tricky ones of ectoplasm and spirit photography. Ectoplasm was the name given to a curious white substance seen extruding from the medium Eva Carriere in 1903. The word was coined by Charles Richet, and competed in circulation with other terms for the same material such as teleplasm and ideoplasm.

Ectoplasm had been known for many years, described as a semi-luminous thick vapour oozing from the side or mouth of a medium, as fleecy cloud, as a whitish-grey vapour, as a cloudy pillar, as a dingy white-looking substance, or as a white diaphanous-looking thing. Ectoplasm provided the raw material of spirit forms or spirit faces. Between 1908 and 1913 a series of tests were carried out on Eva Carriere, and photographs were taken. Doyle was fascinated by the photographs, as he was by anything really weird: 'The pictures are strange and repulsive, but many of Nature's processes seem so in our eyes. You can see this streaky, viscous stuff hanging like icicles from the chin, dripping down on to the body, and forming a white apron over the front, or projecting in shapeless lumps from the orifices of the face. When touched, or when undue light came upon it, it writhed back into the body as swiftly and stealthily as the tentacles of a hidden octopus.' Unfortunately Doyle was not able to view the phenomenon for himself. Eva Carriere (usually referred to as Eva C.) came to London and held thirty-eight sittings for the Society for Psychical Research, but failed to come up to expectations.

Doyle not only believed in ectoplasm, but claimed to have seen its production on many occasions. He anticipated a time when the science of plasmology would deal with different forms of plasm, though these different kinds were not specified. He thought that ghosts were formed of a certain type of ectoplasm, and that the viewer supplied the material. Consequently the cold chill, the trembling and fainting, often subsequent to a ghost's appearance, were not due merely to fear but to the sudden drain upon the psychic supplies. He also thought that ectoplasm played a part in table tilting (a variation of table rapping in which the table tilts in response to questions), being collected from medium and sitters and deposited on the table surface, and that ectoplasm possessed suckers or claws to fulfil its various purposes.

As ectoplasm immediately retracted on exposure to light or attempt at handling, it was difficult to obtain a specimen, but apparently this was achieved; when burned to an ash it left a smell like that of horn. Among the constituents were common salt and phosphate of calcium. Doyle wholeheartedly believed in its existence, and speculated that it might have a hand in spirit photographs, which he also steadily supported.

In Victorian times spirit photography was a widespread and lucrative racket, and snapshots of the departed were on sale in the dirty bookshops of Holywell Street alongside languorous nudes. Before the invention of roll film, photography was a cumbersome business in which there were many opportunities for fraud. A glass plate covered with sensitive emulsion was exposed to the light; when not exposed it was kept in a holder. Spirit photographs could be produced by switching plates, double exposure, trick plate-holders, or tampering in the dark-room. Even when the sitter, with whom the spirit was to appear, brought an observer to see that there was no funny business, he or she was usually too inexperienced to catch a shrewd photographer out. A previously prepared plate, with spirit form ready, was difficult to spot. Photographers used professional models, cardboard cut-outs, any odd negatives knocking around, or painted a spirit on the background of the studio in a substance that could not be seen with the naked eye but could be picked up by the camera. Success went to their heads, and many were caught out through carelessness or through using a photograph of a spirit who was very much alive.

The introduction of roll film took the mystery out of photography for the general public. Spirit photography continued and in 1908 the *Daily Mail* investigated the phenomenon, an inquiry that confirmed everyone in their prejudices and beliefs, and the centres of spirit photography shifted away from London, to Crewe, Bridgwater and Birmingham. Most of these spirit photographers used plate cameras. In 1920 Fred Barlow of Birmingham found spirit faces and written messages on plates that had not been exposed in the camera. Doyle believed that the camera was not essential in the production of spirit photographs.

The business with the Yorkshire fairies only served to confirm him in his belief in the reality of spirit photography, and he became ever more reluctant to consider the likelihood of fraud. In his *The Case for Spirit Photography* (1922) he firmly stated his attitude, and photographers who were detected in fraud were treated as misguided people who had obtained genuine results but who had succumbed to temptation when their powers were at a low ebb. In 1922, photographs were taken on Armistice Day in Whitehall, and among the real people there were, evidently, spirit forms. To attack this photograph was tantamount to treason, blasphemy or at the very least a lack of patriotism that should lead to a sound thrashing. Another sacred relic was produced for the spiritualist cause.

Doyle's principal protégé, William Hope, was one of the Crewe Circle, formed in 1905. Hope worked with Doyle, and on one of the plates there appeared a reproduction of a Greek script in the British Museum with a slight change in the script, showing that it was not a copy. This was tremendously important to Doyle, for it seemed to demonstrate not only Hope's innocence and freedom from deception but the human-type lapse from perfection of what Doyle called 'a wise invisible Intelligence'. Hope also produced a series of slides showing the formation of ectoplasm about the person of William Jeffrey of Glasgow.

Spirit photography enjoys a certain cachet. A photograph is something objective to show a sceptic. At materialization séances phenomena are lacking when an unbeliever attends, but a spirit photograph of the kind produced of Eva Carriere or by William Hope cannot be so easily explained away, however they were produced. The test of a thorough-going spiritualist is whether he or she takes on trust spirit photographs.

Whatever flaws there are in the 684 pages of Doyle's *History of Spiritualism*, it is an immeasurably more impressive production than the science fiction of his later years. If this does show anything, it is that Doyle no longer regarded himself as a great novelist in the tradition of Sir Walter Scott; it may even show a contempt for his calling, and his preference for the shadow rather than the substance, in a fantastic plot, a never-never world populated by pasteboard figures.

Unquestionably Doyle's voracious and diverse reading provided him with much of his science-fiction material, but he is akin more to Poe than to Jules Verne in that he found it difficult to draw a line between the probable and the improbable, even the possible and the impossible. He did not have a sufficiently wide education to assimilate complex data of the kind not touched upon at his university. Fruits of genuine knowledge are seen in *The Lost World*, but a fantasy such as the disintegrating machine kept in a shed in the garden of a Hampstead house is seen for what it is, an unconvincing reminiscence of H. G. Wells's *The Time Machine* (1895). Wells had the requisite scientific background (he studied under Thomas Huxley at the Royal College of Science), but Doyle had not, relying on instinct and his proven ability to grab a reader's attention to get him through. Lecturing on Burns in Edinburgh in 1901 he said: 'The best literature is always the unconscious literature – the literature which takes no thought of grace or style or the right word, but comes in a deep strong stream from a human soul.' These words might serve as an apologia for the strange novelettes of his old age.

Surprising as this work is, it is perhaps less surprising than Doyle's ability to cram it into his full programme of travels, lectures and propaganda. He obtained some relief from his public engagements at a cottage he bought for his wife in the New Forest, following spirit instructions by Pheneas at home seances. Bignell Wood was thatched, picturesque, had a garden gate direct into the New Forest and a stream nearby. Most of it burned down shortly before Doyle's death.

In 1928 Doyle and his family set out for South Africa, a gruelling tour that would have taxed the strength of a far younger man. He was gratified by the sporting achievements of his sons Adrian and Denis on board ship. Denis, a lusty young man of nineteen, was champion of deck tennis, and both were in the tug of war team. Daughter Billy was in the final of the deck bowls championship, and created something of a stir in ladies' cricket by bowling overarm. Sport still had the power to raise enthusiasm in Doyle.

Doyle's views on South Africa were in accord with the general attitudes of the day, which had hardly changed since Cecil Rhodes. He believed in the paternalistic approach to blacks. 'Personally I am not in favour of educating them,' he wrote in his account of the tour, *Our African Winter*, 'though they educated very easily.' His thinking on this was based on the assumption that education would breed 'discontent and thwarted ambition where there was apathy if not content before'. It needs an effort of will to appreciate that the 1920s apathy was considered a good thing, appreciated by the colonial mind not only in South Africa but in India and the West Indies.

He visited the grave of Cecil Rhodes, and his wife conjured up a seance, evoking the spirits of Rhodes and the Boer leader Kruger who had both seen the light and, naturally, were staunch spiritualists. Of Rhodes, Doyle said that he was 'heaven-sent, and heaven-guarded above all human institutions is that British Empire which he did so much to extend'. He prophesied that in a hundred years Rhodesia would be 'the very finest dominion that flies the British flag ... on the whole I know no dominion which is so happily situated'. In the meantime, the boys were out shooting, preferably shooting rare and exotic animals. They 'managed to get a small antelope of a rare variety', perhaps the Thompson's gazelle later mentioned as part of the boys' bag. It seems that Doyle had forgotten, or renounced, his aversion to blood sports.

In his passion for the British Empire, Doyle was extremely annoyed about outsiders who might upset the balance of nature, such as the 'American Missions with their four-square and evangelical dogmas and their hobnobbing with the blacks'. He had suddenly conceived a dislike of America, and American methods. 'Torture was often as much part of the American system as in medieval Italy,' he declared out of the blue. He returned to Britain early in 1929 pleased with his trip and the spiritualistic aspirations of white Africa, though he was aware of the tension between those of British and Dutch descent in South Africa.

In late autumn 1929 he set out on his European mission, visiting The Hague and Copenhagen on his way to Stockholm and Oslo. The Swedes welcomed him, and he spoke on their radio, but he returned to Britain exhausted and had a heart attack. He managed to go to the Armistice Day commemoration at the Albert Hall, and later the same day spoke in the Queen's Hall, but the effort was too much for him, and he was confined to his room all the winter, convalescent in the spring of 1930 and taking an interest in the family pursuit, painting. During this illness *The Edge of the Unknown*, a volume of essays on spiritualistic themes, mainly historical, was published. No one realized that it would be the last.

To the end he was engaged in controversy. On account of an adverse review by Theodore Besterman, editor of the *Journal of the Society for Psychical Research*, of the book *Modern Psychic Mysteries*, Doyle resigned his membership of the society, and he was deeply involved in the Cantlon case. Mrs Cantlon was a medium, and was prosecuted, with two policewomen posing as sitters at a seance giving evidence against her. Mediums could be summonsed on either of two accounts, the Witchcraft Act dating from the reign of George II and the Vagrancy Act of 1824, which stated that 'every person professing to tell fortunes or using any subtle craft, means or device to deceive and impose on any of His Majesty's subjects shall be deemed a rogue and a vagabond'.

Doyle fought hard against this anachronistic and widely disregarded law, and one of the most effective sections of *Land of Mist* deals with the trial of a medium under the Vagrancy Act. Somewhat surprisingly, Doyle ignored the possibilities of the courtroom confrontation in his Sherlock Holmes saga. In July 1928 he had written to *The Times* on the subject of the prosecution of mediums, the use of police informers, and the unpleasant situation of societies employing mediums, equally open to prosecution. 'We are united against those who refuse us justice, and impose upon us a religious persecution,' he concluded.

In 1930 it seemed that at last something was about to be done about a change in the law, and a meeting was fixed for 1 July between a deputation including Doyle and the Home Secretary; Doyle's health had improved since the winter. But this public appearance was too soon, and he was taken back home, a dying man. He died on 7 July 1930. The tributes flowed in to the creator of Sherlock Holmes and the missionary of spiritualism. But without the first there would hardly have been the second. A humble Dr Doyle, M.D., general practitioner, would have had difficulty in getting his voice heard in the boisterous fun-loving 1920s, no matter how sterling and intense his intentions.

POSTSCRIPT

The new dawn never came, though the calamity did. Spiritualism did not sweep the world, but neither did the number of its adherents dwindle with the disappearance of a powerful protector and patron. So far as spiritualists were concerned, the grass-roots believers in Balham and Macclesfield, Halesowen and Tunbridge Wells, Conan Doyle was not important and if he was known he was regarded with as much suspicion as a magistrate who disliked mediums. What did a detective-story writer have to do with them?

The weapons of the psychic researchers became ever more subtle, with infra-red photography and tape-recorders, but whatever they found made no difference to the faithful. Let fake mediums fall, psychic photographs prove to be double exposures, fairies at the bottom of the garden disappear into story-books, spiritualism was not hurt, and although it did not shake the power of the Church it carried on as a sturdy self-reliant religion along with other schisms such as Primitive Methodism and Christian Science, whose believers remained untroubled by sceptics and inner doubts, and were only mildly concerned by the prophets of this or that -ism who stalked, like Billy Graham, through their well-tended pastures.

As the messiah of spiritualism Doyle had but a brief reign and dominion. Audiences in Australia, Scandinavia, Africa and America had seen him, and had goggled, but not at a religious leader but at someone far more interesting – the creator of a legend. Sir Nigel, Brigadier Gerard, sword-waving peasants, these might never have existed. But Sherlock Holmes was a different matter; he was not only a legend but an industry, with Clive Brook in the first Sherlock Holmes sound film, followed by Raymond Massey and Arthur

Wontner ('No other Sherlock Holmes is genuine–accept no substitute,' wrote an American film critic). In 1932 no less than five Sherlock Holmes films were made. A version of *The Hound of the Baskervilles*, now lost, had additional dialogue by Edgar Wallace. In 1939 Basil Rathbone, with Nigel Bruce as Watson, created the definitive film Holmes in *The Hound of the Baskervilles*, Rathbone, of the 'dark knife-blade face and snapping mouth' (wrote Graham Greene), became a star on the strength of this performance, and several other films followed, some of which would have made Conan Doyle turn in his grave, ambiguous as his attitude was towards Holmes. *Sherlock Holmes and the Voice of Terror* and *Sherlock Holmes and the Secret Weapon* brought kudos to no one and only money to the box-office.

Radio and television in the U.S.A. and Britain brought Holmes to those who had never heard of Conan Doyle. There was a wide range of Holmeses, from Sir John Gielgud in 1954 (with Sir Ralph Richardson as Watson), Ronald Howard in 1953–54, Alan Wheatley in 1951, to Peter Cushing in 1959 and Douglas Wilmer in 1965. A ballet, *The Great Detective*, was made in 1953. Sir Nigel Films–quaint touch–a company formed by the Sir Arthur Conan Doyle estate, made *A Study in Terror*, with Holmes solving the Jack-the-Ripper murders. Unquestionably the most stylish of the films featuring Sherlock Holmes was Billy Wilder's *The Private Life of Sherlock Holmes* (1970), with Robert Stephens as Holmes.

During the Festival of Britain of 1951 it was decided to mount a Sherlock Holmes exhibition, and St Marylebone Borough Council provided funds from the rates. Sherlock Holmes societies and individuals who had relished the stories contributed enthusiastically to the success of the exhibition, and the most surprising bodies, including the British Museum and the General Post Office, proved that they could enter into the spirit of the thing. The centre piece was a painstaking reconstruction of the room in Baker Street on the site where it was originally supposed to be.

No fictional character has had such wide exposure, and each rendering brings in a clutch of new readers, young and old. There are many fictional people who are said to appeal to all ages, but this seems to be hyperbole. But there is no question about the universal draw of Sherlock Holmes. Doyle shares with Caesar's *Gallic Wars* the distinction of being perused by schoolmaster and schoolboy alike, though with rather more pleasure. The stories, though dashed off to fill a commission, do exist on a number of levels, as an evocation of the 1890s in town and country, as puzzles, as allegories of right and wrong, and as straight adventure stories in which the villain gets his just deserts. There is melodrama, but no mawkishness, and the motivations are easily understood by spotty eleven-year-olds. The saga is emblematic of order and justice, of a fixed point in a world of uncertainties. The hero has all the right qualities without being a prig or a muscle-bound nonentity.

There are not only films, radio programmes, plays, televised films and plays, books, books about books, and books about books about books, but a whole clutter of ephemera, such as ceramic busts of Sherlock Holmes and Watson at £10 the pair, silhouettes, brooches, cigarette cards from the 1930s, models of hansom cabs, deerstalker caps, Sherlock Holmes bookmarks and key fobs, playing cards, comic strips, jigsaw puzzles, a Sherlock Holmes song from the 1890s and Sherlock Holmes finger puppets. There are specialists in Holmesiana who make a profitable living from their trading in sacred and semi-sacred relics. The volumes of the *Strand* in which the short stories appear are handled, and sold, with something like awe; a copy of *Beeton's Christmas Annual*, 1887, in which Holmes made his first appearance, would have something of the status of a Bible in a Nonconformist household.

Was Holmes an intellectual equivalent of Mickey Mouse, with the same ubiquitous appeal? Hardly. The detective-story writer Rex Stout put his finger on the quintessence of Holmes. He is the embodiment of man's deeply held conceit that he is a reasoning animal. 'Our aspiration to put our reason in control of our instincts and emotions is so deep and intense that we constantly pretend we are doing so. We almost never are, but Sherlock Holmes always is.' Sherlock Holmes always *is* not always *was*. Rex Stout was acute. Sherlock Holmes is alive and well and living at 221B Baker Street. And he still has visitors, to prove it.

Conan Doyle is a different matter. He has been roundly dismissed as a Victorian philistine even by those who love his Sherlock Holmes saga, and he was impetuous, wrong-headed, and held views that were later taken up by patrons of the public bar and which today, to say the least of it, are hardly respectable. So did most of his contemporaries. But he did have the courage of his convictions, a strong sense of honour, and the stern awareness of where his duty lay no matter how inconvenient it was. He did not ditch his first wife when he fell in love with Jean Leckie, he helped to support a body of relatives even when they were not worth propping up with funds, and when he was in the midst of enteric fever in the Boer War he did not decamp back home to safety and a welcoming fire as many of his colleagues did. He saw glamour in war, but so did many others, he saw the light in spiritualism, but this is better than seeing nothing but annihilation as H. G. Wells came to do. He also anticipated retribution on those who did not respond to his call. So did many missionaries of the past. Doyle's Jesuit upbringing, decry it as he did, had its effect after all.

BIBLIOGRAPHY

Adcock, A. St John, *Gods of Modern Grub Street*, 1923.
Amery, L.S., *The Times History of the War*, 6 vols, 1900–09.
Arnold, Julian B., *Giants in Dressing Gowns*, 1944.
Baring-Gould, W.S., *Sherlock Holmes, a Biography*, 1962.
Barrett, W., *On the Threshold of the Unseen*, 1917.
Bell, H.W., *Sherlock Holmes and Doctor Watson*, 1932.
—— (ed.), *Baker Street Studies*, 1934.
Bell, Joseph, *Mr Sherlock Holmes*, 1893.
Bennett, Arnold, *Journals*, 1932.
Blakeney, T.S., *Sherlock Holmes – Fact or Fiction?*, 1932.
Brend, G., *My Dear Holmes*, 1951.
Britten, Emma, *Nineteenth-Century Miracles*, 1884.
Broad, C.D., *Religion, Philosophy, and Psychic Research*, 1953.
Burdett, O., *The Beardsley Period*, 1925.
Burgin, G.B., *Memoirs of a Clubman*, 1921.
Campbell, M., *Sherlock Holmes and Doctor Watson*, 1935.
Carpenter, E., *Prisons, Police and Punishment*, 1905.
Carr, John Dickson, *The Life of Sir Arthur Conan Doyle*, 1949.
Carrington, C., *Rudyard Kipling*, 1955.
Cecil, R., *Life in Edwardian England*, 1969.
Churchill, Sir Winston, *The World Crisis 1911–18*, 4 vols, 1938.
Coates, J., *Photographing the Invisible*, 1921.
Cooke, I. (ed.), *The Return of Arthur Conan Doyle*, 1957.
Crichton-Browne, J., *The Doctor Remembers*, 1938.
Croxton, A., *Crowded Nights and Days*, 1931.
Dakin, D. Martin, *A Sherlock Holmes Commentary*, 1972.
Dilnot, G., *Scotland Yard*, 1926.

Doyle, Adrian M. Conan, *The True Conan Doyle*, 1943.

Drahms, A., *The Criminal*, New York, 1900.

Ensor, R.C.K., *England 1870–1914*, 1936.

Fulford, Roger, *Votes for Women*, 1957.

le Gallienne, Richard, *The Romantic Nineties*, 1926.

Gilbert, Michael (ed.), *Crime in Good Company*, 1959.

Gooch, G.P. (ed.), *British Documents on the Origin of the War*, 1928.

Goodwin, M. (ed.), *Nineteenth-Century Opinion*, 1951.

Gordon, H., *The War Office*, 1935.

Grazebrook, Owen, *Studies in Sherlock Holmes*, n.d.

Green, R.L., *Andrew Lang*, 1946.

Griffiths, Arthur, *Mysteries of Police and Crime*, 1903.

Gross, H., *Criminal Investigation*, 1891.

Gruggen, Rev. G. and Keating, J., *Stonyhurst*, 1901.

Hall, T.H., *Sherlock Holmes – Ten Literary Studies*, 1969.

——, *The Late Mr Sherlock Holmes*, 1971.

Hambourg, D., *Richard Doyle*, 1948.

Hamilton, C., *People Worth Talking About*, 1934.

Hammerton, J.A., *Barrie*, 1929.

Hansen, Ferdinand, *The Unrepentant Northcliffe*, 1921.

Hardwick, M. and M., *The Man Who Was Sherlock Holmes*, 1964.

Harrison, M., *In the Footsteps of Sherlock Holmes*, 1958.

Haycroft, Howard, *Murder for Pleasure*, 1942.

——, *The Art of the Mystery Story*, 1946.

Hearnshaw, F.J.C., *Edwardian England*, 1933.

Henslow, G., *Truths of Spiritualism*, 1919.

Hill, J. Arthur, *Letters from Sir Oliver Lodge*, 1932.

Hind, C.L., *Authors and I*, 1921.

Hobson, J.A., *The Psychology of Jingoism*, 1901.

Hole, Hugh, *Looking Life Over*, 1934.

Holroyd, J.E., *Baker Street Byways*, 1959.

Hope, A., *Memories and Notes*, 1928.

Horn, D.B., *Short History of the University of Edinburgh*, 1967.

Hunt, P., *Oscar Slater, the Great Suspect*, 1951.

Hynes, S., *Edwardian Turn of Mind*, 1968.

Irving, H.B., *Last Studies in Criminology*, 1921.

Jackson, Holbrook, *The Eighteen Nineties*, 1913.

Jerome, Jerome K., *My Life and Times*, 1926.

Knox, Ronald A., *Essays in Satire*, 1928.

Lamond, John, *Arthur Conan Doyle*, 1931.

Lane, Margaret, *Edgar Wallace*, 1939.

Laver, James, *Edwardian Promenade*, 1958.

Lee, W.L.M., *A History of Police in England*, 1901.

Locke, Harold, *Bibliographical Catalogue of the Writings of Sir Arthur Conan Doyle*, 1928.

Lodge, Oliver, *Raymond*, 1916.

——, *Survival of Man*, 1920.

——, *Past Years*, 1931.

Lukacs, G., *The Historical Novel*, 1962.

MacCabe, Joseph, *Is Spiritualism Based on Fraud?*, 1920.

MacCleary, G.F., *On Detective Fiction*, 1960.

MacDonald, A., *Criminology*, New York, 1893.

Mackenzie, Compton, *On Moral Courage*, 1962.

McQueen, I., *Sherlock Holmes Detected*, 1974.

MacQueen-Pope, W., *Twenty Shillings in the Pound*, 1948.

Maitland, F.W., *Justice and Police*, 1885.

Mann, Dixon, *Forensic Medicine and Toxicology*, 1902.

Marquand, L., *The Story of South Africa*, 1955.

Masterman, C.F.G., *The Condition of England*, 1909.

Minney, R.J., *The Edwardian Age*, 1964.

Mix, K.L., *A Study in Yellow*, 1960.

Montgomery, James, *A Case of Identity*, Philadelphia, 1955.

——, *A Study in Pictures*, Philadelphia, 1964.

Murch, A.E., *The Development of the Detective Novel*, 1958.

Myers, F.W.H., *Human Personality*, 1907.

Nevinson, H.W., *Changes and Chances*, 1923.

Nowell-Smith, S. (ed.), *Edwardian England*, 1964.

Osler, W., *The Principles and Practice of Medicine*, 1909.

Payn, James, *Some Literary Recollections*, 1885.

Pearsall, Ronald, *The Table-Rappers*, 1972.

——, *Edwardian Life and Leisure*, 1973.

Pearson, Hesketh, *George Bernard Shaw*, 1942.

——, *Conan Doyle*, 1943.

Phillpotts, E., *From the Angle of Eighty-eight*, 1951.

Pointer, Michael, *The Public Life of Sherlock Holmes*, 1975.

Pond, J.B., *Eccentrics of Genius*, 1901.

Prothero, M., *History of the C.I.D.*, 1931.

Raymond, E.T., *All and Sundry*, 1920.

Richards, Grant, *Memories of a Misspent Youth*, 1933.

——, *Author Hunting*, 1934.

Roberts, S.C., *Holmes and Watson*, 1953.

Roberts, F.T., *The Practice of Medicine*, 1909.

Roughhead, W., *The Trial of Oscar Slater*, 1929.

Savill, T.D., *Clinical Medicine*, 1909.

Sayers, Dorothy L., *Unpopular Opinions*, 1946.

Schofield, A.T., *Behind the Brass Plate*, n.d.

Smith, Edgar W. (ed.), *Profile by Gaslight*, New York, 1944.

Starrett, V., *The Private Life of Sherlock Holmes*, 1934.

Steevens, G.W., *From Capetown to Ladysmith*, 1900.

Summers, Montague (ed.), *The Supernatural Omnibus*, 1931.

Symons, Julian, *Buller's Campaign*, 1963.

——, *Bloody Murder*, 1972.

Taylor, A.S., *Principles and Practice of Medical Jurisprudence*, 1905.

Thompson, Elizabeth M., *Spiritualistic Medium*, 1969.

Traill, H.D., *The New Fiction*, 1897.

Tweedale, Violet, *Phantasms of the Dawn*, 1924.

Usborne, Richard, *Clubland Heroes*, 1953.

Warrack, Guy, *Sherlock Holmes and Music*, 1947.

Watson, E.H.L., *Lectures to Living Men*, 1925.

Wells, H.G., *Experiment in Autobiography*, 1934.

Whyte, F., *The Life of W.T. Stead*, n.d.

Wilkinson, H.S., *Lessons of the War*, 1900.

Wilshire, A.M., *Leading Cases on Criminal Law*, 1942.

Wilson, J.M., *Life After Death*, 1920.

Zeisler, Ernest B., *Baker Street Chronology*, Chicago, 1953.

In addition there are the biographical archives, consisting of genealogical documents, correspondence and material relating to the Doyle family, the Conan Doyle Library, manuscripts of published and unpublished work including short stories and plays. There is also a considerable amount of material concerning Doyle and, especially, Sherlock Holmes in the periodical press and newspapers. The contemporary press is exceptionally valuable for showing that when Doyle in retrospect seems blimpish and jingoistic he was merely echoing public opinion. It would have taken a cooler and more analytical type of man (or a born trouble-maker such as W.T.Stead) to stand against mob mentality.

Among the more interesting newspapers, periodicals and magazines are: *Answers, Blackwood's, Bookman, Chambers's Journal, Collier's Weekly Magazine* (U.S.A.), *Cornhill, Daily Express, Daily Mail, Daily*

Telegraph, Evening News, Evening Standard, Fortnightly Review, Graphic, Harmsworth's Magazine, Illustrated London News, John O'London's Weekly, Journal of the Sherlock Holmes Society, Light, Macmillan's, Medium and Daybreak, New Statesman, New York World (U.S.A.), *News of the World, Nineteenth Century, Pall Mall Gazette, Pall Mall Magazine, Pearson's, Psychic News, Review of Reviews, Saturday Review, Saturday Review of Literature* (U.S.A.), *Spectator, Strand, The Times, The Times Literary Supplement, Titbits* and *TP's Weekly.*

Most important are Doyle's published writings, which cover an immense range, from a preface to Sandow's book on body-building, through the hysterical pamphleteering of the First World War, to the science fiction of his later years. The best guide to his output is H. Locke's *A Bibliographical Catalogue of the Writings of Sir Arthur Conan Doyle*, published in 1928 and therefore not covering the work of Doyle's closing days. There are a number of omissions, chiefly of early pieces contributed to a wide, an embarrassingly wide, variety of magazines including *The National Review, Temple Bar, Great Thoughts,* and the *Sunlight Year Book* (promoted to the glory of soap – Port Sunlight, the model town for happy soapmakers, was founded in 1888).

Most of Doyle's non-Sherlock Holmes books are out of print, but the Holmes stories, long and short, are in paperback, furnished with prefaces by different authors which vary from the flat to the perceptive (Eric Ambler's introduction to *The Adventures of Sherlock Holmes* is the best). It is doubtful whether any of the non-fiction will ever be printed again, even the *History of Spiritualism* which, despite its eccentricities, has not been superseded.

INDEX

AS IT WAS

An Autobiography 1897-1918
Naomi Mitchison

Naomi Mitchison celebrated her ninetieth
birthday in 1987 and is considered one of the
foremost contributors to the literary scene. In
SMALL TALK she plunges us into a child's eye
view of Edwardian life. Girl matures to woman in
ALL CHANGE HERE and Naomi Mitchison
explores her desire for freedom to be and know
herself and her own mind.

CHARLES RENNIE MACKINTOSH

1868-1928
Jocelyn Grigg

An indispensable fully illustrated guide to the
architect, designer and watercolourist who, for his
futuristic vision, was acclaimed father of the
modern movement.

BURRELL: PORTRAIT OF A COLLECTOR

1861-1858
Richard Marks

In 1983 the fabulous collections of *objets d'art* built
up by Sir William Burrell went on show in its
entirety for the first time in a gallery specially
designed and built for it.

This is a unique and lavishly illustrated portrait of
an extraordinary genius.

Other titles in the SCOTTISH COLLECTION

THE BRAVE WHITE FLAG *James Allan Ford*

THE LAST SUMMER *Iain Crichton Smith*

THE SCOTTISH COLLECTION OF VERSE
VOL 1 to 1800 *Ed Eileen Dunlop & Antony Kamm*

THE FIRST HUNDRED THOUSAND *Ian Hay*

DUST ON THE PAW *Robin Jenkins*

THE MERRY MUSE *Eric Linklater*

MAGNUS *George Mackay Brown*

THE BULL CALVES *Naomi Mitchison*

EARLY IN ORCADIA *Naomi Mitchison*

THE CHINA RUN *Neil Paterson*

WHERE THE SEA BREAKS *John Prebble*

A GREEN TREE IN GEDDE *Alan Sharp*

TIME WILL KNIT *Fred Urquhart*

WALK DON'T WALK *Gordon Williams*

SCOTTISH BIOGRAPHIES

BURRELL: PORTRAIT OF A COLLECTOR *Richard Marks*

AS IT WAS (Autobiography) *Naomi Mitchison*

NEIL GUNN 1891 – 1973
THE SCOTTISH COLLECTION

THE LOST CHART
A cold war thriller set in the Scottish city of Glasgow shortly after the
Second World War, '*the Lost Chart*' moves on two distinct planes –
the physical and the metaphysical.

THE LOST GLEN
The famous novel on the decline of Highland ways and values
in the 1920s.

THE OTHER LANDSCAPE
'*The Other Landscape*' returns to the familiar setting of the Highlands
but with a new element of dark humour.

THE SILVER BOUGH
Archaeologist Simon Grant comes to the Highlands to investigate an
ancient cairn. A stranger in a strange part of the country, he finds that
there are barriers to understanding between him and the people
of the community.

SECOND SIGHT
The setting is a Highland shooting lodge, whose occupants are depicted
in stark contrast to the local people. A violent death is foreseen.
But whose? How? When? The drama is played out against a
background of strange mists and elemental landscapes.

OFF IN A BOAT
'*Off in a Boat*' logs the adventures of a man, who at a critical point of his
life, throws caution to the wind, and with his wife as Crew, navigates his
way round the West Coast of Scotland.
Whilst Gunn masters the art of sailing and anchorage, the Crew
explores the possibilities of the camera.